SEEDS IN THE WILDERNESS

SEEDS IN THE WILDERNESS

PROFILES OF WORLD RELIGIOUS LEADERS

MARTY GERVAIS

Marty Gervais
December '94

QUARRY PRESS

The publisher gratefully acknowledges the support of The Canada Council, Ontario Arts Council, Department of Canadian Heritage, and Ontario Publishing Centre.

Cataloguing in Publication Data

Gervais, C. H. (Charles Henry), 1946–
      Seeds in the wilderness: profiles of world religious leaders

ISBN 1-55082-110-5

      1. Clergy — Biography. 2. Christian biography.
 I. Title.

BL72.G47 1994   270.8'2'0922   C94-900603-3

Design by Susan Hannah.

Printed and bound in Canada by Webcom Limited, Toronto, Ontario.

Published by Quarry Press, Inc., P.O. Box 1061,
Kingston, Ontario K7L 4Y5.

"People don't come to church for preachments . . . but to daydream about God."   —Kurt Vonnegut, *Palm Sunday*

"Christ did nothing worthwhile for 30 years. One carpenter more or less in Nazareth could scarcely have mattered. For all practical purposes they were wasted years. And it is precisely to that kind of waste most men are called."
                    — Fr. Matthew Kelty, *monk at Abbey of Gethsemani*

"God, the superbeing who created a universe of some 200 billion galaxies comprising approximately 200 billion stars per galaxy— the same God who created the atom, designed gravity and ignited the spark of life — this god talks to Oral Roberts? Never to an Isaac Newton or a Leonard da Vinci or a Mozart . . . but He takes the time to talk to Oral Roberts."
                    — Bob Guccione, *Penthouse Magazine* publisher

"This is an awful world, just frightening, and we're stuck with it."
                    — Norman Vincent Peale

"I believe in god
who willed conflict in life
and wanted us to change the status quo
through our work
through our politics"
                    — Dorothee Sölle, *Revolutionary Prayers*

"To replace God is an impossible task . . . Nothing can fill the emptiness of His absence . . ."   — Pope John Paul II

"Pray for what you want, and work for what you need."
                    — A fortune cookie message

CONTENTS

PROLOGUE
DIARY AT THE ALTAR OF GOD IN JERUSALEM

1 It is Easter Week, 1985. The gray Mercedes — built like a Sherman tank and carrying seven passengers — roars along the highway from Tel Aviv to Jerusalem. It is an overcast day. Hot. A student from Hebrew University offers her parents and younger brother, just arrived from Boston, a taste of what she has learned about Israel from studying in Jerusalem the past eight months. The young girl leans forward and nudges the driver to point out the rusted-out tanks from the 1948 War of Independence. She also tells her parents about what happened then. The burly taxi driver relates how he was just a baby at that time but that his parents had fought to retain their right to stay in Israel. The battered and dismantled tanks lay strewn among weeds and rocky hills along the highway, memorials to the war. When the student explains to her parents what holy week means to the Christians in Jerusalem and how throngs crowd the already congested Via Dolorosa, or the route taken by Jesus on the way to be crucified, her young brother asks, "If Jesus were alive today, would he have had to serve in the army?" What he was referring to is the mandatory service in the armed forces required of Israelis, both men and women. His sister laughs, turns to him and replies, "Of course, he was a Jew."

But whether Jesus, the peacemaker, would have taken up arms is beside the point. Today he would have found a very different kind of Jerusalem from the one he left so dramatically. Today the city of more than half a million sprawls lazily in the sun. Its chalky white stone buildings are strung out among the hills like the mother-of-pearl beads sold by Arab hawkers in its alley-like streets. In Christ's time, the Holy City was only a fraction of what you experience today. It was a city tucked away in the northeast and bounded by towering white walls and gigantic iron gates. It was a city, originally built by the Canaanites, 2,000 to 3,000 years before it was even conquered by King David, who made Jerusalem his nation's capital. It was a city destroyed time and time again and even renamed by its captors. In the time of the New Testament, Jerusalem was under the iron rule of Rome and King Herod.

Today the city within the enclosed walls occupies only a little more than half a square mile, but in Jesus' time, it was even smaller. Today the Jerusalem with its one beautiful temple — the Second Temple — where the magnificent Muslim mosque, the Dome of the Rock, now stands — is a glut of noisy corridors and fast-food stalls. "It's nothing like what Jesus would have seen," says Professor Halvor Ronning at the American Institute of Holy Land Studies here. "It was far more magnificent, with large stone streets and colonnades much different than the asphalt alleys you find today. Jesus would have been shocked with today's Old City."

First night in the city. Ronning, who teaches biblical geography, is the first to be contacted. He explains that when Christians mark Good Friday a day from now, commemorating the death of Jesus, they will be inching down the Via Dolorosa, a route nothing like the one Jesus would have taken. "And he certainly wouldn't have recognized it," adds Ronning. That first night, I am instantly aware of how difficult it is to take a casual stroll into the Old City — and not come out the owner of something that inevitably will hang in the closet for a generation, without ever being worn. One street hawker makes chase in an attempt to get me to buy a camel-skin hat. "Why?" I protest. "Because it looks good on you!" Arguing does no good — it is best to make tracks.

The next day I meet a forty-two year old Muslim, who earns his living by giving tours of the Old City. He laughingly agrees Jesus wouldn't have been able to find his way to the present city, because the circuitous route he took to Calvary is nearly obliterated by, not only the vendors with their gold pendants, ceramic tiles, rosaries, and Bedouin clothing, but fervent Christians who have thrown up churches and cathedrals and shrines all through the labyrinthine city. Of special interest to the throngs visiting the Old City during Easter are the fourteen Stations of the Cross —

monuments that mark Christ's journey to Calvary as well as his crucifixion and burial. On Fridays, people gather at the Tower of Antonia near St. Stephen's Gate at about 3:00 p.m. for a procession conducted by the Franciscans. On Good Friday the crowd will be here first thing in the morning for a solemn procession that starts at 10:15 a.m. For them, it is the beginning of a long day that won't end until sunset because, for those patient enough, it means taking part in lengthy but vivid burial ceremonies at the Church of the Holy Sepulcher, the holiest site in Christianity. It is believed to be on the site of Golgotha (*Calvaria* in Latin, hence Calvary) where Christ was crucified. The church also encompasses the site of the burial and subsequent resurrection of Christ. The church was first built by Constantine in the fourth century. His mother, Helena, discovered the tomb of Jesus and three crosses believed to be those of the crucifixion. The church was destroyed and later rebuilt by the crusaders, using the original fourth century foundations.

On Good Friday — or for that matter any day during Holy Week — it is impossible for pilgrims who have stormed this city to get near the church. If you're fortunate enough to meet up with the enterprising John Sankhoud, who resides in the shadow of the church, you'll have little trouble getting access to the tomb of Jesus, the tomb given to him by Joseph of Arimathea. When I meet this aggressive, but smiling, mustached Sankhoud, he displays the kind of moxie we'd all like to draw upon. I am amazed at how he pushes through the hundreds who line up for access to the Chapel of the Angels, the antechamber to the room holding the tomb of Jesus.

"Come, let's go!" he beckons, then gently nudges the old women and men who inch closer to the dark entrance with their canes and bags. Somehow, I manage to bypass the queue. I ask, "How are you doing this? What are you telling them?" He has been speaking to them in a number of languages. Sankhoud smiles mischievously, "I've told them you're a priest, and a *very* important person, and that you only have this brief moment to spend in Jerusalem, and you'd like to see where your God is. I told them you have to catch a plane." Suddenly I feel conspicuous, awkward, introverted. Then again, there I am after only three or four minutes practically crawling on my hands and knees into the dark tomb, lit by hanging lamps and candles. Once inside the tomb, I pause for a moment but suddenly realize Sankhoud is right behind me: "There you are . . . Now pray to your God!"

I am there among a half dozen others who stretch their hands over the place where the dead Christ was believed to have been wrapped in a winding sheet. When I leave I try to get around an old widow who kneels in prayer at the entrance — her forehead touching the floor and one arm reaching out to the stone slab that held the crucified Christ. "Those people will be standing there long after you're gone," Sankhoud tells me. "That's why I pushed you in."

But would Christ have recognized any of this? Most will tell you it's really difficult to visualize because so little of the original Calvary remains. According to Ronning, it's "not conclusive" that the present site of the Holy Sepulcher is the location of the crucifixion. Part of the problem, he spells out, is that any evidence there was for this claim lies behind the resplendent trappings of the church. In addition, Sankhoud maintains that the church, divided among the Franciscans, Greek, Armenian Orthodox, Coptic,

Syrian, and Ethiopian denominations, is not ready to permit anyone to penetrate its mysteries. In fact, the denominations jealously guard their liturgical practices from one another. If that isn't confusing enough, outside the Old City lies the Garden of the Tomb purported to be the actual site of Golgotha. "But that's not it," insists Sankhoud. Ronning tends to agree. Their wish is the same as most — that the life of Christ would be better defined and delineated in the city. Why isn't more done to accomplish this? It should be obvious. In reality, the city may be a "Holy City" but it serves very different purposes. It's home for both Jews and Arabs. Christianity is in the minority. Indeed, it is a "Holy City," but it is holy to Jews, Arabs and Christians. As for the Christians, its significance splinters still further into bitter divisions. "God must be smiling at all the confusion," Sankhoud said. "It seems nobody can agree — and yet your God, the God of the Jews, and my God are one and the same. But then like any possession, we guard it, and keep it for ourselves. We don't want any intrusions. We don't want to share it. God must be shaking his head in disbelief. What has He done with the human race?"

To most scholars and experts, even from the Stations of the Cross, it is difficult to grasp a picture of what Christ faced in Jerusalem or what Jerusalem was like in that period. Even if the Via Dolorosa was the actual way of the cross, Ronning allows, it would have differed dramatically from today. In Christ's time, the streets were wider. They were covered with massive flagstone, and they were lined with columns and pillars. Another unmistakable difference between the past and today, explains Sankhoud, is that today the way of the cross is considered by the tourism ministry to be notorious for pickpockets and thieves. "It hasn't always been like that," contends Issa Kouba, a Jerusalem-born Greek Orthodox tour operator who also sells chocolate bars, newspapers, magazines and pocket novels on the side. "It's really been bad just in the past five years, but I don't blame them (thieves). These people can't make a living any other way. It's a pity this goes on in such a holy city."

Some things have changed little in Jerusalem from biblical times. For one, Christ would not have been surprised to find soldiers at the entrance of this city, whose history has been marred by wars and marauding armies. As I approach St. Stephen's Gate, high on the hill among the grass and the gravestones I notice boys chasing one another and paying little heed to the goats they're supposed to be watching. "In Christ's time this was used as a grazing area for sheep," Ronning explains. "Even today a sheep's market is held each Friday close to this area." On the road that snakes around the eastern side of the Old City and offers a panoramic view of the Mount of Olives, two boys, maybe nine or ten, struggle to hitch a cantankerous donkey to a makeshift sled loaded down with sacks of flour. The boys peer up at passing tourists, their youthful eyes clearly begging for help.

During the busy morning in the Old City, women balance baskets of sweetbreads on their heads and set up shop on the stone streets, selling lettuce, tomatoes, apricots, figs, oranges, sabras or prickly pears. And if you can peer beyond the American Express and Visa signs, you can read signs for "money changers" whose facilities in some instances resemble ordinary residences. If you make the wrong turn you find yourself among the dirt and the beggars. Some are shrouded in black and lean against the wall in a cavernous alleyway . . . That unmistakable voice routinely blasts out at the streets over the loud speaker, praising Allah — something that certainly would have surprised a returning Christ.

It is practically dusk, and the sun clings to the towering medieval wall of this Old City. Sitting in the high green grass and tapping a wooden cane against a rock is a young boy, perhaps twelve or thirteen years of age. Just beyond, a flock of sheep moves idly through a graveyard. A man with a toddler huddles close to the fire that crackles loudly in the still air. Somehow I can't help but make the connection to David, the Judean shepherd boy who was inspired by God to kill the legendary Goliath and whose ancient city beyond heaped upon him much glory and consternation.

2 Some things haven't changed. Shepherds still move their wandering sheep through the grassy slopes that border this ancient city, whose roots go back 5,000 years. Now and again, it isn't uncommon to turn around and spot a young boy on a donkey ambling around a corner, trailed by twenty or thirty sheep. He shouts strange guttural sounds to the animals as they move recklessly through the streets. This is modern Jerusalem. The city today is also one of Coca-Cola trucks edging through the narrow streets, of television aerials mounted on chalky white buildings, of Mars bars, French fries, and even hamburgers sold by none other than the Golden Arches, except here it is has been renamed "McDavid's."

Even so, some things never change. Somehow picking up the English-language *Jerusalem Post* is a reminder of entering a city where politics and religion are intertwined in daily life. Where else could you find advertisements in support of troops at war defending the homeland as well as notices on where to find a good buy on life-size wooden crosses? All this is part of Israel's long history — from the time of Moses and Joshua when they charted their way across the vast expanse of desert to the Promised Land. Their movements, guided by their God, led them headlong into worship and war.

Today the Old City simmers in conflict. Although it has been almost two decades since the Israelis recaptured the ancient city from the Arabs, the two are still at odds with one another. Geographically, they are at opposite ends of the Old City, but the two districts reflect the disparities between the cultures.

The Muslim quarter is cluttered with tiny shops, while the Jewish quarter is redeveloped into something resembling Toronto's huge indoor shopping mall, The Eaton Center. Somewhere between the two in ideology and tradition are the Christians, a minority who feel slightly awkward and out of place, even though most are from an Arab background. If you talk to anyone, you hear bitter stories and resentment, each complaining about the other. The Arabs tell you they are a people without a country, that it was pilfered from them. By contrast, the Israelis boast of their "miracle in the desert," emphasizing how they transformed a desert country into a land of progress and wealth. Finally, if you chat with the Christians, they maintain a stony silence, resolute about not taking sides, wishing only to tolerate the differences and survive peacefully in such a milieu.

Beyond the politics, the state of war, and the presence of machine-gun-toting guards on rooftops, the city is hallowed ground for three major religions. Muslims saunter through the markets with their beads, counting God's graces and gifts. It is not uncommon to step into a shop in the Muslim quarter of the Old City and discover a shopkeeper at the back of his store, prostrate on a carpet, facing Mecca and wrapped in prayer. Unabashed foreign pilgrims, who would certainly be ostracized for praying in the street in their own country, are lost in prayer before the Stations of the Cross amid market crowds along the Via Dolorosa, or Street of Sorrows, where Christ shouldered his wooden cross to Calvary. If you head into the Jewish quarter, just below the Dome of the Rock — that towering and glorious mosque that rises above the old walls on the site of the Second Temple — you will find hundreds of Jewish pilgrims standing before the 2,000-year-old Wailing Wall, the retaining wall of Herod's temple. Here, they press foreheads to the stone wall and meditate, or shove messages of hope into the ancient masonry.

I quickly learn that while this may be the City of David, it is also the city where both Christ and Muhammad ascended into Heaven. It is a city that has been under constant conflict, under constant siege since the days of David. Today, Israeli soldiers guard it with their lives — as the jewel of their new homeland.

At dusk, I run into a neatly-dressed Muslim outside a souvenir shop near the First Station of the Cross along the Via Dolorosa. He is ushering around a young German girl. Most of the tourists have fled the Old City, but Bagat Gawdat, a thirty-seven year old freelance guide, urges me to accompany them to the Church of the Holy Sepulcher. Arriving there, he finds the young woman can't pay him, so I put out a few more shekels to pay for her. But in doing so I demand a favor of him. I want to interview him. Gawdat invites me to his house, but says first he must take the girl to her parents. She is barely fourteen or fifteen, and doesn't know how to get back to her hotel. But she is incredulous at Gawdat's offer to accompany her to her hotel across the Kedron Valley. Gawdat suggests that crossing the valley itself would cut off at least a half hour of the walk. Balking at the idea of traversing the dark valley with this stranger, she tells me, "I'm not going to go with him — he's a Muslim! I'd go with you, but not him." The fact that he is a Muslim should have nothing to do with it, I protest, but agree to accompany her anyway, partly since Gawdat has invited me for tea at his home across the valley. In fifteen minutes, we cross the valley and climb the hill, and the young girl seems relieved as she returns to her family at the hotel.

The congenial Gawdat resides in a modest duplex. His wife carries out trays of goat cheese, tea and fruit. His children cling to him as he speaks about Jerusalem, his birthplace. His father still lives in the Old City. I ask him about his life there. "My father is in a business that makes people feel good about themselves," Gawdat begins. I assume his father must be a psychiatrist, or social worker. In a sense, he is the latter. His father, Gawdat tells me, settles private disputes that arise in the community. In most cases, the disputes are resolved through threats of violence. But Gawdat defends his father, arguing that in nearly every instance, these are situations where people are clearly cheating other people. "He is merely rectifying injustices. He repairs relationships."

Once Gawdat bought a television from a shop and when he got it home, it failed to work properly. The vendor blamed it on the lack of an aerial, and wouldn't refund Gawdat's money, or assist him in any way. "So my father went to see this man . . . He said to him, 'My son is not a liar, and you must give him a new television . . . If you don't, I'll break everything in your shop, and I'll burn it to the ground.'" Gawdat related how the man gave him a new television set without hesitation. "In fact, he gave me a larger one. And I felt better about it. So did the man . . . My father knows so much about human nature." Sadly, the custom of dealing with people in this way is vanishing as youths defer to the police, Gawdat pointed out.

3 If you want to meet a man whose roots go back to the seventh century and whose family has, for more than 1,300 years, kept the long iron key that unlocks the Church of the Holy Sepulcher containing the tomb of Christ, then just go into the streets of the Old City and ask for him. That's what the Muslims tell you here. If you inquire among shopkeepers or freelance guides, or, for that matter, among enterprising young children scrambling to make a few shekels, or preferably, American dollars, you will find out where this man lives or the address of his neighbors or which shops he frequents. Because he is so approachable, it doesn't mean he is unimportant to these people. Far from it. He's a man whose privilege of unlocking and locking the church is considered to be the "holiest" in all of Christendom. He is actually envied not only by Christians, but by his own Muslim community. Muslims, too, regard Jesus as a "holy man" and a prophet.

Wageeh Nasselbeh, a thirty-three year old electrician by trade to whom this ancient tradition has fallen, is not what you would expect. He dwells in the new city, modestly, in a two-story home. It is open to strangers who wish to hear the story of the lengthy tradition of his family since AD 630 when the city surrendered to the armies of Caliph Omar. This I learn from chatting with souvenir shopkeepers on the Via Dolorosa, the route traditionally known as the way of the cross. They know the stories and the legends of Omar and of Nasselbeh's family. Some even know the man, but I am told he hasn't been seen for hours.

I ask my new friend Gawdat if he could help. Certainly. He knows of Nasselbeh. We inquire at a few more shops, and one man, wearing a striped hatta, calls out across the street to say he knows one of Nasselbeh's neighbors, and that we should go there. The guide thanks the man and we're off again, this time weaving down the narrow dark and scrappy cavernous streets from the church and through the Muslim quarter and beyond the Damascus Gate into the New City. Gawdat locates the home, advises me to wait, and knocks at a door overlooking a courtyard. In a few minutes, with new directions, we are finally at Nasselbeh's door. His wife unlatches a leaded window in their two-story home to inform us that he has gone to console a neighbor whose father died earlier that day. She isn't sure which family it is, however, but reports that her husband should be back in an hour. Gawdat suggests we ought to wait.

Meanwhile, he furiously paces up and down the street, stopping taxi drivers and neighbors in the hope of locating which family may have lost a parent. He thinks then Nasselbeh could be found and persuaded to return home. I don't think I want to bother the man at a funeral. But Gawdat assures me it would not be impolite. Soon I have the feeling that in minutes I may find myself in the awkward situation of standing in an Arab home that is in mourning. Sure enough, Gawdat's sleuthing turns up the address of the family, but he realizes that an hour is nearly up and, because the family lives near Mount Scopus, it is much too far away and there isn't enough time to go there. We return to wait outside the Iron Gate at Nasselbeh's house.

In just a few minutes, Nasselbeh returns home. He is a man with a warm smile and eyes that lead you to believe he is shy. He wears a black silk suit and flannelette shirt. Nasselbeh guides us into his house and through a bedroom to a parlor. In the bed are a neighbor's three sleeping children, whom his wife is babysitting. Their own children are upstairs, also asleep. Nasselbeh jests sarcastically, "How did you find me?" knowing Gawdat's persistence had paid off. He smiles and mutters something to the guide in Arabic. Nasselbeh speaks English, having acquired it from his parents and from working with tourists in the Old City. He is surprisingly approachable, insisting he isn't bothered in the least by the intrusion. I sense his sincerity, for within a few minutes, his wife has squeezed lemons for juice, followed by a silver tray bearing hot cups of sweet tea, fruit, and candies.

Nasselbeh points out that next week when the Eastern Rite churches celebrate Holy Week it will be impossible to get hold of him. Celebrations are far more demanding and colorful than those of Roman Catholics who mark Easter in a few days. This week, Nasselbeh has merely to open and close the church, and it is done with far less pomp. On Good Friday, Nasselbeh locks and unlocks the church five times as the Franciscans commemorate the death and burial of Christ. Long before dawn today — at 3:00 a.m. — the church has to be unlocked again for special prayers in the Holy Sepulcher. On Easter Sunday, Nasselbeh will be there to open the church at 6:30 a.m. That is not so bad, considering that every other day during the year, the church is open for a mass at 4:00 a.m.

Nasselbeh long ago gave up the exact practice of following his forefathers. Since the Israelis recaptured the city from the Arabs in the Six Day War in 1967, it has become increasingly difficult to carry out the tradition. For a brief period after that war, Nasselbeh indicates, the Israelis dispatched a horse with a guard to escort him through the gates of the Old City to the church. Now, instead of rising before dawn and winding his way through these ancient streets and past the Israeli guards, he has hired a Muslim who resides near the church to open and close its doors. "I couldn't have hired anyone else. It had to be a Muslim."

During special ceremonies at the church — like tomorrow — and at various times through the years, Nasselbeh is there to continue the tradition set by his forefathers in AD 638. Nasselbeh's dark eyes actually sparkle when he relates the story of how Caliph Omar visited the Holy Sepulcher after taking the city. Omar tossed a stone to one side of the church and asked that a Mosque be built there. Today that mosque still stands. The Greek Patriarch offered the keys of the church to Omar and petitioned him to keep the church safe from destruction as a place where people of faith would have freedom to pray. Omar, in turn, offered the key to Aboda Ben Summet, a soldier who had accompanied Omar. "This, I guess, is like my great-great-great-grandfather — I don't know how many greats that is."

Since then, the twelve-inch key has been passed from one generation to the next, except for a period of about 100 years when crusaders seized it from Nasselbeh's family, contending that Muslims shouldn't hold the key to the holiest of Christian sites. In 1187, Saladin captured Jerusalem from the crusaders and the key was returned to Nasselbeh's family — this time for a different reason. A squabble over liturgical rights in the church had divided the Christian denominations which had attempted to dominate the holy place. It was believed that if a Muslim became "the keeper of the key," he could exercise the much-needed control over the church, thereby putting an end to the bitter disputes. The only wrinkle in this long tradition, maintains Nasselbeh, is that about 400 years ago, during the Turkish rule of Jerusalem, a dispute arose over whether his family should have exclusive access to the church. It was decided then that the Judai family would become "the keepers of the key" while the Nasselbehs would regulate the opening and closing of the church itself. This means that to this day, Nasselbeh must go to the Judai family in the Old City and ask for the key. During the early days of Israeli occupation of Jerusalem in the late 1960s, it became a bothersome process. First, a horse would pick up Nasselbeh at his house, take him to the Judai house to collect the key, then a guard would accompany him to the Holy Sepulcher.

There is no financial reward for Nasselbeh to carry out this tradition, unless that is how you describe the donation of $10 a month from the Roman Catholic, Greek Orthodox, and Armenian churches. Certainly this isn't why Nasselbeh continues the more than thousand-year tradition. "This is the holiest of places and I am very proud to hold the keys to this place." The honor he feels is enhanced by the fact his cousin holds the key to another holy place — the Kaaba, the Mosque at Mecca considered by Islam to be the holiest spot on earth. "So this is very special for me." He is particularly honored by the Greek Orthodox Church inviting him as a "witness" for the Holy Fire ceremony on the eve of Easter. This will occur next week. He is asked to go into the tomb of Jesus to witness the absence of fire, then is directed to seal the tomb in wax and place his own inscription on it. "Can you imagine a Muslim doing this? A Muslim in a Christian holy place?"

He explains that his religion regards Jesus as a prophet, but Muhammad as the last prophet. Islam even acknowledges Mary, the mother of Jesus, but Muslims draw the line at the crucifixion of Christ. Islam believes that someone else may have been been nailed on the cross in Christ's place. "So, we have much in common with Christianity . . . and even Judaism where we have our roots. We believe, as the Jews do, that our father was Abraham . . . and although we may not agree with the Jews over politics, we believe as they do in the same God."

Nasselbeh is proud to celebrate Easter with Christians in the ancient church. The Church of the Holy Sepulcher was built by Constantine in the fourth century after his mother had unearthed the tomb of Christ and three crosses believed to be from the crucifixion. The church was later rebuilt by the crusaders using the original foundation. To him, Easter is a holy day for it is the moment when Jesus was taken to heaven, as was Muhammad many years later. To be a part of it, he contends, is circumstantial in the sense that his roots place him beside the tomb at the Christian Easter. Nonetheless, he is very proud to share this holy day. Nasselbeh views himself, or his involvement in this ritual — not in any selfish way — but as the presence of religious tolerance that is needed by everyone, especially in Israel where Christians, Jews, and Arabs are not always comfortable together.

Nasselbeh, an orthodox Muslim who worships at the Dome of the Rock and keeps to the rigid practice of praying five times a day, maintains he would not hesitate to pray in the Church of the Holy Sepulcher. "As a Muslim, I can pray anywhere: in a garden, a mosque, or even a church." Many times, one will notice Muslims making their own pilgrimage to Christ's tomb. "They will remove their shoes just as they do in the mosque out of respect for the place, just as Moses was asked to remove his own sandals on Mount Sinai." Nasselbeh's grandfather actually used a small room at the Church of the Holy Sepulcher where he kept a carpet for kneeling and praying to Allah. The church's key was passed on to Nasselbeh ten years ago. "And since then, I haven't been able to go anywhere. I have to be responsible to the church while my brothers have all left Jerusalem and gone on to their own careers."

After a night of conversation, it is time to go. It is late, and Nasselbeh leads the way past the sleeping children to the door. Gawdat whispers that a gift of shekels or American dollars would be appropriate. It is done with respect, and Nasselbeh accepts it without reservation. Before leaving his house, Nasselbeh, gesturing to the bedrooms of his own children, informs us that his own son is the likely choice to carry on the tradition. After all, he was named after Aboda Ben Summet, the first of his family to receive the key to the Holy Sepulcher in the seventh century.

4 Bright early morning, heading to Bethlehem, south of Jerusalem. Here there are 32,000 Christian Arabs. On the rocky, hilly landscape are the shepherds — the scene reminding me of David, especially since it is here where he was born. But Bethlehem is also the birthplace of Christ. And the Church of the Nativity dominates the community. Its once-magnificent Crusader entrance is now dwarfish, to the point you nearly have to bow for fear of hitting your head. The twelfth-century doorway, still visible, had to be cut down twice — the first time because the Turks rode their camels into the church; the second because pilgrims rode in with donkeys. Here the disparities between Christians are evident. The church is shared by Armenians, Greek Orthodox, and Roman Catholics — or "Latins" as they are called here. At one time, the Greeks prohibited the Latins from visiting the cave-like manger setting, but the Orthodox priests were unaware the Roman Catholics had dug a tunnel to the nativity scene and secretly used it nightly.

Later, at the tiny chapel of the Ascension at the top of the Mount of Olives, where Christ was said to have risen into Heaven, an Arab ticket collector collects a small fee. The round stone shrine, built 300 years after Christ's death, offers little hope of peace as hawkers outside peer in and unrelentingly petition pilgrims to buy postcards or rosaries. Neither does the Garden of Gethsemane at the base of the mountain that faces the Old City of Jerusalem. Beyond its twisted and fat olive trees a man with a camel entices tourists to take a ride for 20,000 shekels (about $18 or $19), or he'll invite you to take a picture of the camel and then put his hand out for payment. One man, emerging from the garden where Christ was said to have been before being arrested and taken before Pilate, remarks, "How can you keep your mind on anything here?"

There are other reasons for being unable to meditate in such hallowed places. Unaware of what is about to happen, I depart from the Mount of Olives. The next morning the *Jerusalem Post* reports that at the time that I left and right in the vicinity, 132 east Jerusalem students and teachers were arrested after a three-and-a-half hour riot at a high school and junior college. The students had blocked one of the roads, and burned tires and large garbage containers, in support of the inmates at Ashkelon Prison who were on a forty-day hunger strike to demand better conditions. The Israeli police, equipped with clubs and gas masks, fired tear gas at the students.

5 The street vendors must still be asleep at this hour. The sun has only just come up and the narrow, dirty alley-ways of the Old City are uncluttered, empty, peaceful. The gate to the courtyard of the church of the Holy Sepulcher is open. A small gathering can be seen resting in the sunlight, waiting for the start of the Good Friday celebrations. They await a small wooden ladder to be passed out the massive wooden doors, and for Wageeh Nasselbeh to open the church. Within minutes the Franciscan procession is making its way to the Chapel of Calvary. Somehow, the pomp and ceremony is quickly lost and the crowds press into the dark, lantern-lit chapel on the second level of this ancient fourth-century church, rebuilt by the Crusaders in the twelfth century. It is lost partly because a bearded Greek Orthodox monk, whose job it is to police the chapel, decides to move back the gathering around the altar on what is believed to be the location of Christ's crucifixion. But standing on a wooden crate among the tall candles and red lanterns, he encounters little success in shouting at the pilgrims, who merely return blank stares and try to shush him, because this is supposed to be a holy place. Frustrated, the monk steps down from the crate and starts to shove people back from the altar. In the meantime, a woman, practically crawling between his legs, makes her way to the little cubby-hole underneath the altar to kiss the hallowed spot where the cross was said to have been. Amazingly, he doesn't notice. Finally, he relents and retreats to a room beyond the chapel. In five or ten minutes, the monk storms back in, this time chasing some enthusiastic pilgrims out of the pulpit-like balcony that gives them a better look at the Good Friday service.

I can't help but suspect the stories about animosity between Latin and Eastern churches here might not be all that far-fetched. Although the Greek Orthodox, Roman Catholics, Armenians, Copts, Syrians, and Ethiopians all share in the church, the Greek

Orthodox Church actually retains a tight control over Christ's tomb and the crucifixion site. Other denominations are permitted access, but the Greeks jealously guard these "holy spots," and make sure those who utilize them remove their fixtures immediately at the end of the service. The Greeks are adamant in protecting their territorial rights from persistent pilgrims who virtually — to their minds — want to overrun these sacred places. At one point on the site of Christ's tomb, a Greek Orthodox priest being shoved by one nagging woman, retaliated with a hard right hook to her head that sent her into a daze. In seconds, police were at the scene to take the woman away. One Londoner, who had made the trip especially for this event, remarked with a smile, "Not exactly a holy moment, is it?"

Outside the doors of the church, various church groups are making their way down the winding streets of the Via Dolorosa. Here the bedlam is far more polite, as cross-carrying groups step aside for others. Off to the sides are the snarling Arab vendors, who in spite of the fact it is Friday, have opened their shops with the hope of someone stepping in to buy anything: a camel whip, bottled Jordan water, postcards, rosaries, olive-wood carvings of the suffering Jesus, whatever.

In the Holy Sepulcher's courtyard, the mid-morning sun is hot. To one side of the entrance, looking quite proud on this day, is a bearded man in a long black cassock. This is Nikipharos Baltatzis, the new superior of the Church of the Holy Sepulcher. In spite of the pushing and shoving — a common practice here — things have moved along smoothly today. At fifteen, Baltatzis didn't know what to make of this ancient church with its formidable ornate chapels of the reverence and devotion people held for its relics. He had come here to enter a Greek Orthodox monastic order. Today he has sorted out that boyhood confusion. Now a priest, a monk and superior of the church, he faces the problem of finding a moment's peace in which to pray in this "holy place" dominated by old widows and elderly men who come here to pray for their families.

As he speaks, I can spot the pilgrims dipping handkerchiefs into the water swirling about the marble slab just inside the entrance of the church, that marks the place where Christ was stripped of his garments. Suddenly, an old woman squeezes Baltatzis' right arm and urges him to open the relic room just beyond his office. I follow Baltatzis into that room where another monk at a long table scribbles down prayer requests and directs pilgrims to place shekels into a wooden donation box. Unlocking the chamber sends the pilgrims into a swarm around the glass cases that protect pieces of the original cross of Christ, chips of John the Baptist's skull and even the left hand of St. Basil from being damaged. The pilgrims furiously run rosaries, crucifixes and religious chains against the cases in an effort for some special intervention or blessing. A macabre scene to a skeptic, but certainly not to these pilgrims who race about the tiny room.

I ask Baltatzis how it was determined which of the three crosses found in the seventh century by St. Helena, Constantine's mother, was that of Christ's crucifixion. I listen incredulously: "A funeral procession was marching past, and they brought out the three crosses that they had found, and touched the first one to the corpse, the second one and then the third, and when they touched the third, the man who was dead, awoke and lived . . . Then they knew."

Baltatzis' greatest hope is for real ecumenism, and for Jerusalem to replace Rome as the "real center of Christianity . . .This is where it all happened, isn't it? It is here to Jerusalem that people come — and they come to get closer to God." Back outside, things are more relaxed. The Israeli guards now lounge in the morning sun with their machine guns at their feet.

6 The Israeli tour guide on the bus is not unlike most: fiercely nationalistic, pragmatic, well-versed in archeology, myths, and legends. And when he can, he stresses the achievements of the Israelis in the desert. He'll point out a highly socialistic and individualistic kibbutz system, where the national government permits small societies to form and to work out their own social and economic destinies. And he'll emphasize that the Palestinian arabs for years squandered any opportunity to transform the desert into an economic oasis. And when I hear this, I get the impression I've just stepped into that age-old controversy, and the line I'm being fed is part of the propaganda that comes with warring societies. At the same time, the guide, a university teacher, seriously disappoints some on the tour — especially the evangelicals — when he declares that according to archeological finds, Jericho's walls had toppled at least 300 years before Joshua ever got there. (The Old Testament account said Joshua marched around the city seven times before the walls ever crumbled.)

The bus rumbles on through Samaria, north along the Jordanian border and past miles and miles of wire fences and armed Israeli camps and check points. Again, the guide is putting the focus on the determination of the Israeli people to make something of their nation: "Ten years ago, there was nothing here but desert . . . Today the Israelis are piping in water and today there is modern agriculture." I can see the fields of dates, tomatoes, grapes, but I also can't fail to notice the occasional Bedouin settlement of mud buildings and tents that cling to the hilly landscape, not unlike the homes they abandoned at Jericho under the threat of Israeli attack. Today Jericho is a ghost town of hundreds of empty mud buildings.

7 Finally at the edge of the sea. I sit in a café. The wind whips around the tables where I rest, surveying the Sea of Galilee. At the self-service cafeteria they sell St. Peter's fish, a white fish found only in this clear, fresh blue lake that reminds me of Lake Muskoka in Ontario. In this area Jesus spent most of his early ministry, and here he was said to have walked on the water with Peter. It is here, too, that Talmudic sages taught and studied. In about a half hour, I head out on the lake (fourteen miles in length and eight miles across) on a boat that crosses over to Capernaum where stand the ruins of a white limestone synagogue in which Christ may have taught. Nearby is Tabgha, where the miracle of the loaves and fishes took place. Farther down the road is the Mount of Beatitudes where Jesus preached the Sermon on the Mount. As we drive through the afternoon sun, I see the shepherds moving their flocks homeward.

8 Easter Sunday morning. 6:30 a.m. in the Church of the Holy Sepulcher. For the Roman Catholics, it is Easter. For the Greek Orthodox and many others of the Eastern Rite, it is Palm Sunday. The Franciscans, carrying candles and incense, and the bishop wearing the miter, march into the room holding the tomb of Christ, and the crowds are here again surrounding the make-shift altar set up in front of the entrance to the tomb. But such peacefulness can't exist here. Somewhere in the Church, the Greek Orthodox monks are celebrating Palm Sunday, and their music, combined with the chanting of the Egyptians who are behind the tomb area, creates a senseless din in the resonant halls of this holy place.

Equally disruptive are three or four other groups, waving palms, marching on the outskirts of the Roman Catholic mass. There is also the usual amount of pushing and shoving, especially when the mass comes to an end. The tourists yearn to see the empty tomb, and to pray before it, but the Greek Orthodox demand the Roman Catholics remove all the liturgical trappings they have brought to carry on the mass. This is evident as the organizers for both denominations are suddenly embroiled in a bitter fight immediately in front of the tomb. Cane carrying women are shoved aside in some instances. It's an ugly scene.

Nasselbeh, the Muslim who holds the key to the Holy Sepulcher, stands in the sunny courtyard outside. He looks around and concludes that Israel can't possibly untangle itself from such disparities. "But my hope is that there'll be peace . . . After all, we all have the same God, don't we?"

RABBI MEIR KAHANE
1
FOUNDER OF THE JEWISH DEFENSE LEAGUE

He spoke of fear. He spoke of the power of words. He spoke of intimidation, ascendency of thought, domination — essentially whatever it took to press the point home.

The first thing that struck me about Rabbi Meir Kahane was his passion, his obsession with ideas. It didn't surprise me because I had heard how he was the kind of man who approved of his followers daubing swastikas and smearing excrement on the buildings of enemies. When I first met this radical Jewish leader in 1982, he told me his adherents — members of the Israeli "Kach," a nationalist movement consisting of extremist vigilante squads — were battling to drive out Palestinians from the occupied West Bank and East Jerusalem. He couldn't apologize for it — it was his mission. It was what he set out to accomplish.

Today, developments in Israel accommodating the Palestinians would have sent Kahane raving. In November 1990, the rabbi was gunned down in a New York hotel by an Egyptian assailant. His followers continue to keep alive his mission, but somehow the group has lost its voice, its significance. At times, its members seem desperate, shrill, grave. While Kahane may have raged against his enemies, and while he may have offered nothing but obstreperous views, there was pride in how he pitched his ideas, how he carried himself. Perhaps it was authority. Dignity of a twisted sort, nonetheless, a bearing that demonstrated he knew what he was talking about. Today, slogans have replaced the hypnotic grasp Kahane once had.

I met Kahane in Detroit. He had planned to see me on the Canadian side, but because of his deportation to the USA in 1971, he was denied entry to Canada. He had been turned back on his way to Ottawa where he intended to protest the visit of then Soviet Premier Alexei Kosygin because of the persecution of Jews in Russia. Kahane had also been barred from going into England and Holland. He believed he was "a marked man." That predicament, however, didn't rankle him. He had other plans up his sleeve.

The Brooklyn-born Kahane, founder of the Jewish Defense League, was forty-nine when I interviewed him. He was fresh from his release from prison in Israel for holding on in the Sinai, defending those actions that had brought him international attention. He declared that Israel should never have given up the Sinai. He regarded the treaty as military and political suicide, and pointed out that Egypt had violated it. Kahane also emphasized that the plan was nothing more than a diplomatic maneuver on the part of Egypt to obtain what it had failed to take during the Yom Kippur sneak attack of 1973. As leader of the Jewish Defense League, the right-wing thinker had been a thorn in the side of the Begin Government in Israel. When his followers sealed themselves in a bunker and threatened to commit suicide in protest of the plan to restore these lands to Arab control, their leader rushed to join them in Yamit in the Sinai Peninsula, but with the view to persuade them not to take such drastic action.

Though Kahane would have liked to see an end to hostilities with Egypt, he didn't think withdrawal from the Sinai, as part of the 1979 Camp David agreement, was the means to that end. He would have rather continued the battle. Indeed, he did, both in words and deeds. Kahane never thwarted his followers from wrecking cars belonging to Arabs and UN personnel. These squads also broke into homes and and beat up residents. In Kahane's mind, it was war. Guerrilla warfare, open and honest. Necessary. Justified.

Author of more than a half dozen books, a graduate of New York Law School, and holder of a degree in International Law and Relations from New York University, Kahane has been surrounded by controversy since the 1960s. His life seemed destined for what the *Washington Post* writer described as "confrontational, sometimes bigoted." In 1947, at the age of fifteen, he was arrested for throwing rocks at a limousine carrying the visiting British foreign minister. It was part of a protest against the British occupation of Palestine. Early in his life, Kahane joined the Zionist youth group Betar and traveled to the Catskill mountains where he underwent ideological and military training. He looked up to his father's friend, Zev Jabotinsky, founder of the revisionist Zionist movement. It was after he had earned his degrees that

Kahane changed his name to Meir. His first job after graduating from rabbinical school was as an Orthodox rabbi in Queens, New York. There he founded the Jewish Defense League in 1968, originally with the aim of lending help to elderly Jews who were being mugged on the streets in the city. He exhorted Jews in New York to arm themselves. The slogan for the Jewish Defense League became: "Every Jew a .22." For a time Kahane was the editor of the Jewish Press in New York.

It wasn't long before the Jewish Defense League broadened its scope to combat anti-semitism, and later to champion the cause of transforming Israel into a purely Jewish state. In those early days Kahane began to flag attention to the treatment of Soviet Jews; after his death Jewish leadership acknowledged debt to the slain leader for having raised the issue.

In 1971, Kahane was arrested again and convicted in New York for making bombs. He fled the country, and settled in Israel. In 1975, he was brought back to the USA to face trial and serve a year in federal prison for parole violations. But prison didn't bother Kahane. Over the years because of the Kach, which he formed in Israel, he was in and out of jail so many times, he lost count. He indulged himself totally in politics and war. He ran three times for the Knesset or parliament in Israel and finally won a seat in 1984 with 26,000 votes. In 1988, however, the Israeli Supreme Court barred him seeking re-election, ruling that the Kach leader was racist.

The message he brought was the same everywhere — Israel should annex the Sinai and West Bank and settle both with Jews. Jews everywhere ought to return to Israel — not only because it was their Biblical obligation, but also because the world was plummeting straight ahead into yet another Holocaust, worse than what took place during the Second World War. Kahane crisscrossed the Atlantic, accepting speaking engagements in the USA, and raising money for his causes, where he gathered up to more than $50,000 at a time. He would go anywhere to speak in large halls or even in private homes. He told me some couldn't understand devotion. He insisted it wasn't a *political* act in the normal sense — it was a religious commitment.

Kahane was a renegade to many Jews. In 1990, Richard Cohen, then president of the Conference of Presidents of Major American Jewish Organizations, compared Kahane to Malcolm X, the slain Black nationalist. What the radical leader declared at meetings, press conferences, and in private homes offended whole sectors of the Jewish population. They admired him, but feared him. When he was elected finally to the Knesset, President Chaim Herzog was so incensed that he refused to carry out the customary practice of shaking the hand of the new parliamentary member. To make matters worse for Kahane, the parliament passed laws to prevent his re-election, including one that specifically prohibited anyone with a dual nationality to run for a seat.

But in private Kahane sounded reasonable, not at all inflammatory. He spoke in a quiet voice, reiterating themes of hundreds of talks, speeches, and writings. He pointed out that to be Jewish was "a wonderful thing — Jews are a special and chosen people of God." To permit Jews to be beaten and oppressed was "an abomination and a desecration of the name of God." As Kahane stressed, "We are obliged to help each and every Jew by commandment. When all else fails, we are allowed and obligated to use any means — including violence."

Some Jews might not quibble with that, but talk of violence rarely has won wide support from Jewish communities elsewhere. In Canada, for example, there was stiff opposition to Kahane's public appearance. The Canadian Jewish Congress, according to the religious leader, preferred to forget he ever existed. "The thing that I saw frightens Jewish leaders," acknowledged Kahane, who encountered paranoiac Jewish leaders "wrapped up in fear over what effect these statements or actions will have on the general public, or to put it bluntly, on the gentiles." Especially when interpreting the Talmud as telling Jews to strike before being stricken. Kahane stressed that Jews ought to use violence against violence. For that reason, he argued, the war in the Middle East was justified. So were the efforts of his people to take what he considered to be "holy Jewish lands."

The reaction of Jews in North America was one of confusion, even revulsion. To them worse still was Kahane's forecasting the next Holocaust would be spawned in North America. But the Jewish leader shrugged at the reaction. He described Jewish leaders in Canada and the USA as being "small people with small minds — they're not really *bad* people, they're just *tiny* people who have to grapple with gigantic problems and they're not up to it. They just don't have the vision or the courage." Most Jewish leaders, Kahane complained, came from a higher social and economic level, and therefore, were out of touch with what people really thought about Jews. "Now, if you want to know what people really think about Jews you have to go into a bar . . . That's where people talk, and as the whisky goes in, the words come out." The Jewish Defense League to Kahane was "the grass roots movement" buttressed by lower/middle class Jews. "We're in intimate contact with anti-semitism."

Early on, Kahane prophesied that North America would be plunged into economic and social woes, to the degree that there would be a dramatic "loss of faith" and "a growth of cynicism" in the system. Watergate was evidence of this. So was the civil rights movement. These, coupled with a slumping economy, will "pave the way for an extremist to take over," Kahane predicted. It hasn't happened yet. But some might argue that a backlash has occurred. Kahane had indicated that such a political environment would send people in search for scapegoats, and Jews have traditionally been the target. This fact, he concluded, made it all the more imperative for Jews to return to Israel and settle there.

Kahane reiterated it was difficult for the Western press to grapple and come to terms with this philosophy. They saw it more in "political" terms, whereas he interpreted his actions as those of someone engaged in a "Holy War." He insisted his views were theologically rooted and his fight was one of redemption. "The key to redemption of the Jewish people," Kahane conjectured, "is a choice between the sanctification of God's name or the desecration of God's name. You sanctify God's name by the belief that he controls the world, and that by our faith and trust we need not fear what the world says. . . . Therefore we should go and do what we have to. If not, we bring on ourselves another holocaust, this time far, far worse. That's the key to it." Most rabbis, Kahane contended, lacked "courage" to assert this. The decision to forfeit the boundaries in Israel was fuelled by what the USA suggests. "In that lies the total lack of faith and belief that there is a God in Israel who controls the world. That lack of faith will cost us dearly."

Violence against violence may not appear to be the answer, Kahane told me, but the fact is that for 2,000 years Jews preferred pacifism. The result? "Crusades, inquisitions, holocausts big and small!" The Jewish vision, Kahane pointed out, was that nations should "beat swords with plowshares — that's a great dream, but if my enemy has a sword, I don't want a plowshare." He maintained the Talmud was clear on this: "It tells us, 'If one comes to slay you, slay him first,' and that to me is just plain logic." The idea of martyrdom was never integral to Judaism. "There's no commandment to be trampled upon and to be killed. Where does it say that? Is it ethical to be killed? No, it isn't ethical. It's insane to let yourself to killed. Take a look at the Bible. . . . Moses killed an Egyptian who was beating a Jew and David went to war. You pick up a Bible — it's all there."

Unfortunately, Kahane said, the average Jew was ignorant of his own roots. He believed it was rare if they even read the Bible. "The average Jewish leader in Canada or anywhere in North America," he maintained, "doesn't know anything about Judaism." He added, "Our sickness is ignorance. We wrote the Bible and the Baptists study it. Well, I know my Bible, and I studied it, and I know what's in it, and I know when Abraham's nephew, Lot, was kidnapped, he went to war. He didn't sit and say psalms. Of course, Jews have got to pray and Jews have got to have faith, and before you go out to battle, you have to pray because only He wins battles for you. But then you have to go out!" Kahane cannot countenance the philosophy of non-orthodox Jews. He defined them as Jews "by emotion . . . They come from orthodox homes, and they remember the Sabbath. There's a nostalgia . . . But if you stopped the average non-Orthodox Jew, and asked him what it meant to be a Jew in 25,000 words or more, he probably wouldn't be able to tell you. Why? Because he's a Jew by emotion." In effect, Kahane added, "If someone is not a religious Jew and insists upon staying Jewish, he's really being a racist."

He scoffed at those who reason that they can't just uproot, leave their jobs and homes in North America, and settle into a new life in the Holy Land. It could bring hardship and chaos to their lives. Kahane snarled, "It *is* a Biblical commandment for Jews to live in Israel. You don't stop and make deals with the commandment. If it is true, too, that there is only a dark and terrible future in this country for Jews, then it makes sense to go there. If I were in a home on fire, and if I had no other home to go to, I wouldn't sit in that house on the theory that I have no other house to go to. Finally, it's a question of faith. If you do the difficult and dangerous things that God wants, it'll work out. You'll go there and work hard."

It was no idle talk on the part of Kahane. He spoke with conviction, a trace of anger, even a little out of fear, consternation. He knew his own life was at stake. Indeed, the day before his assassination, the Jewish extremist leader warned Danny Tadmore's *Voice of Israel* radio program that he anticipated assassination. He foretold that if it occurred, it would be at the hands of a Jew, not an Arab. He told the radio host, "I don't have a problem with the Arabs. I have a problem with the Jews. And if somebody's ever going to kill me, it's going to be a Jew, not an Arab." He was wrong of course. It was an Arab. Tadmore also reported that Kahane had been "fatalistic" about assassination. "If you're a religious Jew everything is pre-ordained."

At Kahane's funeral in New York, some 20,000 Israelis turned out. Today, Kach, the organization he had started, only has seventy-five to 100 hard-core activists. There may be another 1000 in Israel. Nonetheless, according to Dov Goldstein, a Maariv newspaper columnist who was quoted by a Toronto newspaper, "It's an open secret . . . that in the hearts of many ordinary Israeli citizens hides a not-so-little Kahane."

TERRY WAITE
2
HOSTAGE OF WARRING FAITHS

In November 1993, when Terry Waite was sitting at a book-signing table in Ottawa, he looked up to catch the grinning face of a Canadian general who had helped to win his freedom. Without batting an eye, the steel-gray bearded Englishman remarked, "Oh, it's lovely to see you." He then clasped Butch Waldrum's hand warmly. The Canadian brigadier-general had just retired, and had decided to come down to see Waite. Again, the Englishman remarked, "Simply lovely. I really do want to have a chat with you." The two spoke briefly, and made a breakfast date. As Waldrum started to turn away, the tall, imposing Waite smiled and waved: "Thanks for everything."

While the two may never have met until that day in Ottawa, Waldrum spent fifteen months in the shadowy underworld of the Middle East working in a multi-national effort that led to the release of Western hostages in Beirut, including Terry Waite. It had involved some questionable exchanges of prisoners — and even dead bodies — between Israel and its Arab neighbors. Waldrum told a reporter that day in Ottawa that his handshake with Waite "was worth all the work . . . The fifteen months got paid off in two seconds at that table."

It wasn't the first time Terry Waite had been to Canada. I remember him at a meeting in Mississagua of the heads of the Anglican Church from the around the world. Waite had accompanied the Archbishop of Canterbury, Robert Runcie, to Toronto. That was 1986. When it was learned that Waite, considered one of the best negotiators of hostages in the Middle East, having engineered the release of prisoners in Iran and Libya, was in attendance, there was a flurry of excitement. All the media wanted to talk to him. But we were told to stay away. We were advised he didn't care to meet with anyone. This tall, commanding personality stalked the hallways, rarely smiling, usually pushing past others. "He won't talk to you, and if you do want to speak with him, you'll have to see me first." The instructions were issued from an Irishman who was handling all the press interviews for the Archbishop of Canterbury, Robert Runcie. But the man he was referring to was Terry Waite, the Anglican Church leader's special envoy. I remember how infuriated this press secretary was when I rushed out ahead of the archbishop during one session and barricaded the washroom door. My hunch was that he was going there for a break. When he moved to the right to get past me, I stopped him dead in his tracks. "Excuse me, I have a question." He was so taken aback by my boldness that he finally just smiled, and remarked, "This is an unusual spot for the press to ask a question . . . But I guess I have no choice but to answer it, or try to answer it, if I wish to go the loo." I can't remember what it was that I wanted to know. But I managed to detain him at the door to the washroom for a few moments.

The press secretary was incensed. He stammered and complained that I had overstepped my boundaries. After a while, his whining could no longer be taken seriously. Especially after we began to see a different Terry Waite emerge from the sessions. It was particularly funny one day when he was sharing a press conference with Runcie. The head of the Church of England was fending off questions of relations with the Catholic Church when suddenly a nearby telephone interrupted the proceedings. Waite picked it up dutifully, and without batting an eye, quipped, "It's the Pope for you!" The response seemed to lighten the mood and ease the tensions. The next day a picture of the day appeared on the front page of *The Toronto Star*. It was also included in Waite's autobiography, *Taken In Trust*, published in 1993.

The truth was that Waite's personality may not have invited interruption, but as the days wore on, this side of him began to show. Less serious, mischievous. He was bored by the events. One afternoon, when I was working away at a laptop computer, a small Tandy, he suddenly loomed over my shoulder. When I peered up, there was Waite staring down. "Isn't that something?" he remarked, pointing to the computer. He was amazed at its compactness. "Do you like working on those?" I told him I did. He then asked, "Can you show me? May I try?" He moved a chair next to mine, and took the computer from me and placed it on his lap. I gave me him some elementary directions. He typed his name. He was delighted. "How much is something like this?" I told him I wasn't sure, but he could pick one up at a Radio Shack store in Toronto. Later that day, he returned, waving a Radio Shack flyer. "They're *very* reasonable, aren't they?" he asked. Without waiting for a response, he went on, "I'm going to get one of these." At that point, Runcie strolled into the room. "You should look at these," he informed the archbishop, pointing to the laptop I was using. But the head of the Church of England appeared detached, weary. "Yes." That was all. Waite laughed heartily, perhaps understanding his boss' decided lack of interest in new technology. "We should pick up a few before going back, don't you think?" The archbishop didn't disagree. He just walked away.

When the press finally got to sit down with Waite, he balked at nothing. He was loquacious, frank, candid. He was keen to talk about anything. He agreed his height perhaps had something to do with his success in negotiating in the Middle East. "I use it to my advantage." And smiled. Afraid? Indeed, his work wasn't to be taken lightly. He knew he took risks, always did. At this point in Waite's life, he seemed to skirt past the dangers that befell others. He believed it was because he could be trusted. He represented not a country, or political position, but rather a church that sought justice. Little did he realize that less than a year later, he'd be kidnapped on a trip to Beirut. He was taken January 20, 1987. He was held hostage until November 18, 1991. In 1993, his autobiography about that ordeal, and about his childhood years and professional life leading up to that event, was published. It was a book that he never could have envisioned when he was in Toronto. While in prison — some 1,763 days — he penned the book in his head, revealing the inner strengths that carried him through that ordeal.

In Mississauga in 1986, such thoughts about inner strengths, or being a hostage himself, were preposterous. Waite spoke about the nature of hostage taking, maintaining that it was a manifestation of something much deeper, that it pointed to a disorder in the world that was something that North Americans or Europeans might not be able to comprehend. Certainly the world had to learn how to deal with terrorism, but the real challenge was finding its root cause. Waite told a news conference that, in effect, the world had permitted international terrorism to proliferate. "People in the Palestinian refugee camps have been there for years," he said, "and these are breeding grounds for violence and terrorism."

His feeling at that point was that terrorism wasn't going to come to an end over night. In retrospect, Waite was right. On his next visit to Canada, I wasn't able to see him, but I caught interviews in papers and on television wherever he went. Controversy surrounded him. Excerpts from a new book about the Lebanese hostages quoted Runcie, who has since stepped down as the Archbishop of Canterbury, as stating he felt Terry Waite had misled him and compromised his own status as a negotiator for the church. *The Sunday Telegraph* also quoted Runcie as saying, "We both agreed that he would not be working for the church once the (last) Beirut trip had been completed." The newspaper was publishing excerpts from Con Coughlin's *Hostages:The Complete Story of the Lebanon Captives.* The former spiritual leader of the Church of England was further quoted as saying Waite was genuinely committed to helping. Runcie reportedly accepted blame for not keeping better track of Waite. "He did not feel inclined to let me know what he . . . was up to," the church leader maintained.

Waite heard reports about the new book, and Runcie's statements, when he was in Lexington, Kentucky for a speaking engagement, but told the press that he doubted its accuracy. On the other hand, he admitted withholding information about death threats because he thought the church leader would pressure him to stay away from Lebanon. He denied intentionally misleading the archbishop about his work. Runcie believed Waite to be a significant factor in the release of Benjamin Weir, Lawrence Jenco, and David Jacobsen. "In those circumstances I could hardly tell him to stop working for the release of the other American hostages . . . He never told me he had been ordered out of Beirut by the kidnappers," Runcie said. The excerpts claimed that Waite's mission was "dealt a mortal blow" in December 1985 when, as he was trying to secure the release of six Americans held hostage in Beirut, the kidnappers gave him twenty-four hours to leave the city or die. "But even though Waite's direct line to the kidnappers had been cut, in public he continued to give the impression that his mission was continuing and that he was directly involved in the release of the hostages, even though in reality, each release was preceded by Lt. Col. Oliver North's arms shipments to Tehran," the excerpts said. "(Waite's) love of publicity and lack of sophistication about what was being worked on him by the Americans were the cause of all his difficulties," the former archbishop was quoted as saying.

During his own book tour, Waite was clearly irritated by the accusations, especially those that labeled him as a CIA agent. He felt impotent defending himself. He felt his book had said it all. He told the media that although he would never want to relive those years in captivity, he still didn't regard them as "wasted years." In an article in *The Toronto Star*, Mike McAteer, religion editor for the paper, found a more resigned, reflective Waite. The former hostage agreed that his attitude was no longer one of taking things for granted. He reiterated that his life had been on the line, and that it caused him to run over his life, its biases, joys, and emotions. For one thing, he began to doubt his own faith. "Doubt is very much a part of faith," he pointed out. "There is a need for questioning. It's an honest way to grow and develop, otherwise there is a tendency to layer over the experience with religious language. Which might be very fine but it is covering over."

Waite also spoke about faith as "common to all human beings . . . It seems to me one of the purposes of religion is to provide a set of symbols by which your faith is enabled to be channeled and used for creative ends. It's when you lose hope and when you feel there is nothing worth surviving for that you begin to die," he added. "In my case, I was fortunate to have Christian faith because it provided me with a frame of reference."

ARCHBISHOP ROBERT EAMES
3
PEACEMAKER IN NORTHERN IRELAND

He walked into an empty press room, surveyed the seats, then settled down in one of the chairs. It was the end of a long evening of conferences. But while his colleagues were making their way to their rooms, he just wanted to sit and talk. He had found someone, who happened to be the only other person in the room, and just wanted to slouch in a chair and reminisce. That's what he did, and his voice wasn't tiring to listen to. It had a smooth, unctuous tone, the kind to ease troubles and win hearts. And when you heard him, you were sure that's why he became a priest — that he had the right voice to go with the role. And you were sure that's why he was where he was in the midst of trouble because a lot of talk was needed to settle things down.

The man was Archbishop Robert Eames, spiritual head of more than 450,000 Anglicans who belong to the Church of Ireland, most of whom live in Northern Ireland. He has a broad, handsome face. The day I met him in 1986 at meetings of the heads of the Anglican Consultative Council in Mississauga, Ontario, he wore a blue pin-stripe suit that looked stunning against the traditional lavender blouse. Meticulous, good-natured, with a decisive air about him, he was someone in command, organized. And when he stopped to speak to someone, his eyes didn't rove. He looked at them intently, listened closely.

Eames, whose early years as a priest were spent in Belfast where he was born in 1937, preferred to talk about anything but trouble and confrontations. In fact, I remember how he would head you off immediately by saying, "Let me ask you some questions." And he wanted to know all there was to know about word processors, especially the portables that reporters carried about with them to meetings. He said one of his aides wanted to buy one while in Canada.

And before you could get in a question about his homeland, Eames would throw back his head, stare at the ceiling and begin talking. Eventually the conversation made its way around to his fascination and friendship with the Kennedys. He recounted once walking into Ted Kennedy's office, how he found his eyes following a path of family pictures — mostly joyous — across one wall until the pictures ended with the shocking photograph recording the assassination of Ted's brother, President John F. Kennedy. It brought Eames back in touch with what he had confronted all his life: the violence that had snatched away the lives of dozens of people he'd known over the years.

Eames, called "Robin" by friends, had been primate of the Church of Ireland for only a few months when I met him. He had been a clergyman since 1963, but rose quickly in the Irish church — being appointed Bishop of Derry and Raphoe in 1975 and Bishop of Down and Drumore in 1980. He was then elevated to Archbishop of Armagh and primate of All Ireland and Metropolitan. Today Eames continues to play a leading role in the life of the worldwide Anglican Communion. He was appointed Chairman of the Archbishop of Canterbury's Commission on Communion and Women in the Episcopate, and in 1991 presided at the International Anglican Doctrinal and Theological Consultation in the USA at the request of the Archbishop of Canterbury.

Eames may be more down to earth than many others in the English Church. He views himself as "open" to people, eager to meet and share life stories. Indeed, in a book entitled *Believing Bishops* by Simon Lee and Peter Stanford, published by Faber and Faber, Eames maintained that when he was elevated to primate of the Church of Ireland, he recognized he couldn't be "an austere primate figure." Rather, he saw himself as one "amongst (his) people, giving them a lead." It is not uncommon for Eames to declare that his door is "always open," or to drop what he's doing and invite you in for tea. During the debate over women's ordination, he was besieged by media from around the world who demanded an explanation to his report on the issue. As Lee and Stanford related, Eames informed the press to stop by any time. He remarked good-naturedly, "We can eat, drink, and sleep women priests." Part of his success has been due to being both "a good talker," and a "good listener." He is someone who fancies a good yarn, and believes this is a gift to any clergyman, for it permits them to get to the heart of problems in parishioners' lives.

That's why, ultimately, he won't back away from the inevitable questions about the violence plaguing his own country. He agreed it was preposterous trying to "sell" another image when his countrymen were murdering one another. He acknowledged there was really no exaggeration to the state of affairs one reads of in the papers. "It's all true, and you don't get used to it, not really . . . I mean you hear about it, and if it doesn't happen to you, it may not hurt as much, but you still *feel* it, somewhere, deep down. I mean these are my countrymen. They're Christians. They're relatives. They're people, ordinary people, not bad people." Eames himself claimed to have officiated at funerals of some fifty-nine murder victims, all members of the Irish church. He revealed to Lee and Stanford, "You cannot be in close pastoral touch with people like that without realizing the price in purely human, personal terms."

Regarded as "the peacemaker" in his war-ravaged country, Eames maintained he wasn't concerned with politics — only the welfare of his people. He isn't as hard line as many Northern Protestants who dig in and won't compromise or even tolerate Roman Catholics. As leader of his church, Eames has forged an easy coexistence with the Latin church. As Lee and Stanford stated in their book, this Anglican bishop gravitated toward a pluralism in ideas and concepts, and this may account for his own province standing as "a showpiece of cohesiveness." The love for his country and its people is undeniable and sincere. A few years ago, Eames wrote *Chains To Be Broken: A Personal Reflection on Northern Ireland and Its People*. He prays for and believes in a solution to the violence, the hatred, the divisiveness. If he didn't, how could he justify believing in God?

When Eames arrived in Canada to attend the Mississauga meeting of Anglican primates from around the world, he dazzled the media. He sat in an empty meeting room, put his feet up on a chair, and leaned back to tell reporters that when he looked at the two Irelands, he saw signs of peace. "It *is* possible," he said confidently. Though it seemed unrealistic because of the intense hatred between Catholics and Protestants, there still existed a sincere desire among all churchmen to work together on specific issues, such as nuclear arms, the environment and the poor. Miraculously, these two fiercely divided people — Catholics and Protestants — have "worked together" at raising funds or joining in protests against the superpowers' drive to destroy the world through nuclear arms.

Eames described the social, political and religious worlds of the two Irelands as "a cauldron," but when it came to the poor, the Irish were the most generous givers in the British Isles. This was proven, he said, by the money raised for Ethiopia. But divisions between Roman Catholics and Protestants are far from superficial. These people, Eames said, *feel* their divisions. While there may be a "longing for greater co-operation," political pressures upon these two groups make it difficult "to bridge the divide . . . and that's what it is: a divide." Ireland, explained Eames, is "a story of two communities — the RC minority in Northern Ireland and the Protestant minority in the whole of Ireland." The irony is that while North Americans might describe the work on nuclear arms, the environment, or Christian aid as "issues of peace and justice," the Irish regard it merely as an opportunity for the churches to share Christian charity. Unfortunately for the Irish, "peace and justice" are "tainted" by political party beliefs, maintained Eames. Most Protestants in Ireland are "unionists" and associate with the variety of political parties seeking ties to Great Britain. Catholics on the other hand associate with the "nationalist" parties. "Justice and peace for you and me sitting here in Canada are basic concepts for the Christian family, but in Northern Ireland, they take on a 'party/political' label . . . A Roman Catholic will talk about justice and peace in terms of the problems he feels — he feels alienated from the state, and wants more justice . . . He wants more peace . . . And a Protestant will say, 'Well, you're getting justice, you're getting peace, but you're the one upsetting it.'"

The history behind the dispute dates back to the era when Protestant England conquered Catholic Ireland. Catholics were not permitted to own land, or to vote or hold political office. Catholic priests caught worshipping were hanged. Although the decree against Catholics was suspended, Catholics found themselves powerless. An uprising in 1921 resulted in Catholics seizing power and Ireland becoming independent. Protestants in the north refused to bow to this and sought independence from those in the south. This led to the formation of two countries, with the northern half remaining British soil. While there was little violence from the 1920s to the 1960s, dissatisfied Catholics in Northern Ireland — the minority — organized marches and protests. They claimed the Protestants were still very much in control, and kept a tight hold on jobs, housing and political power. Naturally, this opened up old wounds that still festered between Catholics and Protestants. Soon war became a reality once more in Ireland. So did the counter-terrorist army, the Irish Republican Army (IRA). Britain, seeking to maintain the peace, dispatched troops to keep the two religious factions apart.

Eames has found it "incredibly difficult" to explain the nuances of the religious and political strife in his country as much as he felt he couldn't hold back from speaking his mind. The situation differed from that of South Africa where churchmen were "restrained" in speaking their mind. "I don't feel like that — I don't feel restrained at all," Eames said. He admitted the expression "Words Can Kill" took on real significance in the Irish situation. He knew two who died because they were branded by others as "enemies." The unfortunate thing was that both victims were innocent of the charges against them. The Irish archbishop pointed out that the process leading to their violent deaths began with "inflammatory words."

Eames pointed out how difficult it was to leave Ireland and try to forget about what's taking place there: "You cannot shake that off crossing the Atlantic." No matter how "desk bound" a clergyman may be, "It's not easy — you can't shake off what's happening." Whenever Eames spoke of the situation, he did so passionately. His eyes flashed, but there was a curious patience in his voice that could not be construed as resignation. He couldn't envision giving up, or abandoning himself to the situation. That was impossible, since it was always there, like a slap in the face.

While some in the church try to ignore the contentious issues of faith or theology, like the ordination of women, Eames finds it awkward to explain faith in a world dominated by violence. "Just about anything but what's happening here would be better to talk about."

Nonetheless with the subject of his own homeland and the deep divisions between the Protestants — his own people — and Roman Catholics, Eames rarely holds back. It's a part of his role. It's expected of him. It's what it means to be a Christian in Ireland. Eames has come to realize it encompasses a political awareness. It means taking sides, holding opinions, fighting for causes that often put him, and the church, in precarious positions. What bothered him was the Anglo-Irish Accord, aimed at the unification of Ireland. He won't come out "totally for or totally against the accord."

The Church of Ireland, Eames stressed, has officially "welcomed any move that will increase, encourage and stabilize and bring about reconciliation." It has also urged the Irish to put aside their differences and give "serious consideration" to the accord. "You see," said Eames, "there were those who had their minds made up about it even before the ink was dry . . . The reason was that many Protestants in Northern Ireland see any involvement by the Irish republic government as a step toward a united Ireland, something to which they're totally opposed."

While Eames supported his own church's statement that Irish Protestants should open themselves up to reconciliation, he maintained, "Now let me say a word in defense of those who feel threatened by the accord: they've had sixteen years of continued violence. That violence has been directed against security forces, the majority of whom would be Protestants. Secondly, it has been directed against Protestant families in isolated areas. Now, the overt purpose of terrorist organizations of the sort that I mention is to have a united Ireland. If you are in a position of constant threat you will not allow yourself psychologically to distinguish too easily between one method of achieving that and another: namely, violence or constitutional means . . ." Eames stated that although the accord's writers sought a means of reconciliation, the reality was far from it. The objective was to eliminate the alienation felt by the minority, or the Catholics, in Northern Ireland by giving them "a sovereign voice" through an inter-governmental conference. There, grievances by the minority could be aired.

"In all honesty, the reaction to the Anglo-Irish agreement among the vast majority of the Protestants in Northern Ireland . . . has been so violent that the job of reconciliation is at this moment very difficult." Ironically, the Irish archbishop pointed out, the Protestant majority feels alienated. "Before," Eames said, "you had the minority — the Catholics — talking of alienation . . . Now you have the very dangerous and potentially disastrous situation where a majority say the accord has alienated them." The Anglican archbishop feared that "the constitutional politicians" were being "bypassed by the men of violence."

The role of the church should be that of "an enabler," or agent in moving people back to talking to one another. He acknowledged this would be difficult, especially when those in his own church couldn't agree about the proposed accord. "I am often asked then whether I represent a church that is weak — because we are divided on this issue . . . My answer is, 'No, it's not . . . When I speak to the British prime minister or to party political leaders, I can represent so many aspects of the problem . . .'" Eames insisted it wasn't a matter of his church waffling on the issues, but rather striving to understand all sides: "The doors are opening and we're going through those doors and we're introducing politicians to each other . . . and we're doing what I believe is the God-given job of the church — namely being the enabler, to get people to talk together. I believe the answer to Ireland is discussions, dialogue and trust."

BISHOP K.H. TING
4
ARCHITECT OF THE NEW CHINESE CHURCH

It was nearly 10:00 p.m. His colleagues were still lolling about the coffee trolley outside the chapel. He wasn't interested in talk after a day-long session of debates and negotiations over church issues that really had little effect upon his own church. But that wasn't the point for China's Protestant church leader who was then seventy years old. He merely yearned for the peace of that small bedroom in the retreat house where he could ease himself into silence, perhaps read a book, perhaps just lie there. Just a few moments way from finding that peace, he could be seen in pajamas racing down the long hallway to the bathroom, dodging colleagues in their liturgical lavender shirts and dark suits.

This was Bishop K. H. Ting. He arrived in Canada in 1986 for a meeting with the heads of the Anglican church from around the world. At the time, he headed the China Christian Council, an umbrella organization that in the 1980s became the newest denomination in China, finally and officially eclipsing all the scattered Protestant churches that have existed there for a century and a half. In effect, it left the Roman Catholics as the only other Christian church in the country.

When I met Ting in 1986, in some ways he seemed really out of place at the meetings of Anglican church leaders from around the world, who assembled in the idyllic Oblate retreat house near Port Credit, Ontario. While still considered a bishop, and wearing the traditional Anglican clerical colors, his connection to the Anglican Church was rather tenuous, for the church no longer formally existed in mainland China. Moreover, Ting was not the Anglican primate. Nevertheless, the quiet, soft-spoken man had come to Canada at the personal invitation of the Archbishop of Canterbury, who, perhaps, viewed him as one of the architects of a new church in that country. Ting's presence didn't go unnoticed, and it wasn't so much from what he had to say, for little of it concerned himself or his country. It was more in his manner, which was peaceful, contemplative, cheerful. He didn't go unnoticed, either, because of what he represented. He had witnessed the birth of vital ecumenism at the grass roots level, where factions of Christian churches began to speak as one voice about the same

God, something that has yet to occur in North America. And Ting knew something of North America. It was after the Second World War that he had been invited to Canada — to Toronto specifically — to take over the leadership of the Student Christian Movement. He had also been back to Canada several times since then, where he had witnessed firsthand the efforts of Anglicans to reconcile themselves with the rest of the Christian community.

Ting also knew why ecumenism had worked in his own country. It wasn't entirely the result of a sincere effort on the part of denominations to appreciate each other. In truth, the church had its back to the wall. There were forces at play that made the church come to terms with itself, and the bottom line became survival. In spite of that, there was also a willingness to understand God in "Chinese" terms. Ting explained that unless people had some intimate knowledge of his country, they were not going to understand that. Essentially, the Chinese have always resisted the imposition of a Western religion upon its people. Only since the church has had to function as "a Chinese church," and only since it started to adapt itself to Chinese culture, has it begun to flourish.

Surprisingly absent from Ting's voice was the pride or conviction that so often can accompany the details of such success. With Ting, there may have been pride in the kind of Christianity that existed in China, and he may have been a man of conviction, but he wasn't about to overwhelm you with how well his church had managed to cope and stay alive. He sat, Buddha-like, in a corner chair, and merely stated the facts in a flat, small, monotone voice. The only emotion was a slight trace of smile on his broad, tanned face, about the absurdity of life itself, its political dimensions, its theological equations. There was also this tremendous sense of peace that filled the room. He was at peace with himself, his surroundings, new friends. Behind his words, however, were the veritable struggles of his church. He related them freely. The first problems arose when the war in Korea resulted in the end of Western missionary work in China. Many Western churches no longer could dispatch funds into the country. The churches, now cut off from the Western headquarters of their denominations, struggled to survive financially. What emerged was "The Three Self Movement," where the churches began to transform themselves into institutions that would become "self-governing, self-supporting and self-propagating."

This movement pushed the Christian church into "a post-denominational state" where the old denominations — such as Anglicanism — no longer existed as formal entities. Anglican priests continued to work in their own churches and refer to themselves as Anglicans, but, in fact, the church as an institution had disappeared. But even before the churches could develop independence from their Western roots, Mao Tse-tung's Cultural Revolution dealt Christianity — or religion, generally — another blow by expropriating the churches, temples, and seminaries in the country for other uses, thus driving religion into a "underground" situation. This occurred in 1966 and lasted until 1976. At that point, Ting had been teaching theology at a seminary in Nanking, and found himself without a job. Like other clergymen, he started meeting with others in small groups in private homes to keep the church alive. They lived in fear of being discovered by the "red guards" who were dogmatically opposed to faith of any kind, other than that of the revolution. In 1976 when the ban was lifted, the church somehow emerged even stronger, Ting pointed out. It may have been because it had survived the worst.

The irony was that in those years before the church was censored — nearly two hundred years of evangelization by Christians — the Protestants could count only 700,000 in China. Roman Catholics numbered about three million. Since the Korean War, and since religion has had to survive underground, China's Protestants could boast more than three million adherents, while Roman Catholics, five million. In spite of the prodigious increase, Christianity still had little impact on the lives of Chinese, Ting maintained. Today Christian churches represent only .08 percent of the total population, by far the smallest religion in China. By contrast, Buddhists claim 100 million adherents and represent about a tenth of the population, while Islam, the second-largest religion, has twenty million followers. Taoism is the only native religion, but is withering away and sometimes is confused with Buddhism. Nonetheless, while mainline churches in the USA and Canada are suffering drastic drops in membership, the church in China is expanding at such a rapid rate it can't supply enough clergy to handle the increase. However, as Ting commented, the deficiency of clergy isn't for lack of candidates. In fact, the seminaries are having to turn away most applicants. Only one in ten can be accepted. Ting stated that because the Cultural Revolution shut down the theology schools for nearly a decade, the church lost valuable time in not only training people for the priesthood, but in furnishing suitable theologians and teachers for their seminaries. Ting affirmed that Christians are actually proclaiming they would like to see the church continue to grow, "but not too fast."

The conversions the churches are making aren't from the other religions, he pointed out. Very few Buddhists or Taoists are joining the ranks of the Protestants or Roman Catholics. "Most of the converts are those who had no religious faith at all." Again, unlike most other countries of the world, China is a nation of agnostics: "The Chinese are not very religious people," Ting stressed. Still, nearly two thousand years of Confucianism has provided the Chinese with a built-in system of social, political, ethical, and religious thought, based on the teachings of Confucius. Ting himself came from a family where his father was an agnostic and his mother an Anglican. It was through her efforts that he was provided with a religious education. Another influence was his maternal grandfather who was an Anglican clergyman. Ting believed that while his father may have disagreed with Christianity, he didn't stand in the way of his education. When he referred to his mother, he reached into a pocket of his coat and furnished a picture of her. She was 100 years old, still healthy, "And proud that I'm a priest today," Ting added with a smile.

It wasn't until he was twenty that Ting resolved to go into the ministry. At twenty-seven, he was ordained a priest in Shanghai and worked in Anglican churches in China until the end of the Second World War. Before returning to China in 1952 with his wife and child, Ting also attended Union Theological College in

New York and worked on the staff of the World Church Student Federation in Geneva. When he returned to his homeland, Ting was surprised at how the livelihood of the people had improved "remarkably" since the take-over of the Communists. "We found the people were wearing shoes . . . In old China many people walked about barefoot, even in winter."

When Ting refers to Communist China, he is very precise in explaining how wrong it is for Westerners to transfer what they know of Communism in the Soviet Union to that of China: "In China there is no active anti-God society." Unlike the former Soviet Union, China isn't striving to sell atheism. The lesson learned from the Cultural Revolution was that it was "counter-productive to offend people's religious feelings."

Today Ting is still at the theology school in Nanking. But since his return in the 1950s, he has seen his country and religion undergo vast changes: "Christianity in China was pretty much a Western thing . . . Chinese people call it a Western religion, or foreign religion . . . Much of it was a replica of western Christianity . . . Today it is much more Chinese . . . We're giving Chinese expression to our faith." This is manifesting itself in theology, art, and music. The only constant is the basic framework of worship, which has persisted to this day, Ting said. What differentiates the Chinese service from the medley of Western rituals, however, is the music — about a quarter of the hymns now used in the churches are of Chinese origin, not just translations into Chinese. A new technology is developing, too, in the churches, but the process is sluggish. Ting said the church is still very young.

Another development is a type of ecumenism among the Protestants. Ting speculated that a new church would be born in China, and it would be the outgrowth of the China Christian Council. He stressed the only factor arresting it was a small fundamentalist sect that calls itself "The Little Flock." This group opposes many of the beliefs held by the other Protestant denominations. If an agreement cannot be worked out, the China Christian Council will probably proceed with the formation of the new church. Ting expected the name of the church to be called

"The Church of Christ in China."

That hasn't occurred as yet. In fact, the China Christian Council still exists, and Ting has remained at the forefront, though Bishop Shen Yifan is its new general secretary. Ting is also the council's staunchest supporter. As recently as the spring of 1994, he lambasted Communist cadres who "exceeded their functions" and forced the country's unregistered Christians underground through repressive tactics. He claimed that the gulf between the government-sanctioned Protestant Three Self Movement and the millions of Chinese unregistered Christians was being exacerbated by these "cadres who still harbor a bias toward religion." Ting has been urging cadres to refrain from the "arbitrary labeling" of unregistered Christians as "illegal."

Ting felt that in matters of faith, if this new church ever evolved, it would be much the same as its Western derivations, "but in China we emphasize very strongly that the churches in China should be Chinese, just as the churches in England are English." Ting reiterated that the church in his country suffered from being Western, and today the incentive is to band together to ensure the church sustains a meaningful connection to the people there.

Ting said the Chinese really don't see themselves as "models" for the rest of Christianity: "Christians in all other countries believe that denominationalism is not good. But how to get rid of denominationalism is a very difficult question. We got into this post-denominational stage, not by choice, or by the long process of discussion . . . We got into this stage by circumstances." As a footnote to the exhortation to make a more "Chinese" church in China, Ting explained how Chinese Christians actually regard a Jesuit mathematician as a kind of saint in their history. The irony was that if Christians had continued to adhere to the model set down by Ricci, the Jesuit missionary who settled there in 1583, they might have developed along the lines that the church is moving today.

Ting explained that Ricci had gone to great lengths to adapt Chinese culture to Roman Catholicism, and concluded this was "not incompatible with Christian faith." Unfortunately the Vatican didn't agree. The Pope rushed in the Dominicans and Franciscans to convert the Chinese and sever the link between culture and religion. One of the first modifications to be made in Ricci's approach was in changing the name of God from "Shangti" or "the King Above" to "Tienchu" or "the Lord in Heaven." Ricci employed this name because it was used for God in the Chinese classics, and people easily related to it. On the other hand, the name given by the Dominicans and Franciscans was foreign and nowhere to be found in their cultural stories. Today the word for Christianity is "Shangti" and refers exclusively to Protestantism, while the other applies to Roman Catholicism.

Another irony is that Pope John Paul II broke with his predecessors and upheld Ricci's line of thinking, believing that while the church must preserve its universal connection to Rome, it must also develop in its own peculiar fashion. Ting stated that this change of heart from Rome has brought much relief not only to Roman Catholics but to all Christians: "If we want to propagate the Christian gospel in China, we must seek a common ground."

POPE JOHN PAUL II
5
SUBJECT OF PRAISE AND BLAME

For years I used to joke about how I had met Pope John Paul II, that we had had our pictures taken together on a street in Dublin, Ireland. I'd tell them how I stood beside the Pope and shook his hand . . . then I'd show them the color snapshot. Some believed it. Some actually resented it, mostly because I kept it on my desk at the newspaper, the way some might keep pictures of their kids. Some thought I'd lost my perspective, that I'd sold out to Christianity. After all, why was I having my picture taken with a religious leader? Was he some kind of hero? In truth, the picture was a hoax. Hawkers on a street in Dublin, Ireland got me to stand beside what was a cardboard character. The only part of my story that was true was that I did get to shake his hand, actually on a few occasions, in Canada, the USA, and once in Italy . . . But I was there among thousands of others, as he passed by to give his blessing.

Over the years of covering religion, though I never did meet Pope John Paul II personally, and never managed to wangle an interview, I did have the opportunity to write about him, and to be a part of the official media tour covering his visit to Canada. At times I was awed by the pontiff's wisdom; at other times I winced at how idiotic and puerile his judgments could be. He was an enigma — easy to praise, easy to damn, but difficult to comprehend. There was no denying his charismatic draw. There was no denying that he had changed people's lives. There was no denying that the political map of Europe had been transformed because of his indomitable spirit and his unwillingness to compromise. What follows are notes toward an understanding of the man as I followed his life for more than a decade.

1 When I walked into the office at *The Windsor Star* a little late that day, someone remarked that the Pope had been shot. "Sure," I chortled. Then I noticed my managing editor's irate glare through the glassed-in office because he knew I had been loafing somewhere in a café, reading . . . I realized it was no lie — it was true Pope John Paul II had been shot in Rome. I figured I'd just missed the biggest story of the year. The office had been searching for me so I could get some feedback from local church authorities, the usual stuff about how terrible it was, what a great loss this Pope would be. The local angle. That was Wednesday, May 13, 1981.

After a few frantic calls, I remembered seeing a phone number in a Canadian Conference of Catholic Bishops directory for a college accommodating Canadian priests studying in Rome. I wondered if there was anyone there from the London Diocese. As it turned out, yes, there was one from the Chatham area. I telephoned Rome. Within a few minutes, this young priest was on the phone, wailing about how awful it was that the Holy Father had been shot. After fifteen minutes, I concluded there was nothing more I was going to get. I thanked him and agreed that indeed it was a great tragedy that the head of the largest Christian church in the world had been shot. When I reiterated how I hoped the Holy Father would survive, this only prompted the priest to go on again at length. I was just about to hang up when he remarked, "Yeah, it was terrible . . . I heard the gun shots."

"Excuse me?" I interjected. "Gun shots? What gun shots? What are you talking about?"

"The gun shots. Yes, I heard the shots, and I saw the Pope."

"You did? You were there?"

"Yes, I thought that was why you were calling me — I thought you knew."

I kept him on the phone for another twenty minutes to get the full story.

"It was unbelievable. I was just standing less than 100 feet away . . . and I heard two shots . . . and then the Holy Father slumped down and I knew he had been hit."

That was the way Rev. Jacques Charon, a Catholic priest from Pain Court, Ontario described the attempted assassination of Pope John Paul II by a Turkish political dissident at St. Peter's Square. The thirty-four year old clergyman had served in Windsor and was then studying moral theology at Gregorian University in Rome. He was among an estimated 10,000 people in the square who had gone to see the Pope on May 13, 1981. "It was really odd. I was just standing there, and only a moment before the Holy Father was shot, I noticed one of the Swiss Guards looking around as if he noticed something. I turned to my friend beside me, also a priest, and I said, 'Look at the way that guard is looking around . . . as if there might be an assassin somewhere . . . and no sooner had I said that when I heard the shots. It couldn't have been thirty seconds after I said that to my friend . . . there were two shots. I couldn't believe this was happening. I saw the jeep in which the Pope was riding pull away, and I saw the Holy Father collapsing in it. He didn't fall down suddenly, but gradually. I kept saying, 'I can't believe this. It's not true.' I saw the Holy Father's two secretaries grab hold of him and put him down right away."

2 In May 1981, when the world prayed for Pope John Paul II, he was a kind of hero, a religious leader who had breathed new life, not only into his church, but into the Christian world itself. Thirteen years later, Catholics — both laity and clergy — are reeling in bitterness, feeling cheated, angry, confused. At times, he addresses them wisely about the poor and the oppressed; at other times, he's an embarrassment to his own church, stating boldly that women will never be ordained in the Roman Catholic Church, and so should stop asking.

No one can downplay the impact of Pope John Paul II on the course of European politics, notably his contribution to ending the Cold War between the East and West. From the moment of his election, the Polish-born Karol Wojtyla turned his attention to his old enemies — the Communists. He lived to see their ideology pass from the scene, not only in his own country, but in all of Eastern Europe. He watched the Berlin Wall topple. He watched the USA offering help to the Soviet Union. While former Soviet chief Mikhail Gorbachev may have been the architect behind ushering democracy into Eastern Europe, it was Pope John Paul II who was the catalyst. He stood firmly against the Communists, persisting in his war of words, decrying the political repression that had been endured for some seventy years. It seemed unbelievable that Gorbachev would win the 1990 Nobel Peace Prize

— the first Communist head of state to be so honored. He ended the Cold War, but without a doubt, in the background was Wojtyla. His direct, uncompromising and challenging words — and perhaps his prayers — certainly had something to do with it.

A Trappist monk I knew from the Abbey of Gethsemani seemed to have the clearest thoughts about this dilemma over categorizing Pope John Paul II. He shook his head in disbelief at the reaction of people when the Pope in the spring of 1994 declared that the church would never ordain women: "I'm not surprised. I mean, what do people expect to hear from him? Why should they be surprised he'd say women would never be priests? He's been saying that all along. It came out as if he had just said something new . . . Did they really believe this Pope would permit this sort of thing? I mean surely before he'd ever allow women to be priests, he'd let priests get married, don't you think?" Good point. The church's patriarchal structure wasn't about to make exceptions for the obvious. Before anything else, it would press for enhancement of its own male clergy, instead of permitting women to join their club. From the beginning of his papacy, and throughout it, Pope John Paul II has been consistent on a variety of issues that keep re-emerging for debate. From day one, he has opposed the ordination of women, abortion, lifting the ban on the use of artificial birth control, and the involvement of priests in politics. Nothing's changed since his election. It's unlikely he'll ever budge from his position on these matters.

Bewildering to critics and Catholics around the world are what appear to be such glaring contradictions. For one, wherever he travels — and he's the most traveled Pope in the history of the church — Pope John Paul II preaches that the church ought to look to women for leadership. Then why not make them priests? Not necessary, contends the Holy Father. To back up what he has said, he recently named a Sister to one of the highest administrative offices at the Vatican. In other instances, the Pope has gone to Latin America and openly scolded priests directly involved in the operations of government, though he himself has proven to be one of the most *political* figures in the world. In particular, soon after becoming the Pope, he ended the customary Vatican policy of neutrality, as it didn't suit Wojtyla when he became embroiled in international political controversies. In Poland he'll go to great lengths to uphold the right for free speech, yet Hans Küng — and other theologians — have felt the sting of Pope John Paul II's censorship.

Elected in 1978 as Pope John Paul II, Karol Wojtyla, son of working-class parents, was the first Polish prelate elected to the papacy. He was also the first non-Italian Pope in more than 450 years. Wojtyla, born May 18, 1920, entered Jagiellonian University in Kraków in 1938 where he studied literature and philology until the Nazis shut down the university. He worked as a laborer, then studied theology in an underground seminary. He also wrote poetry and performed in a number of anti-Nazi underground plays. He assisted the escape of Polish Jews from persecution. After the war, he attended the seminary in Kraków. Ordained in 1946, Wojtyla then went to Rome to study philosophy at the Pontifical Angelicum University. Upon his return to Poland, he taught ethics and theology at the Catholic University of Lublin. In 1958 Wojtyla was the youngest Polish bishop to be named auxiliary bishop of Kraków. In 1964 he was named archbishop, then cardinal in 1967. In those early years with the Polish Church, Wojtyla pressed for greater freedom of worship. He also stood firmly on the side of his people and openly spoke out against the Communists. His election as Pope on October 16, 1978, stunned the world since it had expected yet another Italian. Wojtyla was fifty-eight.

The new Pope adopted both the name and the style of his predecessor, Pope John Paul I. He also showed a similar regard for people. To ensure his investiture wouldn't conflict with a soccer match, he scheduled it for noon. He was also the first pontiff to wear pants under his vestments. He was open, free-wheeling, forthright. He opted to move the papacy out into the world. For one, he started traveling, often going into countries where authorities would have preferred him to stay away. He was also the first Pope to visit a Communist country, and the first to meet with the president of the United States in the White House. By the early 1990s the "Pilgrim Pope," as he was being described, had visited some forty-four countries, and had addressed the United Nations General Assembly.

Over the years, however, Pope John Paul II has proven himself to be a hard-liner when it comes to tradition. He isn't easily swayed, and he doesn't tolerate dissension. He gave his approval to the first revision of the church's canon laws since they had been codified in 1917, but the new code changed little of the more contentious prohibitions of the church. Wojtyla remained impassive to demands for a change on birth control, to the issues of celibacy for priests, and to the ordination of women. The Pope made it clear early in his papacy he wouldn't tolerate division. He was swift to punish bishops, priests, and theologians who disagreed with him.

3 When I went to Rome in the spring of 1982, I stayed with the Resurrectionist Fathers at their motherhouse near the Spanish Steps. It was they who suggested getting an "audience" with the Pope. Somehow, I managed, and took along a colleague — a man raised in the Anglican Church who harbored an anti-Catholic bias.

An audience with the Pope really means being shoulder-to-shoulder with 5,000 others. Our ticket — handed to us by the head of the Resurrectionist Fathers— entitled us to a position right alongside the aisle. The irony was we didn't stand a chance of remaining there once Pope John Paul II stepped into the hall at the Vatican. As the Holy Father approached, we quickly found ourselves swallowed up in a raging sea, mostly of nuns with tears streaming down their faces. They elbowed and clawed their way past us and others, clambered up on the chairs to get a better look, and pushed right to the rope barriers, calling out "Papa! Papa!" My friend's suspicions were confirmed: "They're nuts! Give me a break! I mean, this isn't Jesus!"

4 The thing that stands out most about 1984 was that I was on the road as part of the media tour with Pope John Paul II when the Tigers clinched the American League East title. In fact, I was in Yellowknife, in the North West Territories. It was also the day before my eldest son's birthday September 18. We had been en route to Fort Simpson, but were forced to land at Yellowknife because of bad weather and there we were, stuck at this tiny airport. The Pope had come to the North West Territories to lend support for Native self-government and for a "land base" for Natives. He planned to urge Native communities to encourage their youths to become priests. When it became evident that we were unable to leave, the Pope disembarked from the plane to speak to a hastily assembled group of representatives of Native leaders. Townspeople in pickups and cars sped from downtown to the airport because they'd heard the Pope was there. It wasn't really the police who kept them from going into the airport terminal — it was sheer numbers. There were 130 reporters and photographers in the place, and some 100 policemen. No one could get past the doors. As it was, there was almost no room for the pontiff.

Probably the most dramatic, spontaneous and sincere public gesture on that twelve-day tour occurred when Harry Daniels, a quick-witted Native leader, removed his stained and well-used moosehide coat and handed it to a surprised Karol Wojtyla. The Holy Father hesitated a moment, then asked, awkwardly, "Is this for me?" Daniels assured him it was. Later the native leader remarked, "I guess I'll have to find myself another coat." That gesture somehow epitomized the tour, the overwhelming response by Canadians to the visit of Pope John Paul II. When the Air Canada jet carrying Wojtyla departed at the end of a nearly two-week visit that was full of fanfare and adulation, it was evident he had touched people's hearts. He caused people to think, especially his own bishops. In a final meeting with them in Ottawa, the Pope made it clear that while they may be doing a great job, they could do better. He warned them to pay more attention to the rise of broken marriages, common-law marriages, and the ever-present disregard of the ban on artificial contraception. There was also the need for a revival of the practice of "personal" confession. It was a serious-minded chat, and one that reminded church leaders in Canada that they had their work cut out for them in a world suffocated by secularism.

Some bishops were amazed by Wojtyla's intuitiveness; others were alarmed at how that message would get translated by the laity. After all, the Canadian church's response in 1968 to Pope Paul VI's encyclical, *Humane Vitae*, which banned the use of artificial birth control, stated that the ban didn't "exempt a man from the responsibility of forming his own conscience according to truly Christian values and principles." The bishops here knew Pope John Paul II wasn't open to such compromise. Somehow during his tour of Canada, it didn't matter. In their midst was a Holy Man. He was a man of mystery, bewildering words, grace and charisma. "This is a man who means business," remarked Bishop Remi De Roo of Victoria, British Columbia. It wasn't just the warnings and unabashed criticism of the social order and injustices that still echoed from stadiums, outdoor parks and cathedrals across the land. As Anglican Bishop Louis Garnsworthy said, who met the Pope at St. Paul's Church, the country's largest Anglican Church, Canada was visited by a man "of care and compassion."

Gathered beyond the red-carpeted steps of cathedrals were masses of average Canadians, the people he had come to see and those who made pilgrimages to see him. Among them, Pope John Paul found nothing but affection. These were people who had closed up their shops, or absented themselves from work or school, to stand for hours along roadsides to catch a glimpse of the papal motorcade as it wound its way into cities and towns across Canada. These were the people who endured the cold and rain, many of them ignoring the mud and cloudy skies to cheer the Holy Father as he strode to the altar to bless their patience and stamina. It was the same everywhere. Wherever Karol Wojtyla travelled, thousands gathered to listen to his baritone pronouncements, or just to stand and see him and receive his blessing. Somehow all the tacky paraphernalia associated with the trip didn't detract from his message. In just about every curio shop in any city, or town, or on the fringes of where he was to be, you could pick up letter openers, china, crosses, key chains, ashtrays, buttons, all bearing the face of the Holy Father. (I picked up an ashtray for my cigar-smoking managing editor who had a deep devotion to the Roman Catholic Church, and told him, "Now every time you butt your cigar, you'll be showing the Pope how much you regard him!")

No matter how much Pope John Paul II may have rankled some with his immutable and unwaveringly conservative attitudes, most Canadians regarded him with awe and devotion. In Moncton, New Brunswick, people ran down back streets and alleys to bypass the RCMP lines, in order to catch up with the motorcade as it wound its way down through the city to the cathedral. In Winnipeg, as Pope John Paul II was getting into a limousine, he made an unexpected rush to a crowd across the street. When he did, a small boy broke beyond the RCMP barriers and leaped right into the Holy Father's arms.

But behind the glittery fanfare were the hard statements, the urgings and pleas of Pope John Paul II: recognition of rights of the disabled, youth, senior citizens; a change in attitude of big business that would put people before profits; support for Native self-government; firm backing for the ecumenical movement; greater involvement of women in the church, but not as priests; stringent morality laws, including a ban on abortion and birth control; church involvement in the peace movement; encouragement to priests to critique social injustice and government abuses, but a ban on priests running for political office; a change in roles for laity to increase their involvement in the socio-economic activity and church liturgy.

While some newspapers and media — including the CBC — took issue with the Pope's pronouncements, as Pope John Paul II departed, the response from the people themselves was one of overwhelming approval. They thundered it out in stadiums across the country.

Such grace and affection did not go unnoticed by the Pope,

according to Monsignor Emery Kabongo, his assistant private secretary. He said the pontiff was pleased with the reaction, and that he had found the time to scan some of the papers during the tour. The Canadian bishops were pleased, too. Bishop J. Michael Sherlock of London, then president of the Canadian Conference of Catholic Bishops, remarked effusively and simply, "Isn't this great!" Certainly they were satisfied with the performance of Pope John Paul, and buoyed by how he addressed the concerns of Canadians. More than that, they were overwhelmed by his honesty and sincerity. Bonnie Brennan, then media director for the bishops in Canada, was moved by how profoundly gentle and sympathetic he was with the handicapped, the sick, and how attentive he was to children.

Certainly, some wondered why he spoke with a liberal mind about social justice and peace, but before coming to Canada had harshly criticized advocates of Liberation Theology in countries torn by war and oppression. There was disappointment, too, over the strong stand on birth control, abortion, and divorce. There were women who were upset that in beatifying Sister Marie-Leonie Paradis of Montreal, Pope John Paul was holding up the stereotype of a woman serving men as an ideal. Sister Paradis was the foundress of a religious order that provided domestic care for priests.

As Brennan pointed out, in spite of such confusion, one couldn't help but feel affection for Pope John Paul II. What he accomplished was a debate in the church, a discussion. People began to take religion seriously, as the start of something new and significant. In a way, that might have been Wojtyla's intentions all along when in Montreal he stated, "To replace God is an impossible task . . . Nothing can fill the emptiness of his absence."

5 Three years later, I was covering Pope John Paul II again, this time in Detroit. I was watching the American scene closely. It had been an odyssey of surprises. Some predicted Wojtyla would come to discipline, that he would descend upon them like some biblical prophet to recite old laws, chapter and verse, and demand unwavering obedience. He surprised everyone. Instead of wagging a finger at a dissenting Catholic population, Pope John Paul II, then sixty-seven, took the time to listen and to pray. He didn't dismiss priests in Miami who informed him they wanted the right to marry. He didn't shut his ears to the nuns in San Francisco who declared a desire to be priests. He refrained from playing the stern father rushing in to reprimand. Instead, he wore the guise of the caring pastor, eager to hear complaints and concerns. As he proceeded west, some of the dioceses caught the momentum. In San Francisco, Rev. Miles O'Brien Riley noted that a wide variety of demonstrators were accommodated in the same way the elderly and the disabled were, given special areas "in order to see the Pope and so the Pope could see them too. We're not red-necked and we're not violent and angry," Riley said. "We're just people with a lot of opinions."

Archbishop Edmund Szoka of Detroit (now working in the financial secretariat at the Vatican) said the Pope was prepared for protest. It was felt that this dissatisfaction with papal policies among Catholics wouldn't mar Pope John Paul II's journey, providing he knew in advance what to expect. After all, he had been in the USA in 1979 and was confronted with a surprise challenge from Sister Theresa Kane who demanded women be considered for "all ministries of the church." The Pope appeared stunned by the question, and gave her no response. This time it was different. This time, there seemed to be overwhelming adulation. When he made his way up the aisle of the cathedral on Woodward Avenue in downtown Detroit, hands stretched out to touch him, reminding me of the Canadian trip, when a young Quebecoise mother handed her baby over heads in the crowd to the Pope. He cradled the baby for a moment, appearing a little perplexed and awkward as to what to do next. An aide rushed forward, and returned the infant to the mother.

The message the Pope brought was to take responsibility for the poor in our midst. The next morning when the Pope addressed thousands who filled Detroit's downtown streets, he had a clear view of a city in ruin, its buildings bombed out, crumbling, and among the rubble were children and families eking out a living. What about a better standard of living? What about racism? What about human compassion? Those were the questions that mattered. Forget women priests, gay rights, a married priesthood. What about earning a living, what about violence in the homes? What about family life? Then again, as for the dissenting opinions, Pope John Paul II in no way compromised the truth, claimed London Bishop J. Michael Sherlock. He commented that it was almost a contradiction for the Pope to be listening so well to dissenting views of American Catholics, then affirm the principles with which they disagree. "Some think the Pope is one of those free-ranging tough anti-Communists who arbitrarily imposes tough laws. Well, he isn't the master of the truth — he's the servant of it."

Malachi Martin, former Jesuit, and now a critic of the Catholic Church, said the Pope laid down the law when it was clear that's what was being asked of him but he also let people have their say. He showed a measure of humility, such as when he was asked in South Carolina whether AIDS was a punishment from God. The Pope said, 'Who am I to tell what is a punishment of God?'" According to Sherlock, Pope John Paul never watered down church dogma to suit the whims of dissenters. "He is a custodian of the truth of Christ, and he can't mess around with what God has revealed."

6 When I went to Nicaragua in the late 1980s, I remember a street late at night — no street lights on that humid June evening — and I peered into homes along this dirt road. In a small kitchen where three men were sitting at a table eating and drinking, there were some pictures tacked up on a wall: a baseball player I didn't recognize, a large American car, perhaps a Cadillac, and Pope John Paul II. Incongruous as it may appear, he fit in with what was important, what was significant in the lives of this family. In that instant, I came to understand another side to the man and his travels. He came to them with a message of hope. This whole business of Liberation Theology with its Marxist leanings may be pure in heart, but here was someone who stood for purity, who championed it, who gave people hope for the transformation they needed to make life better here and now. In that instant, all those other concerns — those of the West, about women priests, divorce, and birth control — seemed to fall away. Here the poor simply wanted a better life, something to hang on to. This tiny curled colored picture torn from a magazine, or newspaper, was what this family clung to that night in Nicaragua.

HANS KÜNG
6
ANOTHER GERMAN REBEL

He arrived that afternoon in the fall of 1981 feeling he could say anything he liked. Naively, he didn't consider that anyone from the media was in the room. Invited by the Ann Arbor School for Ministry to speak at St. Paul's Episcopal Cathedral Hall, he had been advised that it would be a kind of low key appearance in Detroit. As he emerged in the lecture hall, he smiled, remarking that he no longer found it ironic to be making a speech in a Protestant Church. It was happening more and more. He acknowledged that he felt a little like Martin Luther — no longer welcomed by his own flock. Even though he was still very much a priest, he was no longer committed to what he branded as wrong-headed Catholicism on the part of Pope John Paul II.

Nearly two years before, Hans Küng, a Swiss theologian, then fifty-one, had been barred from teaching by the Vatican "in the name of the Church" because he had cast doubt on papal infallibility. He also questioned whether Christ was the "son of God." A holy man, yes, but the son of God? Not a chance.

With a tape recorder in hand, I questioned Küng about the edict from Rome that warned him of speaking out against the church. A stiffly self-conscious priest, no longer wearing the Roman collar, the theologian said that he believed the church was making "blunt contradictions." For one, Küng believed it was incongruous that the Pope would find it so intolerable that his own people, the Poles, were denied the right to speak out, then turn around and muzzle one of his own priests. "Why can't I say anything? What freedom do I have?"

Küng's invitation to address the Ann Arbor School for Ministry was his first American appearance since his appointment as a visiting professor at the School for Divinity at the University of Chicago. In that speech, he didn't hold back in attacking Rome for its "abuse of power and authority." He told the gathering that although the Pope was ever vigilant in raising the issues of social injustice in totalitarian states like Poland, ironically he stifled critics within his own circles. Küng also attacked then Archbishop Edmund Szoka of Detroit for declining the church's representation at the Ann Arbor School for Ministry.

The hardline conservative bishop refused the invitation because Küng was not complying with the Vatican's December 1979 ban on teaching and had gone ahead to accept this engagement in Detroit. Szoka insisted he refrain from such participation. "What happened here is not at all something that is forbidden by Rome," argued Küng. "I am allowed to teach, but the people must know I have no Catholic license. But here they try to hinder me from teaching."

Küng's talk spared nothing. He enjoyed this status of a renegade priest. He openly accused the church of one inconsistency after another. He maintained that although the church was quick to condemn social and political injustices, it held back from signing the European Council's Declaration of Human Rights. He believed the church, too, ought to take a stand now on ecumenism by acknowledging Protestant ministers not merely "as lay people who basically have pious intentions," but rather as "real ministers of the church." (In fact, the Roman Catholic Church is doing that today — even to the extent that some married clergy are permitted to practice as Roman Catholic priests. The Pope extended such privileges to some Anglicans. The most notable was Graham Leonard, retired bishop of London, who was welcomed in April 1994. Then again, the high profile Anglican bitterly opposed the ordination of women in the Anglican Church.) Küng also suggested the Roman Catholic Church recognize the Eucharist in Protestant denominations and make it clear it no longer regards it as something "invalid and not fruitful."

At the time of his Michigan visit Küng headed the Institute for Ecumenical Research, and had been teaching ecumenical theology at the University of Tubigen, in what was then West Germany. It was there that he was barred from representing himself as a spokesman for the Catholic Church in matters of doctrine. Rome's Sacred Congregation for the Doctrine of Faith withdrew his privilege of teaching in the pontifical Catholic chair of the university. He fell into a controversy with the church for questioning not only the Pope's infallibility, but also the church's doctrine on priesthood, and the virgin birth of Christ. It was at Vatican II, however, that Küng, ordained in 1954, really caught the attention of the world. Then a young superstar theologian, he served as an advisor to the Second Vatican Council from 1962 to 1965. By the time he was sent to Rome, Küng had already made a name for himself. His doctoral thesis of 1957 (published later in English under the title of *Justification*) examined Calvinist theologian Karl Barth. The book went to great lengths to demonstrate that the theory of divine grace presented by Barth was in line with Catholic thinking. Barth himself was so pleased with it that he contributed an introduction to the book. In it he wondered aloud whether Küng would broaden his theories to tackle such matters as "transubstantiation, the sacrifice of the mass, Mary, and the infallible papacy." As it turned out, Küng later wrestled with these issues, too.

Küng's book, *The Council, Reform and Reunion,* published in 1962, was his first international bestseller. Two years later, Küng issued a challenge to the Vatican: "The world expects absolute and concrete sincerity of the church. The world expects the church not so much to pronounce these truths as to engage in truth without compromise." According to Michael Novak, a former professor of religion at the University of Syracuse, it appeared as if Pope John Paul II did not shy away from that challenge. The pontiff, apparently, "looked Küng in the eye and told him 'without compromise,' and with 'absolute and concrete sincerity' that however brilliant and well-intentioned he may be, he does not speak with the official voice of the Roman Catholic Church." That was that. The two would never find a field of agreement. But it wasn't only Pope John Paul II who was irked by Küng. Long before Pope John Paul II was annoyed with Küng, Pope Paul VI in 1973 issued a veiled statement refuting the German theologian's views. He did it shrewdly, without mentioning Küng by name. Instead, he referred to his dissenting statements about Catholic doctrine as "erroneous opinions."

Küng knew Rome's statements were directed towards him. Two weeks later, he responded publicly. Münich's Julius Cardinal Dopfner, then president of the German Catholic Bishops'

Conference and also a friend of Küng's, called the reply "defamatory." Küng was unrelenting in his battles with the bishops in Germany. Although he was ordered to be silent, the young theologian went on the attack.

The Sacred Congregation for the Doctrine of the Faith finally issued a declaration outlining how Küng's views did not fall into line with Catholic thinking. These included the theologian's argument about the infallibility of the Pope, the diminishment of the authority of the bishops, and the belief that in cases of necessity a non-ordained person could consecrate the eucharist. In 1977, the German bishops went further to pronounce that Küng's book *On Being a Christian* did not reflect the views of the church. Küng retaliated in the press, calling the bishops' statement "a doctrinaire self-justification without self-criticism." It didn't help matters when Küng's own bishop in Rottenburg-Stuttgart later went on record as stating that the theologian's point of view directly contradicted Catholic thinking.

When I spoke with him that day, Küng seemed battle weary. Though he could have sounded the alarm and embroiled himself in controversy, his charisma seemed diminished. His words may have been sharp, hard-edged, reasoned, but he spoke soberly, clearly, almost in a monotone. His deeply-lined face reminded me, strangely enough, of portraits of Samuel Beckett, the Irish playwright. Like the writer, Küng could be just as wry, bitter, and unwilling to hold back. His last words of our interview were, "Wait, are you a journalist?"

"Yes," I replied, asking, "Didn't you know? I *did* identify myself."

"Oh, I see." Pointing to the tape recorder, "Is that thing still running?"

"Yes, it is."

"Okay, now what did I say today?" Küng paused, rolling his eyes in thought, flashed a mischievous smile, then remarked, "I stand by it all!"

DOMITILIA DE CHUNGARA
7
BOLIVIA'S JOAN OF ARC

Domitilia de Chungara is a squat, solidly-built woman. When she sits down, she rests her arms on her thighs so that her large hands indent the full cotton skirt that dips slowly between her legs. She's wearing a blue raincoat that hugs her broad shoulders. Her black hair is pulled back tightly, and her brown skin and chestnut-brown eyes glow. That's how I remember Domitilia from the World Council of Churches meeting in Vancouver in 1983. There was nothing slick, pretentious, or presumptuous about this woman. Then forty-six, she had a matter-of-fact way about her, easygoing, but exacting. She was regarded as a kind of Joan of Arc in Bolivia where she was married to a tin miner and cared for eight children. Some thirty years ago, this same woman organized a committee of housewives to press for better living conditions among families of those working in the tin mines. A year after she started organizing, the army descended upon innocent workers and killed many of them. Two years later, the army was back again, maiming and murdering workers and their families.

Domitilia gained wide renown for her dramatic speeches in Mexico about the Bolivian situation. She had been there as part of celebrations for the International Year of the Woman in 1975. Her words were put into print in a best-selling book called *Si me permiten hablar*, which has been translated into more than a dozen languages. In 1977, Domitilia was elected president of the miners' human rights organization in Bolivia. With the support of other women, she also initiated a successful twenty-one day hunger strike on behalf of political prisoners and for the return of exiles. Her efforts actually led to the national elections in 1978 in which she ran for vice-presidency of the *Fente Revolutionario de Isquierda*, or Revolutionary Front of the Left. Although she lost her bid for elected office, her cause captured the attention of the country.

In 1980 Domitilia was invited to take part in a major non-governmental parallel meeting of women at the Copenhagen International Conference of Women. After she departed for Denmark, General Garcia Meza's military coup d'état in Bolivia forced her to seek asylum in Sweden. During the next two years, she launched a lecture tour of fifteen European countries to address women's rights and the increase of human rights violations in her own country. Domitilia returned to Bolivia two years later. She told me that the situation had improved in her country, but there was still widespread poverty and violations to human rights. She hoped that these interviews outside her country would draw attention to the political realities there. "I would hope that everything we say is listened to and helps people. The efforts to help us are not many. For some people, our efforts are just diversions, but one thing is for sure, people are never going to stop struggling for their rights. It is this struggle for the people that animates us to continue."

The Spanish-speaking Domitilia, who spoke with the aid of an interpreter, leaned forward, hands slicing through the air in a spirited way, explaining her commitment to Liberation Theology: "For a long time the churches have separated themselves from the problems of the people. There are human laws that prevent the fulfillment of the laws of God. We need a liberating theology which will give the common people an approach to God." Domitilia explained that many Bolivian churches preferred to keep a distance from the people. Few tried to bridge that gap. Those keeping that distance predictably urged people to remain silent in the face of injustices. She described this brand of Christianity as distorted: "I think it would be an unjust God who demanded that we suffer injustice in this life in order to enjoy a better life to come in the after life." Unfortunately, she maintained, this is what many churches are telling Bolivians and others throughout Latin America.

Domitilia feared the reaction of Latin America to its future. With the turmoil, paranoia, and human rights violations stinging the population, storekeepers were hiding and hoarding food. "There is no sugar, no bread, no meat, nothing much of anything." The forces of democracy in the country have been strong, she said, but not Herculean in their efforts to prevent the government from becoming tyrannical once more. She pointed out that the Bolivian Workers' Center and the workers' organizations in the factories never let up emphasizing the need for democracy. The role of the church is to come to the rescue of the downtrodden, but that doesn't always occur. "The church has the ability to communicate to the press and to stage meetings — like the World Council of Churches — so we can talk to people throughout the world. The church can also send visiting teams to the areas of the world where there are problems, and if the church speaks the truth about what they see, they can greatly help our people."

To Domitilia, Bolivians still found it difficult to forget their past — it was scarred by dictatorships. It was a landscape bereft of liberty, a free press, trade unions, or political parties. "When there is a military dictatorship, it means the army can go into your house at any time. Generally this is done at midnight or the early hours of the morning when people are in bed. Women suffer rape in this way. Husbands are taken off as prisoners. There is no one there to protect you. People don't learn about what is happening because you aren't allowed to talk about it." Domitilia herself was taken prisoner. So was her husband and daughter: "Because of the torture, I lost the baby I was carrying. Then I was exiled to Sweden for two years."

But before the estrangement from her homeland, Domitilia described how she sought refuge in one of the mines. The army had been searching to imprison and torture her. She was pregnant at the time, and had to be smuggled out to give birth to twins, but one died. Domitilia's father, a trade union officer, was also taken prisoner and tortured, she thought, due to her own activities. Virtually anyone connected with Domitilia was terrorized, because she had been critical of the government's decision to cut wages in half while bumping up salaries to officers and buying them cars.

She had also convinced the trade unions to rebel. When the government failed to convince workers that the situation would be rectified in two years, it sent in its forces to quell opposition. "I remember that night. We called it 'The massacre of the night of St. John.' Many died — men, women, and children. We protested this killing, and that is why they took us prisoner. They tortured us, questioned us, and they brought psychological pressure to bear upon us. They told us that our children were prisoners too. They warned us that if we wanted to save our sons and daughters, we had to sign blank pages of confession . . . There were severe tortures in the prison." Domitilia related the story of a man ordered by guards to sit "with his legs apart . . . They put a fire beneath him . . They put a tin box on top of that, and placed rats inside of it. Then they put his penis into a hole that was in the tin box. The fire burned the rats, and the rats in turn bit him. His crime? He was a trade union official."

What was happening across Latin America, especially in Bolivia, she pointed out, was a movement of rural people going to the cities to find work. In some instances, they were driven to do so by the army or by floods. "But when they come to the city, they can't find work or food. They have to resort to prostitution. Many of these women have lost their husbands, and they have no means of supporting their children."

The church — in spite of its wealth and extensive properties — has really been of no help. Nevertheless, Domitilia has remained religious. She hasn't given up on God. She was raised a Roman Catholic, but joined the evangelicals when her father switched denominations. "Through him, I began to read the Bible and hear the word of God. Then we joined the Jehovah's Witness. We studied a lot and we were very happy and we learned something of 'hope'. Then we started preaching, going around and talking to people."

Involvement in that denomination was brief. Going door to door, Domatilia became acquainted with a widow and mother of six children who made her livelihood from washing clothes, and offered to help. "I wanted to share the joy I felt, and I started washing the clothes for her." Domitilia continued her visits, trying to convince her new friend that she needed "faith" to survive. "I told her all I learned but she was becoming more and more bitter about her life." When the Jehovah's Witnesses advised her against consorting with someone like this, she quit the denomination. "I was told this woman drank when she was working. I told them I wanted to go on talking to her because I wanted to share my joy with her. They told me to quit." Domitilia realized then she couldn't share what Jehovah's Witnesses stood for. "You can't speak to people about God when they don't have anything to eat." Thus, what became important to her was not so much delivering the word of God, but the means to find food, to eat, "to be human."

In terms of her own faith, she finds herself today even "more confused . . . I don't know what the truth is, but I am looking for a church that will identify with the problems of the poor, and as my youngest daughter says, 'Whose side is God on . . . The side of the rich or the side of the poor?' And if we believe in God, we must have a God on our side!"

GUSTAVO GUTIERREZ
8
PERU'S MARXIST PRIEST

"**T**here is a little man in Peru, a man without any power, who lives in a barrio with poor people and who wrote a book. In this book he simply reclaimed the basic Christian truth that God became human to bring good news to the poor, new light to the blind, and liberty to the captives. Ten years later this book and the movement it started are considered a danger by the greatest power on earth. When I look at this little man, Gustavo, and think about the tall Ronald Reagan, I see David standing before Goliath again with no more weapon than a little stone called A Theology of Liberation." The words are Henri Nouwen's, from a book called *Gracias! A Latin American Journal.* They describe the quixotic Gustavo Gutierrez, the undisputed pioneer of Liberation Theology, a theology which said God's justice for the poor was here and now, and not just in the Afterlife.

To be honest, I had never heard of him, nor did I know anything about Liberation Theology, until one morning I was speaking with then Auxiliary Bishop Marcel Gervais in Windsor, Ontario. On the wall near his desk was an icon of a disfigured Christ on the cross, crying out in anguish. The bishop informed me that it was a symbolic representation of the wretchedness felt by the people in Latin America. Further discussion got around to Liberation Theology. Bishop Gervais suggested if I really wished to write about religion in action, I ought to go to Peru, where the London Diocese of the Roman Catholic Church sent missionaries. It was then the name of Gutierrez arose. He told me, "If you ever go, I will give you a letter of introduction — I know him very well."

It wasn't long after that — in 1984 — I was flying down to Lima. I spent a few days in the city before going out to the Zana Valley, and finally into the mountains, to follow these diocesan missionaries in their work. While the poverty was staggering, the faith among these people was beyond anything I could imagine in Canada or the USA. I recall riding in the back of a pickup truck through obscure villages in order to take photographs and gather stories. In one instance, the people of a small community flagged us down because an old woman was on her deathbed and needed a priest. I trailed after the priest into this two-room house and observed the family about the bed. The old woman lay propped up against blankets and towels. She was thin, bony, haggard — the only part of her that seemed alive was her head, shaking uncontrollably. Her eyes glittered with hope. She struggled to smile. What struck me, too, was how important this ritual was to the villagers. When I asked if I could take a picture, not only was it welcomed, it was practically demanded. It might have seemed sacrilegious — but not to them. The priest — having some knowledge of photography — realized the need for more natural light. He asked the family to move away from the window so that I could avail myself of the sunlight. Death was a kind of celebration — it warranted picture taking. In such a context I began to understand a little more about Gustavo Gutierrez, this man of the people. I had met his people, ate with them, talked with them, and sang with them in churches far from the city and in the barrios of Lima.

Unfortunately, my first meeting with Gutierrez did not go well. When I was introduced to him, he barely acknowledged me. He wouldn't look me in the face. Instead, he spoke directly to Rev. Frank O'Connor, a priest from the London Diocese of the Catholic Church, who served as a translator for me. He told this Canadian priest, who was also a good friend of Bishop Gervais, that he couldn't speak with me then because he was too busy with a conference in Lima. O'Connor pressed Gutierrez, asking if he could find even a few minutes for me. The theologian shook his head. Impossible! But I had brought with me a letter of introduction from Bishop Gervais and asked O'Connor to mention this to Gutierrez, who still seemed unmoved, though he acknowledged his old friend from Canada, who had invited the Peruvian theologian to speak in London, Ontario years before. Finally, O'Connor handed the letter to Gutierrez, along with a check for $1,000 — a donation from Bishop Gervais to the cause of the poor. With that, the theologian's interest suddenly picked up. "Sure, sure, there's maybe some time for him next week!" he said without hesitation. I was told I could have a half hour. Again, this was said without a glance in my direction.

When I finally went to see Gutierrez, he seemed less preoccupied. He also spoke English — something that surprised me since he could have spoken to me directly during our first meeting. It became apparent that he was deliberately circumspect over his relationship with the church, specifically the Vatican because it frowned upon his involvement in politics. Gutierrez's guardedness also had a lot to do with the seething violence in his country as the Shining Path was making inroads in its bid to overthrow the government. Though Gutierrez certainly hadn't aligned himself with these revolutionaries, he, himself, was viewed as one. It was true he hadn't taken up arms himself, but he rarely held back from advocating violence to improve the lot of the poor. In essence, Gutierrez was a Marxist with a Roman Collar.

Physically, he seemed a small man. He walked awkwardly. Childhood polio had left him with one leg shorter than the other. Still, he commanded a curious presence when he came into a room. He was ill at ease, fidgeted and moved about. His eyes darted around the room. He found it difficult to look anyone directly in the face. He appeared perpetually worried. But when he smiled, it was genuine and warm. Somehow it undid all the restlessness that exuded from him.

This was the man who had given revolution a name. He was both the enemy and a hero in his own country. Many sectors of the government, the military, the news media and even his own church shunned him and branded him a dangerous Marxist. Even the papers called him "a Marxist priest" when he celebrated his twenty-fifth year as a priest earlier that year. The poor on the other hand regarded Gutierrez as a comforting angel who offered them dignity and worth. He also attracted a following among intellectuals of his own country and throughout Latin America, as well as among the foreign missionaries toiling among the poor. Gutierrez seemed to waver between being blasé and being worried over the controversy he ran up against with the Vatican and the government. Admittedly, he was bothered by it. He hoped the debate over his work would result in some good. He conceded there was always room for such division of thought. It was healthy, necessary, unavoidable.

When I met him, he was just outside his office. He sat on a stool. He acknowledged that he worried over what the Peruvian bishops were going to say about his work and his speeches. He didn't relish being silenced. He didn't know whether he could handle such discipline. He was certain the bishops couldn't dispute the soundness of his theology, only its pastoral implications. To some, these translated into revolution. To others, it meant justice for the poor, by enabling them to improve their lives. Gutierrez wasn't interested in violence or revolution — his objective was justice. He emphasized that whenever he spoke of justice it arose straight from the gospel: "You can call it Liberation Theology, or whatever you want, but it's really just another word for the gospel!"

David Molineaux (at that time director of the feisty tabloid *Latinamerica Press* based in Lima) pointed out the bishops in Peru had wanted to chastise Gutierrez. They were under pressure from the Opus Dei camp, which vehemently opposed Liberation Theology. Opus Dei, a highly conservative element in the Catholic Church, commonly thought of as fanatical, regarded Gutierrez's theology as Communism, and pronounced it to be Marxist-inspired, dangerous, and the first step toward heresy. Opus Dei was firmly entrenched, too, in the upper class of the church in Peru. Naturally, revolution threatened the very structures that kept their families affluent and powerful. Gutierrez was an outsider. He came from the opposite side of society.

Besides the conservatives, Molineaux noted the large block of bishops "in the center who (were) less interested in the smooth-running institution." These church leaders could be persuaded to go either way. Naturally, Gutierrez also had his own supporters, both within Latin America and throughout North America. Several church leaders rallied to his side and sent letters of support to the Peruvian bishops.

At the time I spoke to Gutierrez, he was preparing to respond to the bishops' concerns. He wouldn't reveal how he would address them, or what he would tell them. On record, Gutierrez firmly believed in democracy, but he was also the consummate Socialist, who freely confessed to Marxist leanings. He stressed, however, that he had nothing but distaste for Communistic solutions. He also disliked being identified *only* as a Marxist. The Roman Catholic Church itself, Gutierrez stressed, was Marxist. But what should be understood, he added, was that Marxism didn't necessarily imply Communism. Not in the purist sense. Of course, that's what Gutierrez was speaking about — theories. He classified himself as a philosopher, a theologian, someone who searched for solutions in theory, but wished to see them applied practically. That didn't mean taking up arms and joining the guerrillas. Gutierrez preferred to dream, to write books, to lecture. He had no wish to flee, to hide in the hills with the revolutionaries, and plot the overthrow of the government. His was a revolution in words. His words, were prayers, solutions, solace for the poor and the oppressed in his land.

Violence on the other hand was always an option, a last resort. Though Gutierrez did not prescribe it, he wouldn't rule out its possibility. He cited the case of Nicaragua where the bishops had declared that oppressed people, in some situations, ought to consider violence to correct injustice. He told me that it was always "an option" and conceded the church could certainly find a theology to justify brutal measures. "But that's not what we want here — our effort is really to find more *human* means to get solutions for our situation."

Gutierrez knew where violence could lead. His good friend and classmate — Camilo Torres — died with the Colombian guerrillas in February 1966. Torres had studied with Gutierrez at Louvain, Belgium. Unlike Gutierrez he believed the fight to liberate the poor had to be engaged in the streets, not in the church, and not in the university. Gutierrez shared his friend's zeal, but stopped short of taking up arms. He opted for the intellectual route. "But we have violence anyway," pointed out Gutierrez, referring to the war between the Shining Path and the government, and the ever-increasing numbers of "the disappeared" in Peru. People on the wrong side of the debate were being kidnapped, tortured, and killed. Families often endured years of frustration and sorrow before finding the remains of "the disappeared."

Gutierrez's reputation was built solidly on his intellectual input into the development of Liberation Theology. Its emergence really came about in 1968 at Medellin, Colombia when Latin American bishops met in an extraordinary assembly that saw the church commit itself to the poor and the oppressed. Pope Paul VI, the first Pope to set foot in South America, inaugurated the meetings and not only set the tone of the conference, but the direction of many thinkers and revolutionaries in Latin America. He declared, "We wish to personify the Christ of a poor and hungry people." Gutierrez was among the influential theologians present at Medellin, and helped write documents that forged the way toward a new vision of the poor. After Medellin he wrote his controversial *A Theology of Liberation*, the blueprint on how the church could answer the cries of the suffering peoples in Latin America.

The poor everywhere in South America saw their plight symbolized in the "suffering Christ." In many of these clay crucifixes — as in the one that I first saw in Bishop Gervais' office — the figure was that of an emaciated, tortured, abused man, unlike the gentle-looking savior portrayed in North American churches. This figure represented the cause of the powerless in Latin America. Even the dust jacket of the English translation of Gutierrez's *A Theology of Liberation* bore the image of the anguished Jesus.

At Puebla, Mexico in 1979, the Latin American bishops met again. This time, however, many hard-line conservatives attempted to derail the thrust of Liberation Theology by excluding from the meetings those theologians who subscribed to this new philosophy. In fact, theologians were prohibited from entering the seminary where the bishops gathered. Nonetheless, through the aid of "friendly bishops" they succeeded in getting proposed drafts circulated at the conference, with the result that the bishops committed themselves to "a preferential option for the poor" over the next decade. Once again, Gutierrez was credited as being the architect of the new document.

The Peruvian writer's message has been consistent: "The church has always taken sides in the past . . . It has always invariably been on the side of the rich oppressors. The plea now is not that the church should take sides for the first time but simply that it should *change* sides. Having sided with the wealthy, it must now side with the poor; having been in the support of those with power, it must now cast its lot with those deprived of power; having enjoyed the privilege in the past, it must undergo risk in the future." Gutierrez told me he held out a great hope for change in his own country. Indeed, he envisioned a transformation across Latin America where people suffering from malnutrition and widespread human rights violations and violence would find solace and peace in their lives. The poor shared his hope, but he emphasized that hope didn't always imply optimism. "To be hopeful and to be optimistic are not the same necessarily . . . I think there is hope among my people that it is possible to change the situation here and that things don't have to be so desperate here . . . But my people are not always optimistic."

Indeed, Peru is wracked with violence and chaos. If anything, the situation is worse today than it was in 1984. The foreign missionaries are being driven out of the country because they represent a threat to the government. Conservatism among many Peruvian bishops, who have traditionally sided with the wealthy, has not been without influence. Paranoia reigns. Gutierrez's vision of a better world seemed less distant in 1984 when Gutierrez had reason to be optimistic. Peruvians shared a kind of solidarity, "a need to be together in the struggle." He felt this would carry them to success. "We've been employing that word 'solidarity' long before the Poles were. Perhaps fifty years ago even!" Gutierrez maintained that "poor people everywhere" understood solidarity and the possibilities of Liberation Theology as something to count on, something to strive for.

Gutierrez was disgruntled over the right-wing evangelists who invaded Latin America with a theology that suggested the poor ought to put aside the task of improving their lot on earth and concentrate upon eternal salvation. Why shouldn't they have a better life here? And now? Why wait? Was this what Christ wanted of them? There was nothing wrong with the notion of striving to bring justice and compassion to the poor, and for the poor to struggle to embrace a better life. If anything, said Gutierrez, it was the duty of each and every individual to strive for a greater calling, for a greater life. "More and more poor people," said Gutierrez, "are understanding that the meaning of salvation lies in their daily lives and not just beyond their history on earth . . . Liberation is just another word for salvation . . . And that means social, political, human, and Christian liberation."

ARCHBISHOP DAVID LEAKE
9
AN ARGENTINE ANGLICAN

R ight from the start, when this tall, distinguished-looking cleric maintained that his church was "significant," that it had something to say about the life of his people, you believed him. He spoke with precise authority. He was decisive, unwavering, certain. There was also a trace of pride, or perhaps he betrayed his own intellectual attitude toward it — a temperament nurtured as a boy growing up in a world that was *foreign,* yet fundamentally his homeland.

When I met David Leake of Argentina, I was struck by his grasp of the world-wide state of religion, and where his own church, that is, the church in Argentina stood. Though he may have British roots, he was born in Argentina. His first language wasn't English, but *Toba,* a South American Indian tongue. Today he speaks at least two Indian languages as well as English and Spanish. Leake's parents — both British — had gone to South America in the 1920s and worked as missionaries. Leake was raised among the Indians, and today — in spite of the fact his theological training was in England — he considers himself "an Argentine." He also insists that when he speaks of his church and its work in the "Southern Cone" of the continent, he's speaking with some authority. He's no foreigner. Leake heads the Anglican Church of the "Southern Cone." He is also bishop of northern Argentina. His education is all British, having gone to Norwich City College and London College of Divinity. He was ordained in 1959 at St. Albans, and from that year to 1963 lectured in the UK. Upon his return, Leake followed his parents' lead, and became a missionary. He held that job till 1969 when he was consecrated an assistant bishop of northern Argentina. In 1980, he was named diocesan bishop.

Leake isn't entirely satisfied with the church's history in Argentina. Things have changed dramatically from the 1800s when missionaries fanned out across the "southern cone" to evangelize the Indians. The church then had a divided role. While offering the word of God to the natives, it also had separated itself from this association to serve businessmen who came to the continent to settle and develop industrial cities there. This divided loyalty has now been thrown back at the church, for though its emphasis may have seemed sincere — and in many instances was — it was really one of favoritism on the part of the religious leadership looking out for the interests of the rich before the poor. With the advent of Liberation Theology (associated mostly with the Catholic Church) Christianity has undergone a transformation. The poor now realize they have a right to a better life, here and now, not just in the spirit world.

Leake sees benefits in this leftist theology, especially in that it raises questions about faith, but maintains that his conservative church isn't moved by this thinking. Anglicans regard it as a passing phenomenon, that may or may not have impact. Examining its effects in Nicaragua, Peru, El Salvador, and elsewhere, however, demonstrates it has galvanized people to hope that life can be better, *here,* that one need not wait for the after life. Still, the Anglican Church is steadfast in its conservatism — Liberation Theology will give way to yet another approach. But such a social gospel, according to the dissenting Leake, is essential in the southern cone. People need to feel a sense of worth and well-being. That worth must find expression in the recognition of fundamental rights, even in raising the standard of living. Such theories have struck trepidation in governments, even in church circles, because Liberation Theology implies the overthrow of government can be justified as a means of bringing freedom to oppressed people.

Leake wouldn't speculate whether such a theology had a solid footing. Certainly in the case of Argentina, his own church — small in comparison to that of the Catholics — has sought to recognize Indian people of the Southern Cone. The church has provided a translation of the scriptures into Indian languages, and pressed the government to acknowledge Indian people as citizens. This latter view runs contrary to the government's intentions. In Argentina, the government has dictated that all citizens must carry identity cards. Thirty years ago, Leake explains, about ninety-nine percent of all Indian people were cut off from this. "Well, if you don't have an identity card, you are considered 'a non-person.' You have no rights to vote, no rights to property, no rights to live . . . You could actually kill someone and virtually they wouldn't have existed anyway if they didn't have an identity card." Leake initiated a campaign to provide Indians with these identity cards. Today ninety-five percent are registered. "And if they're not," he pointed out, "it's because of some inconvenience, such as the distance away from the registry office."

Leake said this reflected somewhat the theory behind the Liberationists, but at its roots is yet another important aspect. Leake indicated that because he made the push for this registration, the cause carried more authority — it seemed more acceptable. In other words, without the church as the voice, the Indians might not have these registration cards. "This had been something which I felt I could really push . . . While my parents were British, I am an Argentine, and as an Argentine, I felt it was something I could legitimately push — not as a foreign missionary, but as an Argentine citizen!" Leake pointed out that the church, which has always guarded against involvement in politics because it subscribes wholeheartedly to the separation of church and state dogma, has now found itself in the thick of a debate over the rights of people everywhere. This, of course, is happening, particularly in Argentina.

Personally, Leake enjoys the challenges that confront him as head of the churches in the Southern Cone. His job involves speaking four languages, and dealing daily with such issues as Indian development, land rights, civil rights, education, basic translation of the gospel, and urban evangelism. He must also comfort those who are the victims of horrendous political violence — most notably, the widows of "the disappeared."

Leake is intimately aware of the violence that has seized South America. One woman on his own staff is now a widow because her husband, who had worked with the *campesinos,* or peasants, was snatched from home one night, and later found dead. The only way this woman and her young daughter escaped death was by hiding in a wardrobe. Another daughter was asleep in another room, and somehow was missed in the night raid. Though the political climate has changed, the problem of "the disappeared" is still present.

The Anglican Church itself has never been troublesome to the government, because its dealings have been almost exclusively with the Indian population, a people that has never posed much of a threat to authorities. On the other hand, Catholic bishops, priests, and nuns working among the poor in urban and rural areas are regularly ambushed. "Anyone who was involved with the poor were targets of suffering," Leake pointed out. The role cast for the Anglican Church now is one of making the government take responsibility for the poor. That is why its religious leadership continues to lobby "in the corridors of power to push . . . political leaders to help." Leake pointed out that in cases where the government might provide government-paid physicians to work with the poor in remote areas, the church is willing to supplement this with medical supplies. The government has always made the excuse that it cannot provide both.

The church in the 1980s was also able to cut through some of the bureaucratic red tape by buying up land, then turning the property deeds over to Indians. The fact is that for years the government has made it impossible for Indians to take possession of land. But in addition to that, the Indians themselves are not motivated to own land. "They don't feel as if the land belongs to them; they feel they belong to the land."

STAN McKAY
10
NATIVE CANADIAN SPIRITUAL LEADER

You could tell that you had just entered the reserve area. The paved road immediately gave way to a dusty gravel one. The road wound down through the flat expanses of poplar and white birch. You passed a large white and gold circus tent where the fundamentalists thundered out their message of salvation. Eventually you ended up at a nearly dried-up river. On one side of the river was the blue and white Stevens Memorial United Church; on the other side, the awesome false-fronted grocery store that kept the reserve in supplies through summer and winter. If you took the road across the river and turned south, in a few minutes you'd be at the southern tip of Lake Winnipeg. The stormy, muddy-looking lake was the livelihood of the 900 native people on this eighteen-square-mile reservation. Each morning, the fishermen steered their bulky-looking tugs out along the narrow river and into the cold lake. It was here they hauled in Lake Winnipeg white fish and pickerel.

Rev. Stan McKay, a Cree Indian, married to a white Manitoba school teacher, walked on the slatted wooden pier that jutted out into the stormy lake. This was home. Koostatak, or "Fisher River" as it is known to most people, is about 320 kilometers or 200 miles north of Winnipeg and only a stone's throw from Lake Winnipeg. McKay never masks his pride for this old settlement that became the bailiwick of the Scottish settlers in the nineteenth century, which explains the proliferation of Scottish surnames among the Natives. The old tribal names long ago fell into disuse. In fact, there is only one family on the reserve that has retained the custom.

When I stayed with McKay on the reserve, he was the national coordinator of the Native Ministries Council of the United Church. For eight years, he had been the pastor of the quaint-looking Stevens Memorial Church, which was named after a pioneer doctor. It was the furthest thought from his mind that he'd seek and succeed in winning the position as head of the second largest Protestant denomination in Canada.

As I drove with him on the reservation, this quiet-spoken United Church minister recalled his boyhood there when his father was a trapper and fisherman, and when he used to swim in stormy Lake Winnipeg. McKay was still worried about how his presence on the reserve reminded people of the "good doctor" who worked there, and how Stevens substituted pharmaceutical medicine for the natural medicines and practices of the reserve. In effect, maintained McKay, several of the old home herbal remedies passed down from one family to another had vanished because of Stevens. But one shouldn't consider this to be unusual — the old Native customs, one by one, have been falling away into obscurity on reserves across the country. A critical issue for McKay was how the invasion of the white missionary took its toll on spirituality and religious customs. Christianity virtually stripped the Natives bare of what they had always trusted, and what they always believed possible. In some instances, there was an unwillingness to learn the Indian languages. The clergy ruled over the reserves like despots, fanatically striving to stamp out all vestiges of what they considered evil paganism.

McKay made it his life mission to work against the longstanding movement to eradicate the old spiritual ways of the reserves. He fought for the establishment of training programs for Native ministers. As early as the thirtieth General Council of the United Church, he planned to push for the establishment of all-Native presbyteries but more significantly the creation of an all-Native "conference" or diocese for the church's sixty Native parishes. He succeeded in getting that. He knew that approval would be history in the making, not just for the United Church, but for the Christian community generally. It would be the first Native "conference" or diocese ever set up in the country. He hoped to clear the way for other churches to do the same.

McKay said Koostatak, where he grew up, was a typical reserve that had been invaded by the strident Christian missionaries who had little or no regard for Native approaches to spirituality. The reserve today is dominated mostly by Protestant Christianity. Stevens' influence is still evident. He taught himself Cree, and thus, to this day, older members of the congregation still sing in Cree at the services. Unfortunately, the remnants of that Native culture are evaporating quickly. Being forgotten are the prayers and hymns in Cree. Also disappearing are the skilled tanners, bead artists, and weavers. If there is anything reminiscent of the ancient culture, it is to be found among the old men or women of the tribes who feel uncomfortable or alienated with these gifts because their children and grandchildren aren't interested in learning them.

I remember meeting Margaret Jane Murdoch, a big woman in her seventies, known on the reserve as the old midwife. She sat at the front next to the organist in the airy Stevens Memorial. She was one of the few from the tribe who clung to the old language and ways. Given the opportunity to sing in Cree, she screeched out the songs as the organist attempted to keep up. When she prayed she easily moved back and forth from Cree to English in a high-pitched feverish voice. To many, Margaret Jane was a saintly, congenial woman. When asked about her dedication to her culture, she shrugged "I guess I am."

To McKay, she was the symbol of the past. She was a conspicuous reminder of something else that was missing — the Native spirituality that had existed in the community. McKay pointed out this "gift" was found among people who had no fundamental theological training. It came from people who had always resided on the reserve. They had a propensity for speaking with people. There are certainly some who still have these gifts, maintained McKay, but their abilities are overshadowed and unwanted by the churches. They find themselves making unsuccessful bids to become clergymen. As candidates for the ministry, they inevitably run up against unsympathetic theological schools without patience for home-spun practical philosophies. Disillusioned, these students flee the school, sustaining the weight of their failure. Worse still, they are left questioning the significance of their own natural abilities and gifts. It wasn't that long ago when a Native student at St. Andrew's Theological College in Saskatchewan was berated for weaving Native church history into an essay on the history of the church in Canada.

The fact is, claimed McKay, the reserves have a spiritual

tradition. A few among the tribe are acknowledged spiritual leaders. When he was a child, shaman-like people made the rounds like old Methodist circuit riders, dropping into homes to sit and talk to both old people and the young. McKay's uncle used to keep him in rapture as he unfolded colorful and absorbing tales out of which emerged a kind of down-to-earth spirituality — not at all framed in the traditions of hymns and scripture readings found in the church setting, but rather rooted in the Cree language and myths. It had the effect of opening up the gospels for McKay and making them more relevant. In essence, he saw this relationship contributing to his decision to attend the University of Winnipeg, and become an ordained a United Church minister.

Ever since his ordination in 1971, McKay has been working to integrate the two cultures. It coincides with a general movement among Native peoples everywhere toward the development of an authentic Native Christianity. In essence, such a marriage of cultures and philosophies means a return to roots, to an affirmation of indigenous spirituality. In practical terms, it means the integration of native myths, customs, and songs with Christianity. In an official way, this was fostered by the establishment of a Native ministry school at Plains Presbytery in Saskatchewan where Native candidates would learn the practical application of ministry.

Another dimension is the application of the Latin American "liberationist" philosophy, which ultimately seeks the freedom of the Native peoples from the trappings of colonialism. The remnants of colonialism aren't subtle. In June each year on the reservation, hundreds line up in the hot sun on the "treaty grounds" — a fenced-off area just across the river from the church. Here Indian Affairs officials and a Mountie in red serge and glistening boots preside at long tables while the reserve's residents march past. Upon announcing their "numbers" to the officials, each Native adult and child is handed a crisp $5 bill. Each person on the reserve receives this money, due to them from the Treaty of 1875. At one time they were given flour and bullets but the twentieth century called for something different.

One year, recounted McKay, an attempt was made to distribute the treaty money by check, but tribal elders angrily rebelled and returned them. "They wanted the money!" McKay maintained that what's at issue for his people is the demeaning nature of this practice. It's bad enough that it is only $5 that is being handed out to reserve Natives — hardly keeping pace with inflation. What's worse, though, is that the practice itself stands as a symbolic reminder to his people that they are not in control.

McKay's election as the moderator of the United Church of Canada in August 1992 stands as another symbol. He believes it will give "hope" to Natives everywhere. Since taking over the leadership of the national church, he has gone across the country in an effort not only to represent the church as a whole — that's expected and demanded of him — but to bring to light the reality that faces the Native in Canada. His push had always been for Natives to come to grips with their own traditions and what is valuable in their lives and in their past.

McKay has been forthright in his statements as a church leader, but has not minced words in stating that the Native peoples have suffered "cultural genocide" at the hands of Christianity. He himself was forced into a residential school during the 1950s where his language and culture were banned. It was there, too, that he experienced physical abuse and sexual intimidation. McKay told one reporter that going to that school was "such a clear example of an ongoing process of cultural genocide, a process that removed people from the context of their own community and culture and attempted to shape us in their image of what civilization is . . . It was brutal in the sense that it was very much like incarceration."

McKay has said time and time again, the fact is most denominations fail to reflect aboriginal spirituality. As head of the United Church of Canada, he believed his goal ought to be an effort to recognize the spirituality of others, and to create a climate in which all cultures and traditions are appreciated. The push among Native people to come to grips with their traditions and with what is valuable in their lives is still running up against opposition. "There's a failure in the church," said McKay, "to see anything of spiritual value in the people themselves."

Among members of the United Church, as far back as the mid 1980s, McKay pointed out the push for a Native "conference" or diocese was considered by critics as insulting to the church. He argued that while the idea for a First Nations' conference may have been new to Canada, the United Presbyterian Church had one in the United States. McKay confessed that some in the "sessional committee" of the church had argued vehemently against the move, describing it as segregationist. "They asked us why we didn't want to remain members of the whole church."

McKay, naturally, acknowledged that the formation of a Native conference would have some effects. The formation of two Native presbyteries — at Keewatin and at Plains — proved by the mid 1980s that Native peoples were serious in asserting their rights. The church's sixty Native parishes strung out across reserves from one end of the country to the other had virtually no voice or influence at the uppermost levels of the church. By influence, McKay meant the ability of Native people to bring in legislation that would enhance their values. McKay felt that giving more power to Natives would help prevent Native churches from closing down. Since the 1950s, nearly twenty First Nations' churches have been boarded up.

The quality of Christianity on the reserve has been difficult to maintain. McKay remembered stories of the old days, of how the Christian church swarmed upon the reserves with Bibles, hymnals, and pipe organs. The traditional drums were stored away and replaced with fiddles. Soon the traditional Cree songs praising all of creation were ignored and replaced with "Guide Me, O Thou, Great Jehovah." Yet McKay envisions a change. Like many of the Inuit who tossed away their "dog tags" bearing federal government identification numbers, so the Natives of Canada's Christian churches want to dispense with the imported traditions of white Protestant and Catholic Christianity. It isn't that the Native people want to turn their backs on Christianity — it's that in their own myths, language, and customs, they find a better means to understand Christianity.

"We're an Old Testament people," McKay said simply. More importantly, he stressed, the church must realize that colonialism and paternalism are tinged with racism, and this has all but denuded the Indian of self-respect and spiritual value.

BISHOP DESMOND TUTU
11
GOD IS ON OUR SIDE

"*Yeah, yeah, yeah, I'm glad I'm not God, you know, because sometimes looking at my handiwork, I would say, 'Well, maybe the best thing to do is just to rub the slate clean and start afresh.' Really, if He doesn't laugh at some of the things we're up to, maybe He weeps a bit.*" — Bishop Desmond Tutu

The first time I saw Bishop Desmond Tutu, he was smiling. There seemed to be a charm, and a conviviality, about the man. There seemed to be something alive in him that wouldn't deny the least bit of joy in life. Here was someone who would seize what little good might exist around him, and wave it about as a sign that there was still hope. It was the summer of 1983 at the World Council of Churches in Vancouver, British Columbia when I first met him. He walked into a press room to meet the press corps. He was supposed to have been in Vancouver two weeks before, but the South African government had barred him from leaving the country. The politicians were uneasy about what he would say. Pressure from abroad, however, helped to lift the travel ban on Tutu and let him travel to Canada to attend the World Council of Churches.

As the South African bishop emerged in the auditorium that day, there was the very real feeling we were about to meet a modern-day saint. Yet the broad, engaging smile and abundant energy undermined that expectation. Or perhaps enhanced it. Who knows. Among the audience there was a sense of confusion, uncertainty, awe. Here was someone whose life was on the line. Anything he uttered that day might be cause for his execution. Not a court-decided execution, but rather a covert, "accidental," sudden, barbaric death. He knew it. He smiled at it. He jested about it, but only obliquely.

Tutu exuded dynamism. Head of the South African Council of Churches, Tutu, a South African Anglican bishop, had been at the forefront, vehemently battling apartheid. At fifty-three, he was a year away from being the second black resistance leader to win the Nobel Peace Prize. Albert John Lutuli, former president of the African National Congress, had been given it in 1960. In announcing the award in 1984, a year after I first met him, the Norwegian

Nobel Committee called Bishop Tutu "a unifying leader figure in the campaign to resolve the problem of apartheid in South Africa." He was recognized as the moral conscience of a nation that persisted in policies of strict race separation called apartheid, which reserved the best schools, housing and employment for whites and denied the country's twenty-three million blacks — the largest segment of the country's population — a voice in government.

Bishop Tutu's brief visit to the World Council of Churches was a last-minute concession made by the government of South Africa, which tried to save face in its embarrassing decision to deny him travel outside the country. As I recall, when he arrived the 3,500 people who had gathered for an all-night vigil on a Friday night to mark the anniversary of the bombing of Hiroshima, were pleasantly surprised to have this controversial bishop address them. Tutu began in his characteristic manner, jesting: "Please, take it from me, the age of miracles has not ceased — after all, why am I here?"

It was this light-hearted, cocksure approach that struck me. Here was a man who actually could turn the other cheek. Though his life was in danger, he refused to be bitter, resentful, violent. His anti-apartheid attack was direct, unwavering, disturbing, but he never advocated violence. Rancor was nowhere to be found. His attack on his government's policies, and on the white supremacists, was launched with buoyant hope and optimism that things could change, and would change — just you wait and see. Such words seemed odd, especially since a compatriot, Allan Boesak, a South African theologian and president of the World Alliance of Reformed Churches, earlier described the reality of South Africa as "a litany of death." He had informed the World Council of Churches delegates that "too many are swept away by the tides of war and too many are tortured in dungeons of death. In too many eyes the years of endless struggle have extinguished the fires of hope and joy and too many bodies are bowed down by the weight of that peculiarly repugnant death called despair."

With that assessment of the South African situation, any glimmer of hope seemed absurd. After all, here was a country torn by unrest and violence and racism. There appeared to be no letting up in the struggle. A new constitution had been drafted but there was little joy in its passage. The country was hit instead with even more riots and fire-bombing. The South African press reported the cause of the riots to be a rent increase in the black "townships," another word for segregated ghettos in which most of the country's twenty-three million blacks live. In fact, the violence was an immediate reaction to what has been the world's most brutal and racist system of government. At the center of that conflict was the indomitable Bishop Desmond Tutu.

That day in Vancouver, the South African bishop struggled to be diplomatic. He had a reputation for never letting up his attacks on the government for keeping the vast majority of South Africa's population disenfranchised — serfs without political power or rights in their own homeland. Until the release of Nelson Mandela from prison, and his subsequent ascendancy to the presidency of South Africa, black South Africans stood outside the system of government, unable to make a selection of candidates to govern them. At that moment in Vancouver, South Africa still did not include such individuals in its tri-cameral parliament of three legislative chambers: one for whites, a second for "colored," and a third for Indian representatives. Limited powers were provided to the two minority chambers while absolute powers were retained by the white chamber. That has all changed with Mandela in power. In 1983 it was a different story. Twenty-three million blacks living in South Africa were systematically denied a chance to survive under the system. They were disallowed not only the right to vote, but were also confined to slums and given an inferior education. Millions were uprooted, and exiled to distant homelands they'd never seen before.

I recall the impression Bishop Tutu left with reporters, or for that matter with everyone at the World Council of Churches. His message was that in spite of such back-breaking racism, the spirit of black South Africans would never diminish — not in the long run. A prophetic Tutu promised that people in authority would be uprooted, that attitudes would improve, and finally South Africa would realize that such horrific injustice must come to a halt. He left no doubt that his attitude toward South Africa would remain positive. Throughout his career, Tutu held out hope that life would change for blacks, that they would be given a right to vote, a right to a proper education, a right to a proper home and a right to live as they ought to, as children of God. This was his message all along. He never let up with it. As early as 1981, he told a Southam News reporter: "The history of Christendom is chock full of things that ought to make all Christians bow their heads in shame. Look at Ulster . . . Look at the so-called German Christians who supported Hitler. In some ways, we've got to be gentle with them here." He was referring to the Afrikaner churches, pointing out that they ought to begin shouldering some of the responsibility for the country's ills.

In Vancouver Bishop Tutu would not level blame, or point fingers. Wherever he went outside South Africa, he remained cool and consistent in his battle. When reporters at the World Council of Churches attempted to pin him down and prompt him to fire off a few verbal missiles at enemies, he opened his arms wide instead and declared that some day both whites and blacks would not only resolve their differences, but would embrace one another. He had learned such persistent hope as a boy growing up in South Africa. "I didn't know anything about baseball . . . but I knew all about Jackie Robinson . . . and I grew inches." He gained courage, too, from "the Brown Bomber (Joe Louis) and Sugar Ray Leonard." The Black movement, Bishop Tutu said, had gained sustenance from obvious leaders — most notably Martin Luther King, Jr., but also from those who spoke for everyone by their achievements alone.

The summer the South African church leader stressed that although he was denied permission to speak to congregations and assemblies of his own people in his country, he still fostered hope. Admittedly this was difficult for many to understand, but he pointed out, "As a Christian, I always remain optimistic. I believe in grace. I believe God can change people. I would not be a Christian minister if I didn't believe this." He related the story of a man called "Tom" who had been in and out of jail (in South Africa) "like some of us are in and out of showers." He said, "When Tom came out after eleven months in jail, he said, 'Thank you for your prayers.' Then he said, 'Let's not be consumed by bitterness.'"

Adopting such an attitude never made things easier for Tutu. During that visit to Vancouver he told an incredulous audience that he augured "an explosion" in South Africa because blacks could not tolerate such racist attitudes much longer. It was difficult being positive when families were being uprooted daily, and shifted from one end of the country to the other. The government, he maintained, had uprooted some three and a half million people, and dumped them, "as if they are rubbish," in arid territories, and forced people into begging and prostitution. Tutu decried the "eerie silence" that had reigned over the issue of apartheid. The only sound heard from the West was criticism that violence should not be used in the fight against racism in South Africa. Easy for them to say, Tutu taunted, and smiled. He knew his history. Although he rejected violence as a means to changing attitudes, he knew the West's attitude was inconsistent with the support given to underground forces during the Second World War, when they struggled against fascist governments. In those years, such battles were lauded by the West, but "as soon as we start dealing with black liberation, the call is for non-violence." Tutu has always believed in "other ways" — non-violent means — to deal with the problem. That's why he helped organize a national council of churches, of both whites and blacks, to radicalize attitudes. In such a forum, he believed the folly of racism would be indisputable. "Maybe one day they'll (whites) realize we're all Christians, that nobody hates him (the white man), that the world is really ready to embrace them."

Bishop Tutu's great hope in Vancouver was to put an end to the confusion over speculation about whether apartheid policies had biblical backing. He found it preposterous that so many white Christian leaders tried in vain to justify apartheid with the gospel. "It is no longer enough to say apartheid is inconsistent with the gospel, but that it is at variance with it. And all those who aid or give support to apartheid should be asked, 'Would you give support to Nazism?' because apartheid is just as vicious and evil as Nazism ever was in Germany." As soon as he made this remark during the initial press conference, Tutu flashed that characteristic smile. It was a triumphant moment. He knew the white Christian community no longer enjoyed the theological edge. He smiled broadly: "What's open to them is the doctrine of redemption."

The next time I saw Bishop Desmond Tutu, it was in the winter of 1986. His prophecies seemed slow in coming. He arrived in Detroit, as part of a twelve-day tour of the USA. Moments after he stepped off the plane, a hasty press conference was held. News people pushed their way into a small room to fire questions at the South African religious leader. As always, he was amused, cheery, animated. I sat in a bank of chairs directly in front of the South African churchman. When his press secretary put out the invitations for questions, I rose to pose the first question, because no one else leaped at the opportunity immediately. What I didn't realize was that when I stood up, I blocked the view of the television network cameras. I only got as far as identifying myself as a Canadian journalist when voices from the cameramen drowned me out from the back of the room, "Sit down, idiot! Get out of the way!" Tutu was quick on the uptake: "I can see that you're not getting a very good reception in this country!"

The questions that afternoon were those he had been answering everywhere. Apartheid. Injustice. Mandela's freedom. Though he stayed long enough to field and deflect them, he was off to bigger things at the high-powered Detroit Economic Club, an organization that has been a venue for American presidents and world leaders. He was also scheduled for a rousing speech at Cobo Arena. At this latter event he was the consummate old time preacher. I remember sitting back and watching Tutu on the platform looking out over a sea of faces. Slowly and quietly he delivered a forty-five minute speech that ended with his arms raised and his voice shouting, "We're going to be free! We're going to be free! March with us into a glorious future!" Moments later the audience, almost on cue, were on their feet and swarming around the platform, pushing past a wall of security people to stuff dollar bills into large wooden blue boxes. The money was intended to fight apartheid in South Africa.

That was January 17, 1986. A bitterly cold day in Detroit. It was long before Mandela would enjoy the dramatic and miraculous reversal of fortune for blacks in his country. Back then, Bishop Desmond Tutu, much like the American politician and evangelist Martin Luther King, marched about the country and the world with one message. End apartheid! End enslavement! The money being collected in downtown Detroit was in a part of the city still ravaged and scarred from the race riots of the late 1960s.

This tiny man on stage in the lavender shirt and glasses sparkling from all the lights knew something of conflict, of poverty, of debate. He had been South Africa's fiercest opponent of apartheid, this buoyant and smiling Anglican bishop from Johannesburg. As he departed from the stage at Cobo Arena, which stands perched on the Detroit River overlooking the skyline of Windsor, Ontario, the five-foot-six Tutu, dwarfed by burly Detroit undercover police, waved to the audience filing out of the arena. The song they chanted was his favorite, the anthem of the anti-segregationist movement in the USA in the 1960s, "We Shall Overcome." There was no mistaking what had aroused them. Some said they hadn't heard anything like this in Detroit since Martin Luther King had been there. To them, the then fifty-four year old head of the South African Council of Churches was a reminder of a charisma sadly absent in the black movement in the USA.

Bishop Desmond Tutu had been on a tour to heighten awareness of South Africa's plight, and to raise money for refugees and education. He made few friends among the corporate structures in Detroit when he issued a sharply-worded warning to the automakers that businesses with interests in South Africa might consider putting a stop to this funneling of money to South Africa, and start considering the need for human rights. It was a harsh indictment of the big American corporations, and representatives from the Big Three auto makers weren't happy. Indeed, some fled the arena for their limousines just outside the doors. Tutu had issued his warning in no uncertain terms. He was like Jesus wielding a whip in the Temple with the money lenders. His anger was directed at the investments in South Africa, and what this money had been doing to his people. "They ought not kid us or themselves when they say they're there in South Africa for our benefit. They should say, 'We're in South Africa because it pays to be in South Africa! We're in South Africa because of the cheap labor . . . And it is our people who are providing that cheap labor." Although earlier he insisted he wouldn't "name names," and held to that promise at the press conference and at the Detroit Economic Club, his audience at Cobo wasn't about to be stopped — they shouted, "Chrysler! Chrysler!"

At a morning press conference just before addressing the more than 3,000 executives at the Economic Club, he pointed out that large corporations threatening to pull out of South Africa could determine "whether or not we're going to have 'Armageddon' in South Africa . . . or peace." Tutu stressed he had come to Detroit with the clear message that "the presence of your companies in South Africa is as much moral as it is economic and political. Whether they (American businesses) like it or not, apartheid is one of the most vicious systems the world has known." Bishop Tutu maintained those American businesses ought to apply some "real pressure" to the government by making clear-cut demands and setting a deadline. He urged the release of political prisoners and detainees, the evacuation of troops from black townships and implementation of a system whereby migrant workers could be reunited with their families. At that time most migrant workers were separated from their wives for eleven months of the year. "If these demands aren't met, then these companies in your country can use their economic clout and pull out of South Africa."

However, Bishop Tutu's shining hour was at Cobo, where he declared in spite of the harsh realities of apartheid, "God is on our side!" To a thundering applause, the Nobel Peace Prize winner announced, "We're going to be free . . . We're going to march into a new society where blacks and whites will know they count . . . because they are persons created in the image of God."

Today, those words hold a new meaning. He had told Detroiters in 1986, "The children are showing us the way. They're saying if it means we have to face up to guns, to police dogs, to tear gas, we'll face up to it and carry stones." Tutu told them that compromise was not the answer, reform was not the solution. "You don't reform a Frankenstein . . . you destroy it!"

MOTHER TERESA
12
SAINT OF CALCUTTA AND CASS CORRIDOR

1 Most Sundays only a handful of parishioners fill the large cathedral like St. Agnes Roman Catholic Church in the slums of the Cass Corridor. That Thursday at the beginning of the summer in 1981, it was different. More than 1,500 crowded into the worn oak pews and stood in the creaky aisles of the sweltering church on Rosa Parks Boulevard. This is the street named after the great Civil Rights activist Rosa Parks. It was her stubbornness and refusal in 1955 to give up her seat on a Montgomery, Alabama bus to a white passenger that became the catalyst behind the civil rights movement in the United States. She moved here in 1957 after losing her job as a seamstress in Alabama. That summer in Detroit, Parks — a frail black woman whose unerring silence was a shimmering presence in a city that had fallen on hard times — was there among her neighbors to meet Mother Teresa of Calcutta, someone she admired.

When Mother Teresa arrived she advised M. L. Wilson, one of the organizers and ushers, that she didn't want a reception downstairs in the basement of the church. At least, she didn't want coffee and donuts to be served. The organizers — feeling a little red-faced — had made the mistake of buying up a supply of donuts to offer those who had come out that night to the church. Mother Teresa, in characteristic manner, stated, "Give it to the poor." She wasn't angry; she wasn't disappointed. But she was emphatic. No food. At the end of the mass, celebrated by then Archbishop Edmund Szoka, the tiny, slightly stooped and saintly-looking sister stood to deliver a message. It was what you would expect. Find the poor. Help them. Care for them. Take a look around. Open your eyes. The poor are everywhere. This quiet-spoken sister also called upon people to rally around the family. Restore family values. Fight abortion and contraception. Hold your kids. Listen to them. Be with them. Though many had to strain to hear this frail nun from Calcutta — some even standing on the pews to catch a glimpse of her — what she conveyed caused many to cry. She spoke about the life they knew intimately, the reality of struggling in a place where the economics proved a cruel reminder every day that things weren't going to improve, and that there was no one to turn to, except God.

Mother Teresa told them there were too many destitute, neglected, and left to struggle by themselves. "This has created terrible loneliness." It becomes the duty of everyone to champion the cause of the aged, the poor, the jobless. "Our sisters administer to 93,000 lepers in India, and I still think being lonely, unwanted, unloved, and forgotten is a much greater disease than leprosy." She went on to explain that the work of her religious sisters in Detroit, in the shadow of Tiger Stadium, was one small step to combat such desolation. But she hadn't come just with words of encouragement. She leveled a stinging blow at abortionists, branding the act nothing short of "murder," declaiming it "the greatest destroyer of peace, the greatest destroyer of love, the greatest destroyer of the family."

Following the mass, I rushed down to the basement, eager to speak with this tiny saintly woman. Embarrassing as it may sound, I was also anxious to have her autograph copies of Malcolm Muggeridge's biography of her. Why I succumbed to a friend's wish to get these signed, I don't understand! But this friend — an avid collector among whose archives are hundreds of signed first editions including those of Abraham Lincoln, William Wordsworth, James Joyce and others — had enjoined me to take along these books on Mother Teresa. When she walked into the room, I hastened to her side. I seemed to tower over this delicate, pious woman. When I held out the editions, she waved them aside, shaking her head, dismissing me. My friend had advised me to expect as much, and encouraged persistence. Mother Teresa asked if I would give the books to one of the sisters, promising she'd sign them later. "No," I protested ignorantly. "Just your signature! Now!" She took the books. Arthritic fingers clutching my pen, she scrawled her name across the title pages. Suddenly I felt foolish. Apologized. She remained silent, impassive. Soon the room was flooding with well-wishers who pressed in to meet the sister. Some held up babies for her to bless. In time, Rosa Parks herself came forward, to pay homage to Mother Teresa. Trying to redeem myself, I apologized again. She smiled, shrugged. I asked her about the sisters working in Detroit. She told me "If there is anything the poor can teach us, it's contentment and peace." She reiterated her message: "I want people to learn to share with one another and to love one another."

Again, my ludicrous and insensitive attempts to persuade her to autograph the books began to haunt me. Here she was addressing the concerns of a world that was hungry, where people suffered indignities, disease, poverty and loneliness, and all I seemed to care about was her autograph, as if she were the American League batting champion. I fell into conversation with a General Motors engineer who had spent the last two years, evenings and weekends, assisting the sisters. "The sisters have been tremendous. When she came here, the sisters were going daily into two homes, but they're going into up around sixty homes now." Mother Teresa, founder of the Missionaries of Charity had been in Detroit two years before to set up this community house in a neighborhood that had been the center of the riots in the 1960s, a racial explosion that, in effect, had driven away businesses from the downtown. Mother Teresa and her sisters are among the few who could possibly cut across the boundaries of racial prejudice and create "this kind of trust," the man told me. He asserted, "She's a living saint. She is understanding, caring."

When I studied her from across the room I saw how she patiently met each and every person. It reminded me of my childhood impression of what a saint was. I felt that I was in the presence of someone unique, holy. Archbishop Szoka greeted her, clasped her hands, and whispered something. She smiled. A stout woman extended an infant to her. Mother Teresa took the baby, holding it close. She blew softly on the baby's sweaty forehead, then placed her right hand over the child's eyes, and prayed. The mother was in tears. So were many others. Mother Teresa spoke softly to the mother whose face suddenly broke into a broad smile.

2 Months later, I was back in Detroit. The wind whipped through the dark alley behind the church. Inside the gate, a path took me through a yard to the small porch of a three-story brick house. If you could peer through the windows at the back of the convent at about 7:00 a.m., you would have seen four nuns prostrate on the carpeted floor of their chapel at mass. One sister answered the door, pushed it open, and I stepped inside. She returned dutifully to the front of the altar.

At the back of the chapel — actually just inside an adjacent room — were two visitors, a man and a woman. They also knelt. A warm glow emanated from this tiny room, the only place alive on this dark vacant street in the heart of the city's "crack" district. The church across the alley rested in stony silence. At the point in the service when the wine and bread are consecrated, each of the nuns bowed in front of the altar, foreheads touching the floor. I noticed they were barefoot. I wondered at how cold it must have been for them on the linoleum floors of this convent.

By the time mass was finished, the sun was just beginning to appear over the rooftops on this cold day. From upstairs I could hear the sounds of children and mothers in the shelter. It was after breakfast, and they were bundled up to face the day. A sister called them in the chapel "Come on . . . come on, and say a prayer . . . Come to the chapel." One by one the mothers edged closer to the doorway of the chapel. They wore heavy winter coats, boots, and hats. Two women were Muslims and appeared bewildered by this business of the Christian prayer. But they weren't. Actually, they were more accustomed to it than most at the shelter, said one of the sisters who led them in the words, "Dear Jesus we thank you for this beautiful day . . ." She then broke into a wailing song of only just a few words, "Oh, how I love Jesus . . . because he first loved me!"

This was the Missionaries of Charity House, the house Mother Teresa had come to Detroit to start. Situated at the corner of Trumbull and Warren, a few blocks away from the Cass Corridor, the tough, squalid inner-city harbor of the poor. Each day this tiny religious community wakens by 4:00 a.m. Each day two of the sisters depart from the spare-looking brick house at the back of St. Dominic's Roman Catholic Church to venture among the hawkers and prostitutes and make their visits to shut-ins and the destitute. They carry with them bags of bread and clothing. Sometimes they go out to clean homes, or just to run errands to the corner store. In everything they do, said Sister Regipaul, they bring with them "the love of God." The message is plain and apprehensible — these people are not forgotten, not neglected, not out of the sight of God. Mother Teresa founded the Missionaries of Charity in 1950. To date there are some 2,000 sisters and 300 brothers toiling in various countries. The Detroit house opened in 1979. Since then the sisters have struggled to bring this message of love to the people in the Cass Corridor area. When they first arrived, they used St. Agnes Roman Catholic Church — also in the downtown slums — as their base of operation. Now they have appropriated the Dominican convent.

The sisters wear white wraparound habits that cover their heads and fall to their feet. At the fringe is the familiar blue-stripe pattern Mother Teresa wears. While working, aprons are worn over the habit. In the chapel, their feet are bare. When they're working, or when they venture outside, or to the soup kitchen, they wear shoes and wool stockings. As soon as the women and children have departed from the shelter, pails and mops are carried to the upper rooms where everything is scrubbed down. That morning it was so cold the steam could be seen rising from the metal pails. The rooms in the shelter have hardwood floors. Iron cots and inch-thin mattresses cram the rooms. Here the women and children sleep. Each room is devoted to a saint: one for St. Joseph, another, the Holy Family, another, the Sacred Heart. In each, there is a statue or holy picture. At the end of the hall is a room with two cots where two of the sisters sleep. They take turns at this duty, to keep an eye on the people in the shelter.

By 8:30 a.m. the sisters' work was finished upstairs where twelve beds had to be made up. The floors glistened, and the disinfectant smell of the bathrooms pervaded the air. The work outside the shelter now awaited them. The sisters filed out into the brisk wintry morning, followed the path to the alley, then around the corner to the side door of the gymnasium. When they unlocked the door, a melon-colored cat stretched indolently at the door frame. "That's Queen," remarked a cheerful Sister Emilia, who, along with Sister Regipaul stayed only long enough to collect bread donated from local bakeries. They stepped back out into the cold and headed to the Cass Corridor. Meanwhile Sisters Kironmoy and Ifsta remained in the building to prepare for the soup kitchen, anticipating people would be lining up outside within an hour.

Within forty-five minutes, a huge pot of soup was simmering on the sprawling gas stove, and about two dozen grilled cheese sandwiches were warming on the grill. Upstairs in the cavernous gymnasium the place settings waited in the gloomy silence. I peered through the side-door window, and spotted the men and women queuing outside. One man shuffled back and forth in an effort to keep warm. He kept yapping away at a man next to him about how it was necessary to believe in God and have "a lil'initiative in your life . . . just to git wit'it, man . . . After all, we may not be here tomorra, man!" Ironically, his proselytizing had all the heart and soul of the nuns themselves or the priests next door. His preaching, though not as stylized, actually engaged some of the same language and perhaps even borrowed some of the same well-meaning philosophies. He was no priest. He was a down-and-outer with a torn, threadbare coat and mismatched socks, to say nothing of the hunger that poured from his eyes. There was no denying it — he was at the side door of this old school for a bowl of soup, spaghetti, or whatever might be on the menu. And he appreciated it. Always cleaning up afterwards, always thanking the sisters. When he entered the building, he nodded to the nuns as he turned left to locate a chair in the gymnasium.

One sister finally asked if I would help. I carried down a tray of hot bread. The man took a long, hungry look at it and rolled his tongue over his lips. A broad grin. But no one rushed to the tables where the food sat, steaming and ready. Everyone waited respectfully at the dinner table where coffee cups and knives and forks were set. They waited patiently for Sister Ifsta to stand at the end of one long table to say grace, and lead them in that same wailing song about Jesus that was sung in the chapel earlier that morning.

Plate by plate, with assembly-line efficiency, the food was placed in front of the haunted and hungry mugs of these Cass Corridor homeless. On the menu today, quipped a fifty-nine year old widow who was helping out in the kitchen, is "Mother Teresa's goulash," or a potpourri of ham, chicken, and vegetables. She assisted the sister in carrying out the plates to each table. I returned to the kitchen and flipped a few sandwiches on the grill. One of the sisters passed me a large metal tray with still more sandwiches and entreated me to help in their distribution. I stood behind a table and waited for the hungry to march past. I observed the long emaciated hands reaching for the steaming meals. Few grumbled. Some muttered that they didn't want soup. Others sneered at the cheese sandwiches. Each projected their own middle-class values cultivated from television, former lives, or whatever, upon the situation in the halls of this old gymnasium. Despite the poverty, each clung to their own ritualistic routine. Some demanded coffee fill-ups. Others, without uttering a word, would place the palm of a hand over the rim of the cup to signal they didn't want coffee. But the sisters and volunteers were tolerant, obedient, mindful.

One woman pushed back her chair, stood up, and cleaned out a plate and a cup before putting it into a plastic bin to be washed. "You know, I go to church all the time. I go every Sunday. I'm a good Catholic." The tiny sister knew she was lying. The business of replenishing the coffee mugs and soup bowls followed. Then the clean up, clearing away dirty dishes, washing them in the large metal sinks in a kitchen that reeked of natural gas. During the week twenty-five to fifty-five may stop by, but on Sundays, about 100 crowd into the building at one time. "We need all the help we can get," Sister Kironmoy said.

I could tell the regulars. They cleaned up after themselves, respectfully returned their plates and cups to the plastic bins, and thanked the sisters. They also *worked* the sisters, trying their patience. One man begged for a new belt. "I've got a size 42 pant, but I'm only a 38." When Sister Kironmoy, who knew him, appeared downstairs, she inquired, "Where were you at Christmas — I didn't see you." He replied, "Oh, sista, I's in jail." The nun listened to his plight about the belt, nodded, asked him to wait, and disappeared into another room. After a while, she returned with a wrapped present for the man. She had bought presents for the regulars at Christmas. He hadn't been there, so she kept it for him. He thanked her profusely. Toothy smile and a wink. "I hope it's a belt!" From the window, I watched the man pause in the corner of the building in the windy alley. He ripped open the present and yanked out what appeared to be a pair of woolen socks, or maybe mittens. Something else tumbled to the ground where it unravelled . . . A belt. He grabbed at it on the ice, held it up like a trophy, and let out a cry, "Yes!"

By noon the dishes were washed, the floors swept. The sisters bundled up and made their way back to the house for an afternoon spent in prayer and reflection. At 3:00 p.m., two sisters returned to the kitchen across the alley and prepared pots of hot chocolate for the school children who dropped in after class to be tutored. When they arrived, the gymnasium exploded with sounds as they raced to the tables. Again, prayer. Then hot chocolate. Then the studying began. Retired principal Charles Cromar of Royal Oak, Michigan, dropped in every day to help the children with arithmetic or English. By 5:00 p.m., the kids were gone, and the women were back at the shelter, looking to stay the night.

When I left, Sister Kironmoy asked, "Will you come back to do some more work?" I didn't quite grasp her meaning. I replied, "No, I'm finished here — I've got all I need," suggesting my story about this place was complete. I failed to comprehend what she was after. She had wanted to know when I would return to do some real work, to help out in the soup kitchen. I promised to return. Like so many others, I sensed that, deep down, I probably would never make it back.

AGNES MANSOUR
13
SISTER OF MERCY

A gnes Mansour has always been cool-headed and methodical. She weighs what she's going to say before going on the record, but when she commits herself, she holds nothing back in her delivery. She speaks honestly, almost without emotion, as she tells you how she views her life, and the issues that stand before her.

Mansour is now sixty-four years old. She was a Roman Catholic nun more than a decade ago, but was coerced into quitting her religious order when then Archbishop Edmund Szoka of Detroit forced her hand. He ordered her to resign from her position as director of Michigan's Department of Social Services because her department financed abortions of poor women in the state through its Medicaid program. At the time of this battle, which raged in 1983, the program paid out more than $5.7 million for 19,500 abortions in Michigan. The Sisters of Mercy religious order to which Mansour belonged for some thirty years backed her stand against the archbishop, arguing that she be permitted to remain both a sister and director of the agency. The Vatican ruled, however, that she must either leave the order or quit the welfare agency. She left the order.

The day I met her in July 1983 was unbearably hot. I had driven up to Lansing, Michigan with *The Windsor Star* photographer Randy Moore to see her. With great reluctance, she had agreed to the interview, but secured a promise from me that she would tell it in her own words. There I was downstairs in the lobby — about fifteen minutes early for the meeting — when I spotted her. I hadn't expected to run into her there. Indeed, I had hoped I wouldn't run into her, for both Randy Moore and I had delayed putting on our ties because of the heat. There we were arranging ourselves when she walked past. It made for an embarrassing moment. She didn't mind. She was pleasant, eager, understanding, and thoughtful. Her practical and down-to-earth approach put us at ease.

My first question was deflected, but not in any *political* way. I asked if someone in religious life going through such turmoil can actually expect things to get better. Does faith kick in, and signal to them that everything will be fine? Mansour smiled. "It depends on what you mean by 'better'." She knew what was meant. She had support from many sectors for her war with Szoka. "I had a good deal of support. I had to make a decision based on my best insights in what I considered to be the right thing to do. Whether it was right or wrong." She looked to God for help. But also to "the extensions of God on earth." By that, Mansour meant she sought "objective input" in her decision to leave the religious order and continue helping the poor in Michigan. "I didn't want to push it in the direction I wanted to go. I really didn't want to go in the direction it had to go in. But I didn't have any alternative. I discussed it with people I had great respect for, that I knew would be honest with me. For their best insights."

She relied heavily on the Sisters of Mercy, saying "there was no way I was going to ignore them . . . They're the people I've always dealt with in any ministry placement. The bishop doesn't tell you where you're going to be placed! We always work through our religious community — they're the community where I had my religious formation and took my vows, and it was where I was committed whether I was in or out of the diocese." The fine print behind the vow of obedience — one of the three vows she took when she became a nun — means that one is asked "to discern the will of God. I think there is a misunderstanding. People think you take a vow to the bishop. You don't take a vow to a bishop. We (in the religious order) take that vow in a very collegial way where your insights are also taken into consideration." If the Sisters of Mercy had not backed her decision, things would have been different: "I probably wouldn't have gone in that direction."

But in taking that route, she still didn't feel "at odds" with the church. "There are all sorts of misconceptions about what the Roman Catholic Church is. It's the people of God. There are various models for churches — hierarchical and authoritative models and there are also 'people' models. Anybody in authority, whether in the church or out of the church, has to be in a service role rather than in a controlling, dictating role." Regarding the battle with Szoka (now elevated to a cardinal and dispatched to Rome to reorganize the financial structure of the Vatican, for Pope John Paul II) Mansour told me, "I am not blaming him. I'm not bitter. I'm really not. I'm going about my business, and I don't have any time for negative comments in regard to the whole issue."

At the time of that controversy, Mansour was earning $57,000, and was giving all of it to the Sisters of Mercy. When she left the order, she took only a stipend from the salary in order to live outside the convent, but the balance went to the religious order. She would never rule out returning to live as a nun. "Only time will tell." Mansour said, pointing out she has never permitted others to push her into making decisions. "It seems that we let what happens happen, and then we accept it as we go along. I am most concerned that something be done in the church to respect political ministry. I think it's a very legitimate one and a very needed one and one where a person can, indeed, make a difference."

Mansour had harsh criticism of Pope John Paul II. She maintained that it was hypocritical that he would direct priests and nuns to stay away from seeking political office, when he himself was perhaps the most visible sign of the church's involvement in politics. At that time, the Pope had just gone to Poland, making it clear he opposed the government's policies regarding workers. He also came out in support of the Solidarity Movement. "He's having a lot of influence there," commented Mansour who felt that Catholic religious could do the same if they were permitted to involve themselves in the political decision-making.

Mansour often stated that the Vatican lacked a clear grasp of the American scene. She elaborated: "I don't think there's a full realization of where religious women are in their ministry and how much we have taken seriously Vatican II. We have looked at collegiality and subsidiarity. Our whole mode of operating is very different from the hierarchy of the church — it's more collegial. It has happened to most religious communities." Mansour believed Rome exercised an iron fist in the issue over her job with the Michigan Department of Social Services. She labeled it "intimidation," and described it as affecting a wide sector of priests and religious. Mansour received hundreds of letters of support from clergy and sisters, but few would go on record supporting her publicly. They feared reprisals. Only the Sisters of Mercy came out unequivocally in support.

Mansour's hope was that her fight with the Vatican would not set back the women's movement within the church. If anything, she hoped it would advance the concerns of women. "I think it has raised the consciousness of some. Unfortunately, there will probably be a few casualties. There will be those who will say, 'Oh, my gosh, I didn't think this could happen,' or 'I didn't want this to happen.' Even among those in the hierarchical church I don't think they want these things (like Mansour's confrontation) to happen. They're (church authority) not doing this intentionally. I really think they thought I was going to do what they told me. I'm sure they did. That's why I think they were very surprised. And sorry." As for the future of women in religious life, Mansour couldn't speculate, except to indicate that it all depended upon the new Code of Canon Law. "Some areas of the new canons are very restrictive, giving a lot of authority to the local bishops. Depending upon the local bishops, you can have great differences. You could have some problems, especially with religious communities that have been used to handling their own administrative affairs."

When Mansour looked back at the time when she entered the convent in the 1950s, she could see that women in religious life had become more active. She could not understand why women should be barred from ordination. "I'm in favor of it. Now, I wouldn't want to be a priest. But I think (women's ordination) is needed. I think it's legitimate. I see absolutely no valid reason for not having it. It's totally appropriate. I don't think we should block women from administering in the church or outside the church. We still don't have enough women in politics. But ordaining priests will come. It's just too slow." Often compared to Mother Teresa, whose position with the poor was also highly political, Mansour was told she should follow this other sister's style. "She's opposed to abortion, and I should be doing that, too." Mansour had a different agenda: "You have to do it according to your own insights and your own ways."

As for her stand on abortion, Mansour was clear: "I am opposed to abortion. But I believe we have to address the evil of abortion other than through legislation. We've got to change attitudes. We have to respect the fact that people in good conscience come to different conclusions. I don't think we should assume that we possess the total truth and that we should push the laws that would make them go against their own conscience. I think what we have to do — and if we care about life — is to try to improve the quality of life, and that means finding support systems for people who are having problem pregnancies and finding alternatives to abortions. There are ways other than simply condemning people or trying to get laws changed . . . That doesn't do any good, unless you change attitudes. You don't really address the issue at its heart if you go through all the back doors and confuse the issue. I say you create a greater chasm between the extreme positions."

Mansour felt that some parish priests kept abreast of the issue of abortion and could speak intelligently about it. Others couldn't. It is this latter group that doesn't want "to be pushed into a corner . . . It's a very complex thing to talk about legal rights, personhood and viability and what the trimesters are and what the Supreme Court decision was. Unfortunately they would prefer to have it handled like sin — black and white. But it's not black and white. We shouldn't be trying to find simplistic answers to complex subjects like abortion. That's why it doesn't lend itself easily to legislation. We do have a job to do in terms of attitudes, but any solution has got to allow for some flexibility, and unless people are open to that, we'll create wider and wider gaps between the two extremes, and we won't be able to tighten up the laws and rationally address what is actually going on." It's unfortunate, said Mansour, that the Vatican took a step backwards in terms of social justice issues. While Pope John Paul II may have a good record of championing the causes of some, he also continues to stomp all over others.

She maintained that Vatican II "unleashed" a different kind of church — one that seemed more intensely political, to the degree that it has caused other denominations to go even further than the Roman Catholic Church. There were movements that occurred outside the church as well, citing the Civil Rights movement in the United States, and the revulsion felt by a nation to the Vietnam War. This also led to the battle to end nuclear proliferation. "When you're faced with the realities of war, as we did with the Vietnam War, then we recognized the horror of it, so global injustice became that much more obvious to us with the media explosion, and people began to react to it."

Mansour pointed out that it was Pope John XXIII who unleashed a new consciousness in the church when he wrote *Pacem in Terris,* an encyclical that was addressed, not just to clergy and bishops, but "to all people of good will." It was the first such encyclical to speak to a wider audience. And in it, the Pope raised the nuclear arms issue. "It wasn't just that . . . It hit many welfare issues, that people have a right to food, clothing, health care, to reasonable social services and to leisure . . . And he was talking then about how individuals should relate to individuals, how individuals should relate to the state, how the state should relate to the state, and how nation should relate to nation. He was talking about how we're not going to have peace unless we have a community relationship. And we're not going to have community relationships unless basic needs are taken care of. Yes, he did trigger off the consciousness."

Mansour felt Pope John XXIII succeeded in getting the church to start thinking about the wider community, and taking responsibility for not just themselves, but others. It triggered a kind of political activism in religious communities. In particular, religious women responded by re-organizing their communities, and adapting their ministries "to what was going on . . . It wasn't just teaching and nursing anymore; we started going into social work, we started going into ghettos; we started going into Central America."

Ten years after this interview, Mansour seemed to measure up to that vision she saw in Pope John XXIII's encyclical. She didn't return to the convent, but she did leave her job with the State of Michigan in January 1986 to become executive director of the Poverty and Social Reform Institute in Detroit. As for the spiritual side of her life, which in the earliest days of being in the convent occupied so much of her time, Mansour said, "I don't separate my life. I don't think people ought to compartmentalize their life. My spiritual life is bound up with what I do. I try to be as conscientious and honest as I can be and to be a person of integrity."

SUZANNE SCORSONE
14
THE PRINCE'S TRUST

This petite woman, hair pulled straight back, pushed aside a mug of hot tea and her son's photograph, then gingerly peeled back a precarious mound of correspondence and papers to reveal the desk top. She was searching for something scrawled there a long time ago. A Latin quotation. "Ah, it's here . . . Now this is something for me that's very basic." Then she immediately translated: "In necessary things, unity; in doubtful things, liberty; in everything, charity, love."

When I met Suzanne Scorsone in the fall of 1989, she was forty-four. She said it was this quotation that she used as a guide in the role as director of the Office of Family Life for the Roman Catholic Archdiocese of Toronto. A tricky business, this job of being a voice for the then-aging and ailing, but still very determined, Archbishop of Toronto, Emmett Cardinal Carter. That is, whenever someone enquired about issues of almost any kind, from abortion and divorce to rent review and Sunday shopping, this bright and articulate woman would do most of the talking. Not to say that Carter had relinquished control. Far from it — it was more that this powerful prince of the church trusted what this dynamic woman had to offer.

As a result of such responsibility, Scorsone has had to align herself decisively on the side of the church. She hasn't lost sight of the dangers inherent in this because it can have the effect of turning people away. And that is something she'd like to avoid. It means listening. It means being positive. However, it doesn't mean you stop handing out the party line. As you can expect, Scorsone has been the target of criticism from some quarters who regard her as too conservative, too right-wing, especially in the firm stance she takes on abortion and right-to-life in interviews and speeches.

She shrugs at the labels applied to her. "I just try to do my job." She smiles, stating this, acknowledging that it sounds a lot like a cop-out. In a real sense, however, it isn't. Scorsone doesn't view herself as an iron-fisted enforcer of Catholic dogma. "I try to be a unifier, not a splitter." The bottom line for her, however, is to hold "to the basic beliefs of the church . . . Read me the Nicean Creed, and I'll say yes at the end of every sentence. That defines me. For

Catholics it used to be assumed that that was basic stuff, I mean, I see myself as terribly middle-of-the-road."

The story of the outspoken and articulate Suzanne Scorsone, who was appointed director of communications for the Archdiocese of Toronto in March 1993 but continues to run the family life office, is a curious one. That is, you wonder how it came about that this New York City-born anthropologist and granddaughter of a Pentecostal lay preacher arrived at Carter's doorstep. But after well over a decade as director of the family life office for the archdiocese, you can only conclude, that who better to have than an intellectual, a mother of five, and someone in love with the church?

The account of that meeting between Scorsone and Carter seems almost a part of legend or myth in church circles. Claims are that this willful intellectual barged past stammering officials and stormed right into the oak-lined rooms of the cardinal's inner sanctum and told the archbishop he couldn't get along without her talents. Although it was a lot less sensational, it was still gutsy. Scorsone knows it. Fresh from completing a doctorate on the charismatic renewal, which she was a part of for several years, Scorsone, then in her mid-thirties, dashed off a letter to Carter. "I told him, 'Here's what I can do, and here's why you need me.' And it just so happened that the cardinal was preparing for the (international) synod on the family back then . . . and so he hired me to do a three-month background report on contract on whatever he might need to know about family."

Scorsone threw herself into the task, pulling together statistical profiles of the state of the North American family. After conducting hundreds of interviews with social workers, those in ethnic communities, church officials immersed in dealing with divorce and marriage tribunals, and the clergy in the parishes, she presented the archbishop with a set of recommendations. One of those proposals landed her, curiously enough, with the job of director of the newly created family life office. "I didn't make that recommendation saying I ought to be 'it'," she said, amused now at what transpired. "I did not try to construct for myself a job! But ultimately the office was created and I was put in it!"

Scorsone was the first married woman to be appointed to such a position in North America. In other family life offices, there were religious sisters, priests, or couples, where men were actually on the board. Looking back at that period, she mused that with her background in anthropology, she had some insight into the international pressures and situations with regard to the way societies behave. Her letter to Carter put it simply: " 'Someone like me could be very useful, since you have to go kicking around in an international church and I can give you this kind of background information.' So it was sheer serendipity or providence . . . that the synod on the family was coming up and he could definitely use someone like me."

The tone for Toronto's family life office, however, was different right from the start. Many of these offices function as social work agencies, whereas Scorsone preferred to leave much of those activities to the numerous agencies that already existed in the area. "They didn't need me for that," she said, pointing out that the family life office handled issues. It meant Scorsone began writing briefs to government and making representations to the media. "If someone calls up and wants to know about wide-open retailing on Sundays, then I do that. It's a family life issue. What's going to happen to the single mother retail worker on Sunday? When is she going to see her kids? Where does she find child care when all the schools and day-care centers are shut down? No one is talking about opening them up for her on Sundays. So what happens here?"

The issue that really propelled her name to the public stage was abortion. So much so, in fact, that former Prime Minister Brian Mulroney's office named her as a member of the Royal Commission on Reproductive Technology in 1989. She served as a commissioner till November 1993. When the abortion controversy was raised, Scorsone was prepared to do battle, set to pick apart any statement made that suggested the fetus was anything less than human: "It's human; it's a being; it's not a grape!" She elaborated: "At conception, something comes into existence that was not there before. Anywhere after that, you just have a progression with no clear lines at any point at all."

As for the proposals issued from Ottawa, Scorsone was less than satisfied. It was clear that politicians were at work trying to soothe the ruffled feathers on both sides of the debate. She recognized that neither side would be happy with the result. As far as she was concerned, the issue was far from over. When the final report was made public, it was clear that Scorsone's dissenting opinion was registered on a number of issues. She questioned matters concerning the freedom of conscience, embryo research, issues in the prenatal diagnosis of a disorder, the genetic link in donor insemination, and judicial intervention in pregnancy. Her views on abortion have been published in *The Canadian Catholic Review* and in a book edited by Ian Gentles called *Freedom: Choice or Life?*

Scorsone's enthusiasm still betrays little of the charismatic that she once was. But coming into the Catholic Church wasn't an easy or a quick decision. She described it as "a ten year road," recounting how from the time she was a teenager attending the Presbyterian Church in the United States, she had always been drawn to the Catholic tradition. That attraction emerged through friendship. For years she struggled against her parents' protestations. She's still amused that her delinquency then was not "drugs and alcohol, but running off to pray by myself in Catholic churches." There was a much later period when Scorsone was in university and she seemed to turn away from not only Catholicism, but Christianity itself, embracing other strains of thought, even toying with Judaism. It was after reading C.S. Lewis's *The Chronicles of Narnia* that she really began to understand where her faith lay. In 1969, she finally made a profession of faith in the Catholic Church.

Scorsone said it was only natural, that with so much enthusiasm for her religion she came to embrace the charismatic renewal movement and became so deeply involved in it. She describes herself now as "post charismatic," meaning that although she received "a great deal from it," she has "gone out the other side." Those were years that she "spoke in tongues" and was engaged in activities "half the nights of a month." That became a little more difficult, nearly impossible, when she started raising a family, especially a family of five children. But it wasn't even that so much as Scorsone simply moving on to being comfortable with her relationship with God and her church. When I met her in 1989, she spoke about how nightly she assembled her five children — ages six to twelve — to read them Bible stories. "They all get it," she said, adding that no matter what other story — secular story — they may want, there's always one segment of scripture. Scorsone argued that the stories in time become "so familiar that it is simply part of the air they breathe." One of her twin daughters told her mother she was tired of the stories, but in religion class, they're "acing the courses."

Scorsone has never lived under any illusions that attending church was something kids love. In 1989, she expected it would get even worse when her children become teenagers. "Dragging a four year old to church when the kid doesn't want to be there and he spends his time kicking the pew in front of him is not easy. But you have to be positive and smiling so they know you are a smiling person and so the church will be seen as a smiling church for them . . . even though very often my six year old (daughter) will spend the entire mass on the floor underneath the pew. But that's all right, she's there, and she's quiet and she knows we're still smiling at her."

This commitment to her family never gets in the way of the job. When I spoke to her in 1989, her office readily gave out her home phone, knowing she was juggling schedules, running kids off to the doctor, to appointments, to school, knowing it may be easier to reach her there. It was not uncommon for her to interrupt a reporter on the phone to inform him she had to mediate a small matter that had erupted in the home. All the while, the message was being driven home — Why not? After all, isn't she still the director of family life?

LOIS WILSON
15
FIRST WOMAN OF THE UNITED CHURCH

When I first met her, it was the summer of 1980. She was seated in a corner of the press room at the twenty-eighth General Assembly of the United Church at Dalhousie University in Halifax, Nova Scotia. Not quite five feet tall. Spectacles slipping down her nose and a small notebook on her lap to assess what she should say to a newspaper interviewer who was expected to telephone at any moment. She had just been named moderator of the United Church of Canada, the second largest Christian denomination in the country. "I'm the first," she declared proudly in that sharp, confident voice that some mistake for stridency. But that perceived attitude doesn't describe what Lois Wilson is all about. Long ago, she gleaned what people were saying, and concluded that when you're a woman, and you've got answers to questions that are posed, then it can be taken for abrasiveness, shrillness. That's not her. She shakes her head, wags her index finger like a school teacher. Not me.

The telephone call finally came, and I overheard the conversation — at least from her side. Same old thing. Same questions. After she was through, Wilson confessed to the frustration over the refrain. "What do I tell them? What do I tell you? They ask me, 'What's it like to be the first female moderator?' Well, I've just been elected. I still feel the same. I'm still a woman. I'm still a minister. And I guess I'm now the moderator. But my life hasn't changed. Not yet anyway."

She was fifty-three at the time. I had already heard all the back-room talk about her. If Lois got the job, God help the church! She'll stop at nothing to get it! That kind of thing. She had enemies. Though this may not have sounded like a church setting, that was the chatter. There was little doubt in anyone's mind — if you could own up to the reality — that running for office in the second largest denomination in Canada was a political maneuver. Lois Wilson knew that. And she lobbied hard and long for the job. And so when I met her, I expected someone controversial, biting, grating, unsparing. Her speeches seemed bereft of the unctuous, obsequious, laudatory platitudes of others. She spoke clearly, sharply, often cutting to the quick. Somehow it sounded the right chord.

Here was someone prepared to take on the country. Here was someone set to breathe new life into a confused and tired church.

In private, she was less threatening, more intense, less guarded, even naive. She conversed about her children, and her husband, also a minister. There was fondness for the chaos in her household where grace before meals was said routinely. She wondered whether that little prayer meant anything anymore. Assuredly it must, she nodded, but then winced: "I don't know how much is prayer and how much is ritual and ripped through — I just don't know." Night prayers? They don't always get said. Still, praying is a big part of her life — not every hour of the day, not even every day. Usually when big decisions must be made. "When changes happen in my faith journey, when things go wrong, when things disturb me . . . That's when I pray." God is never forgotten. God is always turned to. But "the rhythm" of her prayer life is never regular. Though there is this down-to-earth, motherly, practical, pious ("Call me Lois, not Rt. Reverend, please!") and realistic side to her, none of this seems to have stood in the way of her vision of what her role was in Christianity. And one realizes that any woman who raised a family of four and then tackled the ministerial life only to succeed in becoming of the head of the Canadian Council of Churches (1976-1979), then leader of the largest Protestant denomination in the country must have some dreams to carry her.

Wilson has a very distinct view of Christianity. It is this which has carried her through to the present. Instead of a Christian putting "on the whole armor of God and the helmet of salvation and feet shod for peace and the breastplate of righteousness," she portrayed the contemporary Christian wearing "a new suit," but not armor — armor was for the Middle Ages. "We need a new kind of clothing for a new kind of combat. We need fish-eye lenses for our eyes, so we can see the world in the round as it really is. We need earphones. That would be extremely useful, so we can listen and really listen to how the world is hurting. Contemporary Christians would probably need flippers for divergence from the mainstream of our culture."

That was the way Wilson spoke in 1980. Fourteen years later, she was still living that description, and zooming off to San Salvador as part of a Canadian delegation to observe the elections. When the voting returns came in, and the governing conservatives fell short of a majority and faced a run-off against a leftist coalition that included guerrillas from El Salvador's civil war, the former moderator was there to flag attention to what appeared to be fraudulent practices. "We feel there is a strong possibility of fraud, though we did not observe it on election day," said Wilson. She called for a massive overhaul of the election rules before Canada should advance any more aid.

In 1992, she was in Colombo, Sri Lanka as part of a nine-member Canadian fact-finding mission checking out human rights abuses among the government and Tamil rebels. Wilson led that delegation, too, and passed on "hundreds of petition of disappearances" to the Sri Lankan government. That's the armor she speaks of — being on the front lines, but with *very* different equipment. It means keeping your sanity, keeping your eyes open, your mind open. It means listening. Then again, it also means speaking and declaring clearly and properly what is right.

The contemporary Christian, Wilson told me in 1980, must be prepared for "the spirituality of combat — a style of Christian witness which is in continuity with the best of our heritage, but also looks to the future in terms of the kinds of ways in which we're going to have to diverge from our culture." To Wilson, it was a style that meant "engagement that doesn't fear dissent or conflict." It must also be rooted in biblical understanding of the human condition and of the concept "of God, nature and the world." Jesus is a good example of that. "When asked a question, Jesus responded with a question!" To Wilson, that's the model of Christianity she has struggled to follow. Occasionally, it gets her in hot water. But Wilson is tough-minded. "It is a style which withdraws from the human condition or society or relationships and says spirituality has to do only with my private life. It isn't a style which delivers a message in a dominant imperialistic style, saying this is what you've got to do."

For the United Church, this has been interpreted in terms of social issues. At the twenty-eighth General Assembly the hottest of these was the task force on human sexuality with specific reference to homosexuality. It was an issue that would grip the church over the decade, to the point that it eventually caused a split in allegiance, and forced many members to flee the church altogether. Wilson took an intractable position to the issue in 1980, declaring how the church had to face up to human problems. It could not and should not seek "the easy way out." Dismissing the concerns of many over the sexuality debate wouldn't have been prudent. No matter how controversial the subject, the church should never "shut its eyes," she said.

The hapless state of affairs that Wilson witnessed in 1980 may have come to pass over the decade. The church simply failed to reach back to its biblical roots. Fourteen years ago at that General Assembly, the former moderator complained of the apparent absence of "Biblical grappling" in the sessions. She pointed out that a Korean clergyman working in Canada noted how so little emphasis was placed on scripture at business meetings of the United Church. "What he was saying was, 'Are you minding your tradition biblically and theologically to know who you are, and when do you do that? I haven't seen any evidence of that.'

"The thing that makes sense about our church is that we are by and large biblically illiterate, not in the sense of quoting scripture passages, but in the sense of understanding from our reflection upon the biblical story of who we are as the people of God, what our bias has been historically, what the story tells us about history and ourselves and what is our role in all that in contemporary world." The new moderator hoped to push through greater attention to scripture at business meetings. What occurred over the decade was a debate that soured the church, and turned people against one another.

Wilson's vision in 1980 may have been naive, but to others it seemed inspiring and truthful. It wasn't so much that she wanted to impose her own lifestyle upon the church — not in any egotistical sense. She considered that heeding scriptures, turning to them for guidance, for inspiration, for simply being "in touch" with one's roots was something every Christian ought to heed. She hoped to set herself as an example.

Perhaps Wilson didn't realize then that others couldn't share that down-to-earth, sensible approach. She was no fundamentalist, no Bible-thumper. "Yup, I read my Bible a lot. I think I've always read it, but more laterally, as one would read poetry. Let me explain. You see, I've never been under the pressure of having to produce a sermon every week. So I've never had the pressure of having to read the Bible in order to get a sermon. So for me, it's been a luxury."

NANCY MANAHAN
AND
ROSEMARY CURB
16

LESBIAN NUNS

Her mother told her if she wrote a book like this, she would be making a big mistake — she would be ridiculed and hurt. She advised her daughter, Rosemary Curb, then an English professor at a Florida college, not to reveal to the world her lesbianism or the fact that a high percentage of women in convents had lesbian experiences. Curb wrote the book anyway. She collaborated with Nancy Manahan. Both had been nuns in Roman Catholic religious orders. Both are lesbians. The book they wrote — *Lesbian Nuns: Breaking Silence* — was published in 1985 by the small feminist press, Naiad Press Inc. in Tallahassee Florida. It became an instant bestseller. It was sold to Warner Books, a mass marketing house, for a six-figure price. The book has remained in print, but the Warner publication has run out, and Naiad has taken over distribution again. I met Curb and Manahan when they were promoting the book in the Detroit area. They were signing copies at a gay bookstore.

The two told me they faced heavy opposition in writing and editing the book which brought together not only their own stories, but those of other nuns or ex-nuns. The most formidable opposition, which ironically resulted in the spectacular success of their book, came from Rev. Peter Conley of the Roman Catholic Archdiocese of Boston. He told a Boston TV station that the appearance of the two authors "would be an affront to the sensitivity of Roman Catholics." The show, as a result, was cancelled. But this propelled the book to national attention. Curb said her mother's worries were shared by many — that the sisters behind the convent walls would suffer the repercussions of their secrets in public. It was now evident, she maintained, that there was a tremendous amount of relief that the story of these sisters finally was out in the open. She stressed that the silent burden in their lives had been lifted.

The two authors' greatest fear was that people who didn't read the book, but heard about it, would go away misunderstanding its purpose. The book, they claimed, wasn't written to titillate, and it did not set out to paint convents as a haven for lesbian activity without regard for spirituality. The book, maintained Curb, wasn't "anti-Catholic in any way." While the two are no longer practicing Catholics, they do not take the view —in this book anyway —that the Roman Catholic Church is no longer a viable religious institution. Curb pointed out that while they may believe the church no longer offered them a way of life to which they could subscribe, those whose stories are included in this book feel quite differently. In addition, Curb went on, although the emphasis in the book may be upon lesbianism, it was wrong to assume that all that was important to the individuals was their sexuality. That's only a part of the total picture. Curb emphasized that many of the women in the anthology were "deeply spiritual individuals . . . and many of them are leaders in their communities . . . We're not saying that all nuns are lesbians or that most are lesbians. We are simply telling the stories of some nuns or ex-nuns who are lesbians." In many cases, too, Curb said, some ex-nuns didn't discover their lesbianism until after they fled the convent. In the case of Curb and Manahan they were unfamiliar with and fearful of their own desires.

Curb, now forty-five, entered the Dominican Sisters at the age of eighteen. She described the experience as "the purest happiness I have ever known." Unfortunately such joy was fleeting. Just before final vows she left the order. She had been a sister for seven years. During those last two years she had had a clandestine relationship with an older nun. Curb said she was totally unaware of what was happening to her. "I had never heard the word 'lesbian' before." It was long after she left the convent that she became acquainted with the term. When Curb left the religious order, she went into teaching. She married an English professor and had a daughter. Her marriage, however, lasted only four years. Today, Curb is "living as a single lesbian mother with (her) daughter."

Thirty-eight year old Manahan is also a teacher. She spent a year among the Maryknoll Sisters. The lesbian experience was entirely mysterious to her. While she was in the convent, she fell in love with another nun to whom she had gone for spiritual assistance. What confused her was a desire for greater spirituality, but also a yearning to share love with another woman. In this book, Manahan makes it clear that when she left the convent, she didn't realize that her decision was linked directly to "being in love with a woman." After her exit from religious life, the nun to whom she was attracted also left, and the two lived together as lovers for seven years.

What many don't understand, say Curb and Manahan, is the bewilderment and frustration felt by people who flee the religious life for what appear to be purely sexual reasons. It's more than that — it's a desperation founded on confusion, pain, hurt, guilt. For years after leaving the convent, many feel "cut off" from their spiritual life. They can't cope with it — they experience a kind of exile from God, but realize it's self-imposed. The attempt to speak to others led to the book, explained Manahan. Only through talking with other lesbian ex-nuns was she able to come to terms with her own emotions. She also discovered how much she loved the convent. These conversations helped Manahan reclaim "the spiritual dimension" of her life. Curb, too, was able "to integrate all the phases of (her) life, which before now had seemed almost like separate lives."

Today, the two have differing views on the religious life. Curb sees no value at all in the vow of chastity imposed upon nuns and priests. She said many of the sisters in the book provided their own justification for engaging in lesbian sex, in spite of the vow of chastity. In one case, there was a nun who had been living with a woman she loved for twenty-five years, but there had never been any sexual activity between them. "Others," pointed out Curb, "do not consider it a requirement of their vow of celibacy or chastity to avoid sexual activity. A few interpret the vow of celibacy to mean unmarried . . . Strictly speaking, if you look the word up in the dictionary or if you speak canonically, that's what it means . . . Therefore it does not prohibit sexual activity. Of course you could go on to say the church prohibits all sexual activity except a sanctioned marriage. So you're in a Catch-22." Curb believed that while some — including the church — may regard such an interpretation of the vow of chastity as a convenient and not very solid argument, "these people are saying they are better people if they are sexually active . . . They say that if they are going to do the good work that they feel called to do as part of a religious community, they can do it better if they are not eaten up with sexual repression . . . That's the choice they are making. I am sure there will be the rigid moralists who will say this is not right."

What is taking place now, said Curb, is "the taking of one's spirituality into one's own hands and not allowing an authority to dictate. Of course it has been traditional within the Catholic Church for the members of the church to be dictated by a rigid hierarchical structure." Manahan wouldn't rule out the traditional view of chastity, but said that it ought to be "a choice." She believed religious communities should make it possible for nuns, brothers and priests to make their own choices on how "best to serve God."

Both said convents have come a long way from the period in which they were nuns, and that while there are still sexually-repressed sisters, the spirit behind the cloistered walls was generally far more open than it used to be. Curb said today's sisters are "a lot healthier," and the reason dates back to the work of Vatican II when the church began to overhaul its structures and examine its theology in the light of new thinking.

THÉRESE GADOURY
17
BRIDE OF CHRIST

Singer, musician, lawyer, businesswoman, teacher, builder of schools — at forty-two, Thérèse Gadoury has accomplished more than most do in a lifetime. Behind the public image is a woman who lugs about a weighty religious statue in her purse, attends morning mass every day, and rises without hesitation when she can't sleep and drives to a chapel that's open all night. It is there, in silence and darkness, that she'll sit, or kneel, and pray. Not so readily apparent, is that while she may be a recognized musician, she has made the religious commitment to become "a consecrated woman living in the world." In layman's terms, it meant taking a vow of chastity; it meant remaining a virgin. It didn't mean becoming a nun or joining a religious community.

"It's really dedicating your life to Christ," pointed out Gadoury. In a very real sense, it meant becoming "a bride of Christ." The seriousness in which the dark-haired, buoyant Gadoury explained this was softened by her smile. She's no quack. She insists her feet are planted firmly on the ground. She started the Académie Ste. Cecile in Tecumseh, a suburb of Windsor. It was meant to be a small school with a modest music program in 1979, but Gadoury prodded it along to the extent that today it has sprawled into three campuses with programs running from nursery school age to high school. She maintained she has been "genuinely happy . . ." and isn't lost in a kind of religious fervor where one loses touch with the world around them. She works hard, knows she must be a tough businesswoman, and knows her role is to inspire, to educate, and to bring people to an awareness of a fuller life. In no way does she attempt to impose her approach to life, or her decisions upon others. She isn't out to proselytize. "I'm at peace with myself."

Before committing herself to chastity, she had dated regularly, and enjoyed the friendship of men. Gadoury felt, however, "there had to be more to life. I thought I could be a faithful wife, and a good mom but really this was the perfect vow for me." Gadoury pointed out that few are aware of the history of the vow-taking of consecrated women, which pre-dates the development of organized religious communities for women. She herself only learned about this practice a few years before she went ahead with those final vows. And when she did, in a wedding-like ceremony at the altar at St. Anne's in Tecumseh, with Bishop J. Michael Sherlock presiding, she felt like the stereotypical bride — it was the happiest moment of her life. "I still feel like I'm on my honeymoon," she confessed, adding, "I know I'll stay on it till the day I die. And when I go to Heaven, it'll be my first wedding dance . . . I can't wait for that moment . . . That love I have for my God is a spousal commitment."

Thérèse Gadoury is no lightweight. Indeed, she's a woman of immense talent and unerring business acumen. At nine, she was studying piano and theory; at eleven, the organ; at thirteen, music and liturgical courses from the Gregorian Institute of America. Today, she has degrees in music from the University of Western Ontario and the University of Toronto. She also has law credentials from the University of Windsor. Gadoury's growth as a vocalist and musician was meteoric. She captured numerous awards and scholarships and gave concerts and performances throughout southwestern Ontario and Michigan. She was also an organist at various churches in Windsor. In the late 1970s, students lined up at her parents home to be tutored in the studio her father had built for her. Gadoury was content with the way things were until suddenly one day everything changed. In looking back at that moment in June 1978, she dismisses the notion that it was mere coincidence. It was more than that. Providence? Heavenly intervention? Intuition? Hard work?

She's talking about the founding of the Académie Ste. Cecile. And when she starts this story, this articulate and confident woman who has boundless energy and limitless optimism, steps into what most would identify as bizarre territory — the unbelievable, the outrageous, the stuff of dreams.

It had never occurred to her to start such a school. On a moment's notice, she reluctantly took up an invitation from a friend to perform at a funeral for a priest who had died in Detroit. She hadn't known the priest, hadn't even heard of him before, and therefore tried to beg off the assignment. She also had good reason — she had a tight schedule. Gadoury arrived at the church in

Detroit feeling resentful. Before going up to the choir loft, she decided to take a glimpse at the cleric in the casket. Emotion flooded over her, and she felt the overpowering sense of being in the presence of a saint. She believed that even more when she sang *Pie Jesu* by Gabriel Fauré.

She had wanted to remain in the church but knew she had to rush back across the border to a student waiting at her home studio. It was during that drive back that Gadoury, preoccupied with the mass, spied an empty lot along one of Windsor's north-south streets and heard herself muttering the words "Académie Ste. Cecile." The name meant nothing. She had no idea why she had uttered it. But when she got home, she announced to her bewildered mother she was starting the Academy Ste. Cecile. "All I knew at that time was that I was going to do this. And my parents weren't about to question me."

Over the summer, Gadoury set out to accomplish that goal. She expected her father, a builder, would assist her. But shortly thereafter, while performing in Switzerland, she received a telephone call informing her that her father had died suddenly. She returned to Canada for the funeral, believing her dream had now vanished. The last time she had seen her father had been at the Windsor Airport. He had comforted her by telling her not to worry about the school — that he would help to find a place for it. Without her heart in it, she went ahead with the bid on the empty lot, but it fell through. She searched without success for a building elsewhere. Frustrated and disheartened, she prayed that her father would give her a sign. "You'd have to know my father — he was so literal."

Suddenly for no reason at all, the numbers 12 and 21 began to figure in this quest. Again she was baffled by this phenomenon. Then at the urgings of a real estate agent, she toured through the old Bell Telephone building in Tecumseh. She hadn't considered the place — it seemed too large. "But when I walked up to it, there it was — I looked up at the sign above the door. It was 12021 . . . That was my dad's humor. That was my sign."

Such coincidences are as nothing compared to those connected with the dead priest in Detroit. The funeral had bothered Gadoury.

Her search to learn more about him led to the knowledge that he had been "a builder of schools." She shrugged this off, realizing she was "reading into" that coincidence. Then Gadoury learned about his extensive collection of statues of the Madonna, and was curious about whether anything there might explain the mysterious impact he had on her life. She asked for permission to go through his collection. It had not occurred to Gadoury that her findings might be connected with the name Ste. Cecile, her confirmation name. When she was granted access to the priest's room, she noticed it was crammed with hundreds of religious statues of the Madonna. On her way out, feeling a little disappointed because she hadn't found anything, she suddenly spotted a small statue of Ste. Cecile.

"Of all those statues, why that one?" Gadoury wondered. "You have to understand how difficult it is to find one of Ste. Cecile. I was stunned." Gadoury sensed then she was on "an adventure . . . I knew I was going to open up a school." When she left the priest's residence that day, she was handed the statue of Ste. Cecile, as well as a small figurine of the Madonna that this priest had carried with him in his suitcase. "It had been all over the world. I promised I would carry it with me wherever I go. That's why I keep it in my purse," Gadoury explained, pulling the small statue from her handbag.

As she related this story she was sitting at a wide desk in her office at the old Bell Telephone Building in Tecumseh, which has undergone more than $1-million in renovations and expansion. She maintained what while she proceeded with efforts to open the school, she also sought to piece together "the puzzle" that she'd come to realize was her mission. Gadoury can always anticipate the questions put to her. Why a music school? Why not a religious school? "Well, isn't music the instrument of peace? If I am able under one roof to have children happily living in harmony . . . It's an opportunity for us to live in harmony."

Today, Académie Ste. Cecile, a private school that operates with tuition funding, is open to anyone, any denomination. It continues with a basis in music, but its programming encompasses all subjects. "We teach the whole child. Who is the whole child? He knows his math dead on, he knows his grammar, knows his français, knows his geography . . . and loves his music. What a gift to give a child!" Gadoury calls it "the balance" that every child ought to have in their life. "We want to send all of them into the world and let them aspire to the best in life, and the way to do that is to give them a strong appreciation of everything."

The problem with many is that they regard music strictly as art. "Sure, it's art, but people think too much of it as an art; it's also a science. Two plus two in music is saying two half notes equal a whole note. That's math." Gadoury views the foundation of music as a means "to waking up the senses." Children exposed to music at an early age witness their skills at "observation and discipline" sharpened. "Just as I don't want to have a non-cultural scientist," maintained Gadoury, "neither do I want an illiterate musician."

She fears nothing about the future. She embraces it. She'll tell you that she's worked hard to achieve her goals. And while some may assume she's been "handed" success, she doesn't see it that way. It's a matter of being in tune with the universe. For Gadoury, it comes down to replying "Yes" to God, "and when you do that, He never leaves you alone." Often Gadoury can't foresee the next step. She remembered while at law school she continued performing as well as being organist at Sunday masses. Simultaneously, she also shepherded the business fortunes of the Académie. "So I had little time for prayer. I was exhausted." To cope, Gadoury found solace at Assumption Church, adjacent to the University of Windsor campus. There, seated in the quiet of the church, in the mid-afternoon, she would sift through reams of legal cases. "A lot of people remember me there. I kept saying, 'Lord, I don't have very much time, and I have to pray, and I have to run a school, so let us read this together . . . and You enlighten me." At the end, getting the law degree made sense. Today, besides running the school, she also handles its legal work, a task far more demanding as the institution swells in size.

Worry? Sure, Gadoury worries. The academy is bursting at the seams. It's gone far beyond the tiny music school she started in the

1970s. "I have lots on my mind." But it rarely gets her down. "The true sign of a Christian is to be joyful. Whatever cross one bears, whatever cross one has to carry, or whatever hardship is given to you, it's important to be joyful. Joy is contagious and eventually the cross is going to be lifted up, and the hardship less difficult . . . There's not a cross too big that God doesn't give you the grace to bear it."

DOROTHEE SÖLLE
18
POET OF PRAYER

Dorothee Sölle looked perpetually worried. She barely had time to eat her breakfast. She picked up a tray and rushed through the line and to a table. No time for small talk. She had a meeting ahead of her. Following that, she was expected to address a small group. This was in Vancouver in the summer of 1983. She was then fifty-four. Frail-looking, intellectual, quiet, intense. Already a renowned theologian in Germany and teaching at Union Theological Seminary in New York, Sölle had been in Vancouver to speak to the Sixth Assembly of the World Council of Churches. Her writings and lectures on the peace movement were what landed her there. When the invitation came, she accepted willingly. The reason was evident in her books — she had an obsession with war, an abhorrence of it. At every opportunity she spoke out against the ever-increasing militarism that dominated world politics.

When I met her, Sölle's concern was over the dramatic confrontation that persisted between East and West. She yearned for an end to it, prayed for it, wrote books, delivered lectures, and engaged in symposiums and conferences, all aimed at raising the consciousness about it, all aimed at changing the minds of people. She smiled, then quipped that at the heart of the matter, too, was a desire to put an end to the letters she had been getting for years. It was that correspondence, however, that made her acutely aware of the fundamental trouble the world was in. People wrote to her about poverty, violence, and injustice in their homelands. In coming to Canada Sölle confided she saw an opportunity to speak about "the madness" that governed the struggle between the Soviet Union and the USA. For Christians, she felt there was no justification for such activity. In one book, she wrote, "You cannot seek God while you prepare yourself for mass murder, just in case." For Sölle, peace built on terror was not peace. That message was reiterated throughout her speeches and writings, but it was something worth repeating.

In her speech to the Sixth Assembly that summer, Sölle, with her scruffy close-cropped blonde hair, seemed dwarfed by the podium in the gigantic building where some 3,000 delegates and official observers had gathered. But her words, carried by loud-speakers, left her audience spellbound. "Some Christians in our countries are saying, 'What's so bad about safeguarding our security with arms? We're not actually going to use the bomb, just the threat of it.' In reality, however, the bomb destroys the fullness of life Christ has promised us. It destroys the life of the poor in the material sense, the life of the rich in the spiritual sense. It has become lodged inside us, it has taken possession of us. We will never know the fullness of life while we live under the bomb. The world I live in is rich beyond measure in death and ever more sophisticated in its means of killing. The bombs lying stored ready for use beneath the earth's surface and under the oceans in submarines, the quantities of explosives intended for every human being on earth, are, I believe, targeted on God. The meaning of the arms race is this: God is to be eliminated."

I remember speaking to one delegate after her speech, and she described Sölle's approach as "religious Bolshevism," because she linked the arms race to poverty in the Third World. Later in discussion groups or private talks, Sölle elaborated: the potential of channeling billions of dollars spent on arms into feeding the world. Sölle claimed the Third World was "living on the edge of death in stark, economically conditioned poverty. There are people who are hungry, who have no shelter, no shoes, no medicine for their children, no clean water to drink, no work — and they can see no way of getting their oppressor off their backs." She told the story of receiving a letter from a Brazilian woman who reported that one day she saw forty-two little coffins with the corpses of children en route to the cemetery. Those children, including two of that woman's own, had died because there was no milk for the babies. Sölle was moved by the experience, and spoke of it as something that continues to bother her. What irked her was this chasm between the Third World — afflicted with hunger and violence — that struggles to survive, and the First World — with all its abundance — that plots its own death with nuclear arms.

There was a disarming simplicity to Sölle's approach. She preferred to keep the issues uncomplicated, elementary, and human, because then they had meaning for others and could be shared. She told me later how she had met a woman from Leningrad whose speech had been nothing but propaganda. The audience actually demanded the woman say something more personal about where she lived. So "stunned" and "hurt" by the reaction, she finally began to open up, and revealed to the audience how she feared the winter ahead, for it meant "standing in the cold in long lineups of food." The words moved Sölle.

Born September 30, 1929, in Cologne, Germany, Sölle studied classical philology, philosophy, theology, and German Literature at the University of Cologne, Freiburg, and Göttingen. She was awarded a philosophy degree by the University of Göttingen in 1954. After graduation, she taught at a number of schools and universities. In 1973, with her husband Fulbert Steffensky, a professor of religion and education at the University of Hamburg, she founded the ecumenical working group *Politisches Nachtgebet,* renamed *Christen für den Sozialismus,* a theological and poetical movement that has since spread throughout Germany, the Netherlands and Switzerland. The author of several theological books and collections of poetry, speeches, and essays, Sölle continues her work in Germany. For a while she divided her time between teaching at Union Theological Seminary in New York and the University of Hamburg in Germany. More recently she has left the American university to spend most of her time writing and lecturing in Germany. Sölle's work has not gone unrecognized. She received the Theodore Heuss Medal in 1974, the first award of this honor for achievement in "civil courage and democracy" given to a theologian. In 1982, she was also awarded the Droste prize for poetry in Meersburg, Germany — the highest honor for a woman poet in the country.

To Sölle, even though the geography of Europe has undergone a major transformation, and the old East-West divisions have disappeared, other difficulties have surfaced. The debate over nuclear arms may not appear to be as urgent, since steps have been taken to ease tensions, but the armaments still exist. So does the war industry. The potential is there. As for the link to social justice, the

Third World is ever present. Poverty persists. So does oppression. Sölle continues to address those concerns. Indeed, it has become her mission, her life's work. She continues to voice her vision in lectures and writings. When I saw her in the early 1980s, I remember how "useful" her prose was in waging theological arguments, posing questions, and analyzing how bad things were. Over the years, she has written a wide range of theological texts, many of them recycled essays or speeches, dealing mostly with the peace and justice movement. In 1993, she published *Stations of The Cross,* a book about her Latin American pilgrimage. Sölle has written on the feminist movement, publishing *Strength of the Weak: Toward a Christian Feminist Identity* in 1984. She also published *On Earth As In Heaven,* a book dealing with Liberation Theology. "But when I want to express more than that," she explained, "such as hope, or love, the poverty of people, indeed a different kind of language, one that is more open, more transparent, that lets the light shine through . . . then I write poetry."

Sölle started writing verse in the late 1960s. It arose out of a need, she said, to express feelings about the issues of peace and justice. *Revolutionary Patience* was published in 1969 in German. It was translated into English and published by Orbis. In 1983, she came out with another book called *Of Love and War,* devoted almost entirely to the peace movement. "In Christianity, everyone's a poet. If you can love, hope and believe in God . . . In other words, if you are given all these supernatural powers, then your language can transcend everything that exists . . . Everyone who prays creates a new language."

ANDREW M. GREELEY
19
SEX FOR THE GREATER GLORY OF GOD

He's a slick well-heeled priest. He likes to live high on the hog. It's not that he refuses to give a thought to the poor in Africa or Latin America, it's simply that if he's got it, why not spend it? I met him at the top of the towering Renaissance Center overlooking the Detroit River. He wasted no time in taking control. There was a rawness to his demeanor. He scanned the menu quickly as if it were a casual letter, then ordered without even glancing at the waiter.

The man was Andrew M. Greeley, newspaper columnist, sociologist, lecturer, and best-selling novelist whose books deal with sex, greed, and power. They're the ones that sell. All the theological and sociological stuff that he wrote since his ordination in 1954 sits on shelves. It might bring him respect, but nothing more. One book, *The Making of the Popes*, however did better than most, making the *New York Times* bestseller lists in 1978. Odd as it might seem, Greeley thinks he can do more "for the glory of God" with his popular titles. In the 1980s, he started bringing out such titles as *Thy Brother's Wife* and then *Cardinal Sins*. The sales surpassed anything he'd done before. In three decades, he's written nearly thirty books and monographs. There's little doubt about what brings in the cash, and what captures public attention.

When I met him in 1982, Greeley was at the height of his popularity as a novelist. Although he continued to teach sociology at the University of Arizona, and act as the senior director of the National Opinion Research Center at the University of Chicago, he was building another reputation for himself — the author of dirty books. And because he was a priest, everyone wanted him on their television or radio talk show. The media swarmed around him, begging for interviews. The thin, balding Greeley, who looked more like Bing Crosby as the good "Father" in the 1944 movie *Going My Way*, loved every minute of it. As always, he wore the Roman collar. He talked a mile a minute in a kind of rough, sharp voice. Witty, funny, at times thoughtful, introspective, but rarely with the sensitivity one might expect to find in a man of the cloth. Greeley acknowledged that his fiction can come pretty close to his own views. Take the line from *Thy Brother's Wife*:

"You can't be a good bishop unless you're an accomplished liar. We lie to Rome about how enthusiastically we receive their bull — we lie to the priests and the laity about how they should enforce such rulings; we lie to the press about what we really think. We even lie to ourselves, although we know that we won't be able to sleep at night because of what the Goddamn encyclical is doing in our dioceses."

Greeley smiled. Sure. But he didn't see himself as a rebel. He claimed his sense of autonomy didn't brand him as a renegade in church circles. He was committed to the priesthood, wanting nothing more than that. At the same time, he was fiercely independent and planned to stay that way. He knew the church could censor him, but remarked, "That's one of the risks I take that at some stage of the game the church might say, 'Stop writing!' and I'd say, 'No, I won't!' And they'll say, 'Well, you can't practice the priesthood!' Well, I'd just go on writing, and I'll go on being a priest. If they don't let me say mass on Sundays and hear confessions on Saturdays publicly, I'll do it privately."

Greeley didn't believe that was going to happen. He wasn't harming anyone with his books. Moreover, his writings didn't veer away from church dogma or criticize it. He didn't see himself as a threat to the Vatican, as might be Hans Küng. "It would be wiser for them (the Vatican) not to (say anything) . . . The notion that my books are scandalizing the faithful is absurd, and I don't think anybody can find any heretical doctrines in either of those books."

It's not entirely true that Greeley's own views have remained unspoken. He has repeatedly contended that Rome has overstepped itself in forcing priests out who may hold differing opinions about official church laws. Greeley also called Pope John Paul II's actions offensive, and described them as "an abuse of power . . . The church has to be reformed, but then the church has always needed to be reformed. The church doesn't know the Renaissance is over."

Ironically, Greeley in the early 1980s came under intense criticism by his own church for writing scenes of carnality and corruption involving priests and bishops. Today these passages in his novels are almost prophetic, as revelations later began to appear in the papers indicating that such behavior was not uncommon among the clergy. "But do you know, some of the scenes are very watered down," he said. "My editor made me cut a lot. You're going to lose both ways. If they are pallid, people are going to say he doesn't know anything about it, and if they're explicit — or more explicit — then they're going to question that, too. I think human passion is the sacrament of God's passion. Well, the reaction is peculiar. One archbishop said to me, 'I like the story a lot, but most of my priests don't like it . . . but they didn't read it! And I think most of the criticism doesn't come from the Catholic conservatives, but it comes from the liberals — the Catholic editors and reviewers. They very much resent a priest writing fiction, especially fiction successfully."

Greeley claimed the "jealousy" was difficult to understand: "They're (priests) angry. The publicity director from Warner Books who came along with me on a couple days of the tour said, 'I have never seen an author subjected to so much hatred!' So much hatred in fact that it scares me a little, the violence of it all. The typical Catholic reviewer says, 'This book is a bestseller but it's a bestseller only because it's a novel by a priest and if it wasn't a priest, no one would pay any attention to it.'" Greeley rejected such claims: "Books don't sell two and three million copies because they're novels by a priest . . . It sells for the same reason any book sells — by word of mouth, because it's a good read, a good story."

Andrew Greeley dismissed the suggestion that wearing the Roman collar was a ploy for marketing books. "I always wear it on public occasions. I don't wear it in classrooms when I'm teaching. I may wear black slacks and a sports shirt. But whenever I'm on television or radio or making any kind of presentation, it'll either be a Roman collar or a black turtle neck. The reason is I'm not ashamed to be a priest — it's part of my identity." Once, after noticing a Jesuit scientist or marine biologist on television, who wore, not the Roman collar, but a brown suit and tie, he concluded, "That's fine if that's his style . . . But it seems to me it would have been so much more effective in making the point that religion and science are not incompatible if you had a marine biologist, obviously tops in his field, showing that he was clearly committed to his religion. That's sort of my explanation for why I do it." So, sure, it's partly for effect, Greeley acknowledged. "I'm making the point I'm a priest, and it's not incompatible for me to write books, too."

Greeley believes that much of what he writes — the sex and all — is no different than Christ telling a story. They're parables. He claimed that the story in *Thy Brother's Wife* about an archbishop falling in love and sleeping with his brother's wife was just that. "It's a parable of God's commitment to us — the Holy Thursday feast (opening chapter) is the story of God's covenant, putting another overlay on the commitment of Sinai (Old Testament story) at the Last Supper . . . and the commitments, however imperfectly made and imperfectly kept, are commitments that are sustained under the power of God so it's not so much that we're committed to Him, but He's committed to us."

Greeley won't mask his feelings about the church. The contentious issue — even today — regarding the artificial birth control ban is something ludicrous. He contended that most priests oppose the church's ban and view it as lunacy on the part of the Vatican. "They (Rome) should have left the thing alone for ten to fifteen years and re-thought the theory. Where it stands now is it's still in limbo. It's in a kind of limbo that comes when the papacy says something and the hierarchy goes along verbally and the lower clergy and the laity reject it. You have this dichotomy between the two components of the church."

Local clergy, Greeley stressed, may repeat the party line, that artificial birth control is wrong, but in private, they'll counsel individuals and advise them to abide by their conscience. "One knows this is the case, and Rome knows it, and the bishops know it, and they don't try to stop it . . . They just keep re-asserting their loyalty to the doctrine." The Catholic Church would have to be blind to assert that the laity are practicing anything but birth control, Greeley said. For the Pope to make statements that married people ought to make a commitment to family may be fine in theory, but it was less than convincing to individuals who find it difficult to make ends meet. "You've got absolutely no communication between the married and the ecclesiastical institutions at the higher level on the meaning of sex and marriage. There's no input at all and that's where they've come to this crisis. Whatever the theory may be, neither the Pope nor the hierarchy is listening to the married couple, or for that matter the clergy themselves who know the problem. There's absolutely no positive teaching on intimacy."

Greeley told the story of a colleague who walked into his office in 1979 with a working copy of a paper for the Synod of Bishops in Rome. It declared that the laity must be warned of the dangers of "unbridled passion." He told Greeley, "Don't the damn fools know? The real problem is bridal passion!" To Greeley, the only thing that kept marriages together today were "the interludes of unbridled passion . . . We need more of them!" He went on to say that the problem with the Vatican was that much of what is done occurs "in the upper floors of the apostolic palace" where few have "a sense of what contemporary marriage is like." Church officials, Greeley stressed, "don't realize the church's biggest challenge is to provide the motivations, the resources, the illuminations that married laity need to keep their love alive over a fifty-year marriage. That's the problem — there isn't a positive theory of sexuality and marriage. It's either warning of dangers or it's such high-flown theory that it doesn't mean anything to anybody."

Greeley may sound like a renegade, but insists he's fundamentally a traditionalist who hopes the Catholic Church would recover its tradition and return "to the old ways of being much more consultative." That means destroying the Renaissance power structure of the Roman curia. "There has to be a Pope who'll say, 'You work for we bishops of the world and you don't dominate us!'"

To Greeley, another problem to be tackled by the Catholic Church is that of homosexuality. He balked at approval of ordination of gays. He scowled, pointing out the fact some priests and bishops are homosexuals. Greeley shrugged. "I'm sure we have many homosexual priests and bishops who not only haven't acknowledged their homosexuality to anybody else, but they haven't acknowledged it to themselves. They just don't find women attractive."

Celibacy is not an issue. Greeley said celibacy is no more a problem for a priest "who is happy in his work than fidelity is for a married man or a married woman who is happy in their family relationship." He maintained that a priest "who likes what he's doing and getting satisfaction from his work is as happy and well adjusted as a married man." It's not to say that priests don't stray, or don't "lust" after women. In his novels, Greeley has described priests as "lusting after every woman they encounter." A sad truth. There's no hiding the fact. Always been that way. Priests are human, like anybody else. "We hear a little more about it today . . . But are there American cardinals who have had children? I don't know. But have there been bishops and archbishops in the USA and Canada who have sired offspring? Yeah. Not a lot. But don't tell me it never happened!"

"But you know, the central problem is the question of identity, or what a priest should be doing. All the sexual problems of priests are unimportant compared to the problem of teaching within the church. Priests are coming out of the seminaries without knowing how to read and write. I would hope there are changes in the seminaries so priests can come out with a taste for reading and learning some of the rhetorical arts that are necessary to write a decent Sunday homily." One of the glaring disappointments facing the American church, according to Greeley, lies in the fact people find the sermons "awful, just awful." He added, "You know, it's the most important thing we do and yet only ten percent of the young people under fifty think we're excellent at it. That's damning!"

The issue of the ordination of women will be a long time coming for the Catholic Church. Greeley couldn't have read Pope John Paul II better. In 1994, the Pope cleared up any confusion on his stance — there will *never* be women priests in the Catholic Church. "But I would ordain them tomorrow," Greeley stated. He argued that in spite of what some church figures claim, scholars can prove that such a tradition exists in the structure. In the early church, there were female priests, even bishops. The reason Rome has been giving is that it's never been done, and that's why it can't happen now. The truth? Greeley smiles, and drives his point home: "We can't do it, because we don't wanna do it! We want women around as little as possible!"

MORLEY CALLAGHAN
20
THE FABLE OF JUDAS

Morley Callaghan sat in his living room in the rambling, gray house on Dale Avenue near Bloor and Sherbourne streets in Toronto. He was wearing brown corduroy pants and a bulky Irish-knit sweater. Callaghan had just finished autographing hundreds of books. A book dealer had just left with several cartons. He now wanted to relax, smoke a pipe, talk. He gravitated to conversation, and when he was excited about something he grew animated, occasionally rising to his feet to pace the room. The thing that excited Morley Callaghan was his newest novel, *A Time for Judas*. He was eighty years old then, author of *More Joy in Heaven*, *The Loved and the Lost*, and *That Summer in Paris*. The new book had just been released by Macmillan and was already a sensation. Laudatory reviews had been pouring in from everywhere. He was pleased.

But what Callaghan wanted to know was what the religious community thought of it. Not that he cared if it condemned his book as heresy. He was just curious as to how religious leaders would regard his theories about Christ's resurrection.

In the novel, Callaghan reconstructed the story of Jesus' death and resurrection. He maintained the resurrection was merely a popular belief at the time of the crucifixion — a belief that has remained with Christians down to this day. In fact, Callaghan maintained, Jesus' corpse was removed from its initial tomb and buried elsewhere. The empty tomb set the apostles abuzz, and they declared their leader had risen from the dead — just as he had promised — three days after the crucifixion. Although *A Time for Judas* is fiction, Callaghan regarded the book "as very true . . . It's a true story!" He maintained, however, that in spite of his claims to the contrary, he didn't think it should "shake anyone's faith in Christ or Christianity." Turning a little philosophical, he observed, "It's a deeply Christian story."

That day in October 1983, when I met him at his house in Toronto, Callaghan confessed he had been awaiting word from Christian leaders. Old friend Emmett Cardinal Carter of Toronto had been strangely silent: "I'll probably hear from him — either publicly or privately. But I am also interested in hearing what some of the Protestant theologians say, too."

Callaghan, raised a Roman Catholic, had always been drawn to the church. When he went to Windsor in the 1970s as writer-in-residence, instead of taking an apartment, he resided with the Basilian fathers. He enjoyed the company, the conversation, the camaraderie. He loved to goad them, to engage in controversial subjects. As for the new book, he predicted there would be this hesitation on the part of the church world to tackle the subject. What he didn't expect was the reluctance from publishers to issue such a book. One American publisher worried over "how the pious people would take this." The publisher told Callaghan that previous novelists, dealing with the subject of Christ, have "written around the apostles and distanced themselves . . . He told me I had made Jesus, Judas and Mary Magdalene real people . . . That's the point, they were real people. And if they weren't, then the gospel has no meaning for anyone."

If people expected a fable in this novel, they were in for a surprise, pointed out Callaghan. "If I'm destroying the fable, then it's time for that, surely." Callaghan reasoned that it shouldn't matter to Christians whether the resurrection was a triumph of the flesh over death. The fact is, the results are the same: people will continue to believe in Christ, and regard him as God's son. To the Toronto writer, whose early career was tied up with Ernest Hemingway at *The Toronto Star*, and later in Paris, what was essential about Christianity was faith, whether you could abandon yourself to trust God. If you could, then nothing would shake that faith. The Judas story, he insisted, should only enhance that faith because it knitted together the doubts that haunt the story in the New Testament.

According to Callaghan, there were so many unanswered questions in the gospels that it was difficult to have faith in Jesus. But his own story, which some critics have called "The Fifth Gospel according to Callaghan," portrayed "a believable Jesus." He didn't mind that tag: "There's something to it, you know." Talking to an Italian Catholic who worked in the consular service, Callaghan was told the book shouldn't surprise Christians. "The man wasn't at all shocked by what I wrote." What the man liked especially about the novel was the redemption of Judas.

Callaghan's account in the novel portrayed an intelligent, compassionate man in the figure of Judas — someone ready to carry out a pact with Jesus, so Christianity would not end. The covenant meant someone would have to betray Jesus. Judas was the one deemed best to carry this out faithfully. The New Testament account on the other hand portrayed Judas as some misguided follower who, in bewilderment, betrayed Christ for thirty pieces of silver. To Callaghan, Judas was head and shoulders above the other apostles, whom he described as "dull." In espousing this, the frail-looking, but still spry and alert Callaghan contended he wasn't "abandoning anything at all," referring to his Catholic upbringing. To others, this was akin to heresy — it went against the church's teaching.

The Toronto-born writer, who was educated by the Basilian priests at St. Michael's College, was always clever in his dealings with the press. He successfully managed to slide about, to avoid being labeled. The last thing he wanted was for the novel to associate him with a whole raft of religious writers, especially the born-again Christian movement. It wasn't a book of that ilk. It was fiction. It was literature. But also at its foundation, it carried a sense of urgency and truth. As to whether he was still Catholic, or whether he still believed in God, or anything, Callaghan side-stepped the question. That was irrelevant — he was a writer.

"Let me tell you a story," Callaghan said with circumspection, puffing on his pipe. "James Joyce, whose whole scholastic background was rooted in that ancient tradition (of the church) once told me how Protestant clergymen visited him in Paris. They told him how they felt quite good about how he had become a Protestant . . . Joyce said quietly to them, 'I lost my faith, not my reason.' " Callaghan paused, and smiled: "So, the question of whether I believe in God or anything is of no importance. Heaven is within us . . . Look inward for it. The Sputniks and satellites don't encounter God, do they?"

But it was still a concern of Callaghan's, and it was apparent that his Catholic education had pushed him to engage the question of morality. It continued to emerge in his fiction. Subtly, artfully — the way Callaghan intended. He shunned the more obvious, the glaring subscription to what the church defined for itself and its adherents. But Callaghan was influenced by Jacques Maritain, the French Catholic philosopher who was at the Institute of Medieval Studies in Toronto. From him, the novelist acquired a Christian humanism or personal humanism which dominated his later fiction. The stress was placed on intuition and moral freedom. As Desmond Pacey notes in the *Literary History of Canada*, Callaghan recognized that the "supremely important thing on earth" is "the human person, and the supremely important thing in the person is his soul or spirit." To Callaghan, the soul found its "fullest earthly development in self-sacrificial love."

This certainly applied to Judas in Callaghan's book — a Judas who gave himself up to propagate a legend that would transform society. Callaghan didn't mind elaborating on this. For him, the key to the gospels — and he found this missing in theological talk — was the new law Christ heralded: the law of "love."

When I left Callaghan's rambling old house on Dale Avenue, he clasped the bowl of his pipe and pointed the stem at me like a discerning professor. "Now read it, and read it carefully — there's nothing in this that should alter what you believe. You can still believe in God, in Jesus, in everything." How the death of Jesus was handled — that was something else again. That was Callaghan's point. And like the old newspaper reporter that he was from *The Toronto Star* days, the writer argued that he was merely going after a story. Why should that change the nature of theology? It's just an interesting story.

NORTHROP FRYE
21
THE GREAT CODE

Novelist Paul Theroux must have been reading Northrop Frye's mind when he wrote in *The Mosquito Coast* that the Bible was "the owner's guide to western civilization." Frye has spent a lifetime demonstrating this in classrooms at the University of Toronto and in his books. He has pronounced over and over again the Old Testament and the New Testament *do* tell us something about ourselves, why we behave the way we do and why we think the way we do. They're also reflected in our literature in a vivid way, and for him it is our literature which is the expression of everything we are.

Speaking to Northrop Frye is not easy. If he doesn't detest interviews, he certainly doesn't place much store in them. On one occasion, one writer decided (wrongly) to ride with him on a train from Toronto to London, Ontario, in the hope of getting to know him a little better for the feature story he was writing. At one point when the journalist posed a question to Frye, he merely turned away to watch the landscape fly by the window. At first, the interviewer wondered whether one of the world's most influential critics was lost in thought, and whether he was pondering how he might answer the query. But no, Frye had decided not to respond.

I decided to speak with Frye over the phone. This was in March 1982. He had just published a new book, *The Great Code: The Bible and Literature,* considered to be his most important work since *Anatomy of Criticism,* which still sells more than 10,000 copies each year. It's not the kind of book that would cheer the hearts of evangelicals who want something more inspirational. Frye might curl a lip at that. His fundamental interests are literature, and the influence of the biblical material on writing. The fact is most evangelicals couldn't care less. What's important to them is finding Christ, making Him their personal savior. Frye's sole purpose in doing the book, however, was to stress the importance of sacred writings on secular literature. To some, no doubt, this is a blasphemous way of dealing with the Bible. A fundamentalist might even brand Frye "an anti-Christ." What might surprise detractors is that this erudite creature who spent a lifetime at Victoria College in Toronto is an ordained man of the cloth. He became a United Church minister in 1936, but went on "permanent leave" almost from day one. Nonetheless, he still clings to the label and hasn't quit the church altogether. Since taking that leave, however, he has written ten books.

Frye was born in Sherbrooke, Quebec in July 1912, but grew up in Moncton, New Brunswick. In 1929, drawn by a national typing contest, he went to Toronto. He finished second in the competition. Soon after, he enrolled at Victoria College. Ten years later, he was on the school's staff, teaching English Literature there. Eight years after becoming a professor, he wrote a book that startled the literary establishment. The book, *A Fearful Symmetry*, raised the consciousness about William Blake. Up till then, the writings of this poet seemed convoluted and difficult. Frye, according to John Ayre in *The Canadian Encyclopedia,* showed readers that Blake wasn't incoherent, that he resorted to symbolism drawn heavily from Milton and the Bible. *Anatomy of Criticism* with its emphasis upon mythic form followed ten years later.

With the release of *The Great Code,* a study of symbolism in the Bible, Frye seemed to invite all the wrong questions. He seemed tired of the refrain about his disinterest in being a practicing clergyman. When I asked him bluntly whether he still believed in God, he paused for such a long time that I thought he had put down the phone. Finally, he replied: "Well, that's a rather strange question." Is that it? I waited. Finally another sentence: "I suppose so." Another long pause. Then: "Well, I am what I am." That was it. Considering his writings about the Bible, the words seemed ominous, Jehovah- like. The words to Moses.

Eventually Frye opened up, but only a little. He described himself as being "a non-conformist" when it came to Christian belief. His view of the Bible, as an example, was eccentric in terms of doctrine, mostly because he seemed indifferent to it. Yet, one can only wonder why. After all, he was the grandson of a Methodist circuit rider on his mother's side of the family. Many of the books he read as a child also were from his grandfather's library. It seemed natural for him to study to become a United Church minister. For a brief period in Saskatchewan, he spent time in student ministry in a three-point charge. But in 1936, when he graduated, he decided to go to Oxford to pursue a career in academia.

"I didn't have any difficulty in belief. My feeling was that I didn't have the administrative qualities and other things that were needed," he explained in that deadpan voice. Ranking high on the list of "other things" was socializing with parishioners. Frye has always gravitated to reclusiveness. He has that reputation for being cold, distant, inhospitable. Indeed, he seemed to foster the classic misanthropic personality, keeping to himself, preferring to stay clear of questions — especially personal ones. He once told an interviewer that he couldn't see himself as a clergyman in some small United Church charge, because he couldn't tolerate "small talk over tea and biscuits, the clergyman's stock in trade." Though he stayed clear of such a life, he has assisted at weddings for friends. The option for a career in literature wasn't something new when Frye chose it. He actually saw the two professions as complementary. Especially in retrospect, because his grappling with the Bible in university actually helped him understand literature.

Frye made the point that he came from a generation where there was heavy emphasis upon the Bible, and when he got to university, there were "a great deal" of references to scripture he had learned in childhood. People today, he commented, know virtually nothing about the Bible. He noticed this in particular in the classroom where students enrolled in English Literature classes went away with little knowledge of scriptures. A regrettable fact, Frye concluded, because Western literature has its foundation in the Bible — the myths, allusions, motifs are there, intertwined around the words and stories. One can't avoid using the scriptures as a starting point to what is being written. "It's certainly easier to teach *Paradise Lost*," pointed out Frye, "if a student comes in knowing what the Bible is all about." He blamed "the general collapse of the educational system and the fear of indoctrination," for general ignorance of the Bible. "My experience with the Bible is that it can be taught without indoctrination. I've taught everybody from Greek Orthodox to atheists. In the classroom environment it can be done. I don't see any reason why it can't be done in the schoolroom."

The general trend has been to hold classes on religion or the Bible given by clergymen. "Those tend to discriminate among students. I don't see any reason why the Bible can't be taught in relation to our own cultural heritage which would make it equally intelligible to everybody." Frye's prescription would to be to send graduates of religious studies into the public classrooms. Because there isn't an emphasis on the Bible in relation to cultural heritage, there is a general misunderstanding among many people when it comes to interpretation. The most glaring example is the feeling that scripture can be taken "literally." Frye has no patience for this. He is irked by fundamentalists who strut about with a Bible in one hand quoting whatever they see in the Old and New Testaments to justify some cause. He pointed out that while they certainly know the contents of the Bible, which is more than he can say for many other people, they have little understanding of its genealogy, its impact upon culture, its relevance to the world at large. Frye's own book on the Bible isn't a theological probe. Then again, he emphasized, "It's not a cryptic attempt to proselytize either."

Some might hold the opinion that the Bible is "inspired," but Frye regards it plainly as "an edited book . . . and the editing was done in a very conscious and rational process." He quickly added that he didn't rule out the idea of the Bible as a "Holy book," or that God may not have had a hand in its telling. Indeed, the work might have been "inspired" by God, but the writers were individuals who knew something about language and storytelling. He maintained that these writers brought all of those skills to bear in the creative process. Most scholars, or for that matter most Bible students, would have little trouble with such a view, Frye said. He indicated that a cursory study would demonstrate that the Bible was compiled by editors, and that it wasn't a direct transfer of the words of God to Man, unedited and without bias. Cultural biases, practices, rituals and thinking are all woven into the writing.

Frye doesn't mind puncturing the theory of "literal" meaning because he sees it as dangerous. "Meaning is not straight descriptive meaning that A means B . . .Their assumption is that the Bible is literally true that it's a straight signal from God to Man . . . It seems to me that the Bible is more deeply involved in all the resources and nuances of human speech, and not a simplistic conception of literal meaning."

MARGARET ATWOOD
22
THE DREAM OF REASON

Margaret Atwood's name is not usually associated with religion. She's a renowned novelist and a poet, and may even be an outspoken critic for social justice causes, but little about her work would suggest she had anything to say about religion. Still, in 1982 long before she wrote *A Handmaid's Tale*, where it was presumed she was making several prophetic statements about the way life was being lived on earth, I spoke to her about her belief, the Bible, the state of affairs in religious thought. Unlike many other writers, the Canadian-born Atwood doesn't shy away from the most fundamental question of all, a belief in God. "Well, I was brought up an agnostic of the old nineteenth-century kind," she explained. "In other words, my father was a scientist and he quite strongly believes you can't make statements about things that you don't know anything about. And my early experience with Christians wasn't that pleasant, let me tell you."

It had nothing to do with her family being agnostic. "They didn't go around proclaiming that . . . I found at that time the kinds of churches in Toronto in the late 1940s and mid-1950s were very, very self-righteous and right-minded and really more interested in form than in substance. I have to say on behalf of the United Church of Canada, which used to be very much like that, that it certainly has changed in recent years. Now it has a very active social program, and it is busy examining itself from all sides. It is undergoing attacks from all sides, even from its own members."

But, Atwood added, it is "no great advertisement" for the church when some of its own members behave in a manner that Jesus Christ preached against. By that, Atwood meant, "self-righteousness and judgmentalism and throwing the first stone.' She wasn't specific, but she didn't need to be, for at the time, the first rumblings over the "gay issue" were just being heard. Eventually this erupted into the debate over the ordination of homosexuals. Atwood witnessed a "true Christian spirit" operating among communities like the Quakers, the Unitarian Church, and those in Latin America, where many have adopted Liberation Theology as a means to solve the crisis in faith and economics. "In general, all one can say is if you try to live an entirely rational life, all that does is to suppress the other side of you and it comes out in strange forms, which Blake paraphrased — 'the dream of reason breeds nightmares.' So I think I've seen it from both sides. Probably because I was brought up an agnostic, I was a religion shopper in youth and I went piddling about to all of them to see just what they were offering. None of them got me, but I went through some strange places en route."

Atwood believed it was important to let children conjure up the "idea" of God, perhaps even read the Bible. In essence, to let children experience the poetry of God. "My father believed the Bible was a very necessary book. So do I. But I can't invest an awful lot of existential belief in the kind of God who orders the generals of Israel to wipe out this town including the women and the children and the animals . . . and all that Old Testament blood and gore . . . Some people still invest a lot of faith in that, and this substantiates them in wiping out this and that . . . I think the misuse of religion has done an awful lot of harm . . . Look at the minister of the interior in the States who thinks the second coming is at hand, so his attitude is, 'Why bother protecting the parks?'"

As for education, or literature, however, Atwood viewed the Bible as essential. "I think these are absolutely necessary stories for anybody to have if they're doing anything in literature. But so is great mythology, and we don't worship Zeus." In terms of morality, Atwood claimed it was difficult to hold a moral point of view about the world without believing in God. "To me, if you do right, it shouldn't be because you're afraid someone is going to put you in Hell if you don't, or because someone is going to give you a cookie if you do . . . It ought to be because it's right."

Atwood argued that while her work may not have an obvious connection to religion, as do the writings of Brian Moore who focuses upon priests in Ireland, or martyrs in Huronia, there are moments when her fiction reflects such a consciousness. "In *Life Before Man*, I've got a funeral scene that takes place in a church, and in *Surfacing*, the Catholic visual symbolism is used quite extensively, plus, of course, one of the essential symbols of our civilization, the offering up of the sacrifice."

To those who may argue the church shouldn't be involved in social issues, and that its prime purpose ought to be spiritual, Atwood stated, "Well, that's someone who believes the spiritual realm and the material realm are separate, and that's a transcendentalist who believes that. Those of us who are imminentists believe God isn't up there somewhere. He's right here, and so when you kill another person in a war, God isn't off somewhere else. He's right there — that's Participaction! Either you believe the spiritual realm is separate from the material realm and has nothing to do with it, or you don't. But if you do, then you must believe man's job is to get from the material realm to the spiritual realm somehow, in which case everyone should just commit suicide or have someone do us in." Atwood added that she found this to be "a great contradiction with the church . . . If life on earth is so crummy and awful, and the flesh is so horrible, why not divest yourself of it as quickly as possible? But that is not, in fact, what Christianity teaches."

The Toronto-based writer's understanding of the New Testament and how she "reads Christ" comes down to the view that he was "preaching concern for one's fellow man, or human beings . . . If you really do love your neighbor, then you've got to be involved in social issues, otherwise it's just hairshirts in the refectory and that's pretty selfish . . ." Atwood hoped her daughter would be inculcated with "the content of the Bible" minus "the guilt" that so often creeps into the soul. "I don't feel guilt ever accomplished a thing, unless you can turn it into art as Brian Moore can . . . But mostly it keeps people from acting in any way. . . They spend all their energy on the guilt."

As far as public education, Atwood favored some form of teaching at the elementary or secondary school level where biblical stories could be taught — not from the point of dogma, but from the point of just getting to know our roots. More like a comparative mythologies course. "A little Babylonian religion, Old Testament, New Testament, some Islam, something else quite different maybe, a North American Indian religion." Atwood believes

North Americans are ignorant of their own religions and mythology. But there was a time when they were familiar with it. Past generations knew the stories, but never thought of these as mythology. "They thought of it as revelation."

To her, it's time to get back to the roots. Because you may feel disgruntled with religion, it's unwise to shut the Bible and not have anything to do with it. "Why throw out the baby with the bath water?" asked Atwood. She added, "In order to read John Milton or Margaret Laurence, or really anybody, you have to know something about the Bible. . . . I do not like the new version. I like the old King James." What Atwood finds curious is how people who read Margaret Laurence's work want to ban it, "because it says something on page 162 that they don't think is right . . . They don't realize her books are in fact very mainline Christian."

Atwood knows the fundamentalists disagree with such a view, but "they don't understand their own religion . . . I think certain kinds of fundamentalists put a lot more stress on the Old Testament than they do on the New, with the result that they ignore the message of Christ, which can be summed up in about two pages, at least the important things that he actually said — the Beatitudes, the Lord's Prayer and the Golden Rule . . . But all that eye for an eye and tooth for a tooth stuff is Old Testament and that is presumably what Christ was coming to do away with or supplant . . . But you know, if you put together a lot of what he said, a lot of it is fairly contradictory . . . I think you could make a pretty good case for somebody having freely added things. When you read him, there seems to be two different voices speaking. He alternates between the new voice and the Old Testament voice."

To Atwood, Jesus didn't come simply to reinterpret and revitalize Judaic law. "He was certainly against legalism, pure formalism," she pointed out, and as a result violated many laws.

"There will always be that conflict in religion. You see it in Islam now as well, those who want to take a formalist interpretation and those who are more interested in the spiritual side . . ." To the suggestion that fundamentalists of Islam may seem more rabid and militant than our North American fundamentalists,

Atwood maintained, " I think we can match them here. Throughout the history of Christianity, we've certainly had people who were just as rabid." Atwood said the fundamentalist movement in North America grew by leaps and bounds in the 1970s and 1980s because it offered people "something they didn't have. I think they're frightened. I think they're frightened of the world right now. They don't feel secure in the way they used to. Their jobs are being threatened. Money isn't as easy to get, and they feel uprooted, not anchored to anything, and this offers them something secure. I think I'd rather them belong to a group that offers them some support, than not to have anything at all."

Atwood's perspective is that in the 1960s people moved away from religion, but found solace in other ways. "I saw that movement as rather religious too. People went around and said "I love you, I love you," thinking you were going to get instant revelation." At the time, Atwood lived in Cambridge, Massachusetts. Timothy Leary was at Harvard. She remembers someone — a Catholic — who was on one of his first LSD experiments. "At that time, no one knew that it could turn you a schizophrenic, and they were doing it in a supportive group. Basically it worked like a computer: i.e. garbage in, garbage out. What she brought to it was the Catholic religion, and that's the form the LSD revelations took. She just connected it to her religion and it didn't turn her schizophrenic — she found it very enlightening."

Atwood contended it wasn't because Leary had started handing the stuff out like candy that people began having these bad experiences. "The reason they had bad experiences was their lives weren't very good anyway, and they had no context in which to put these things. Just all of a sudden a big someone would come out of the sky and squash them. I still think some of the cults that use drugs probably use them quite responsibly and get things out of it they find very useful, particularly the Indians. But if you just go take them for kicks, thinking you're going to get something in a little package without putting any work in yourself, you won't get anything out of it except bubble gum."

Atwood, like other writers and intellectuals in North America, has little use for the electronic church. "I'm against people manipulating other people's emotions to make a lot of money. If I were a Bible Christian, I would point out the passages in the book saying you shouldn't do that. Christ turned the money lenders out of the temple, didn't he? I would like to see what they're using that money for, besides Cadillacs and limousines."

JIM BAKKER, BILLY GRAHAM, JERRY FALWELL
23
TRAVELING GOD'S HIGHWAY

1 For months I had planned the trip, long before the debacle of Jim and Tammy Bakker. In May 1987, I started on my journey down Highway 77, that broad red ribbon on the map that Christian fundamentalists call "Highway to Heaven" or "God's Highway." It runs like a vein down into the deep South, plunging through Ohio, West Virginia, Virginia, North Carolina and straight into the Bible Belt. It took me directly to the land of Bible message billboards, guiding me past the gates of Fort Mill, South Carolina, to the home of Christian scam and scandal, past the pearly gates of Jim and Tammy to the heartland of "the holy war" that was being waged between a righteous Moral Majority and the now-deposed Bakker Empire. As I made my way south, there was only a hint of what this part of America was all about. Quaint, white-frame, steepled churches dotted the lush, green, rolling landscape. At each junction to a town or a city, among a forest of Holiday Inn and Ramada Inn signs, were billboards bidding drivers to "Turn Back To the Bible." Almost each time I encountered someone, they'd nod, smile, and welcome me with "God bless ya" without batting an eye. It was also clear that in God's America things were not right.

Just as it was hard to find something other than gospel or country and western on the radio, it was difficult to ignore the indulgent denials of immorality over PTL or the smooth-talking words of "forgiveness" about the Bakkers. In a way, the country and western music with all its hurtin' and cheatin' was a flipside to the "gospel" fabric that pervaded the lives of the people there, whether they were Baptists, Pentecostals, or Lutherans. I wasn't surprised to find that on the walls of a highway restroom just past Akron, Ohio, someone had crayoned an obscene limerick with reference to Jim Bakker. Above that, someone else had scratched out a line from the Gospel of St. John. This was far from the edge of God's Country. And I wasn't surprised to learn that many of the drivers of these eight-wheelers were card-carrying "Truckers For Christ," and that among the highway maps and operating and regulation manuals, there was bound to be a well-thumbed New Testament. Many also proudly claimed to be PTL partners, or faithful contributors to Pat Robertson's 700 Club, or followers of Rex Humbard or Jimmy Swaggart.

It wasn't long before I had penetrated this landscape that I realized I had crossed some invisible boundary line: I had stepped into the heartland of the Bible Belt. Nothing signaled this — no road signs, no guide books — but there was the sense I'd passed into some territory that was like nothing else I'd ever seen. If it was a Wednesday night and I was passing by a Pentecostal church, I'd spot cars parked bumper to bumper along the shoulders of the highway. If I rolled down the car window, there'd be singing and hand-clapping. Birmingham University history professor David Edwin Harrell, biographer of Oral Roberts and an expert on the Bible Belt, told me in an interview that if you're looking for "boundaries" it's best to begin with the old Confederate states at the time of the Civil War, "and the Bible Belt comes stronger as you move toward the interior core."

There was no mistaking I had entered Bible country once I got near Charlotte, North Carolina. The road signs pointed me in the direction of Heritage USA, the multi-million dollar religious Disneyland complete with its gigantic water slides, the original childhood home of Billy Graham, and a recreated stage set of the City of Jerusalem with Herod's armies and shepherds and camels. I was drawn to the magnificent Heritage Grand Hotel with its glitzy lobby of chandeliers, mirrors, and twinkling lights, and surprised to be handed receipts in the restaurants that declared "Thank you . . . And we love you!" In the lobby gospel singers gathered about a Steinway grand piano for hymns at afternoon tea-time. Behind the registration desk the giant letters "Jesus Is Lord" jumped out at visitors. I found myself in one of the few hotels in the land where the lobby carried romanticized pictures of Christ and the Blessed Virgin. It was a hotel without mini-bars in the room, or smoke shops in the lobby. Smoking and drinking were banned, and the wake-up calls advised you, "This is the day the Lord has made!" Bikini-clad women were forbidden from the hotel pool. It was also a hotel where the message of love and kindness prevailed, even to the extent that the doorman hugged you upon arrival and remarked, "God loves ya, and so do I!"

As soon as I stepped foot in this sprawling 2,200-acre religious dreamland, I knew instantly I'd entered not just fundamentalist, Bible-centered America, but "charismatic" America where people spoke in tongues and where prophecies were as commonplace as cornbread and catfish. Essentially, that's what Heritage USA was — the epitome of the excesses of fundamentalism, betraying an odd commingling of carnival razzmatazz, amusement parks, early American revivalism, and old-fashioned Protestant Bible camp camaraderie. At its base, however, was a genuine spirit of goodwill perfectly reflective of a kind of down-home gentleness, open-eyed wonder, and love of family and God. Then again, it had the veneer of Victorian England, suggesting fierce family loyalties and the sort of church-going practices that were merely part of the cultural fabric, not necessarily out of intense Christian awareness.

The photographer I was with caught a couple of young women who worked at the hotel sunbathing in bikinis in a discreet and not so well-known spot. They pleaded with him not to publish the photographs because bikinis were strictly forbidden by the Bakkers. Guilt. Crime. Sin. It was all there. Even at the very gates of Heaven. Doug Oldham, a singer and then a regular on the PTL show, acknowledged that while there was "certainly just as much crime here as anywhere else, it's part of the culture to think of 'righteous living' and following Christ. You may get it from your parents, or your grandparents, or whatever . . . But it's part of life in the South. You grow up with it. You may not always follow it, but you're aware of it more here than anywhere else."

The hope with Heritage USA was that it would provide welcome relief for the Christian experiencing morality being threatened in open society; that the theme parks, the television show, the shops, the hotel would all point to what life ought to be like. "Granny Jo," an amiable gas station and "junk store" owner at Fort Mill, described the country as "God's Earth," especially Heritage USA: "If you've never been there, it's heaven! Just heaven. Ya'll see!" Along Route 21, the billboards blasted out at you, not the words of St. John or St. Matthew, but the happy faces of Jim and Tammy Bakker. Somewhat ironic considering Jerry Falwell's intentions of eradicating any vestiges of the Bakker dream.

As I penetrated the gloss of Heritage USA, which was plagued with the scandal of adultery and mishandling of PTL funds, I wondered if all the self-righteousness from the Swaggarts, the Falwells, and the Robertses was only another sign that God's America was headed for collapse, that paradise was soon to be swept away.

Jerry Falwell, the highly controversial Baptist minister from Lynchburg, had been petitioned by Bakker himself two months following revelations of Tammy's drug addiction and Bakker's own confession of adultery with a New York church secretary. Immediately, the head of the Moral Majority ordered an end to the era of fat salaries, luxury homes, Cadillacs and Rolls Royces that had marked the lifestyle of PTL executives. Also ended was Bakker's $1.6-million salary. So were the blackmail payments to Jessica Hahn, the woman with whom Bakker had had an adulterous affair. Ousted by Falwell's new team were Bakker's top aides, as well as Rev. Richard Dortch, the ingratiating PTL host and president who had initiated the Jim and Tammy forgiveness campaign. These were sweeping and swift measures targeted to return credibility and trust to the Christian community, including Falwell himself, who said his mission was "to stop people laughing at us in restaurants all over the country." His intent was to usher in a new era of moderation, with less charisma, and more level-headedness. Such actions could be interpreted, said Harrell, as the Bible Belt desperately trying to disentangle itself from tradition and history.

The question at the time, however, was whether Falwell would push the charismatics off stage. He himself insisted: "I'm not going to make a Baptist camp out of it. I'm going there for the purpose of seeing that it is always a Christian camp . . . I am there to do my best to prevent it from falling into the hands of a secular group."

Fear of the secular world encroaching upon the values of the South was really the motivating force behind the Electronic Church, explained Harrell. The Picture-Tube Church, consisting primarily of Southern-born leaders, brought with it a philosophy and theology that was a throwback to the South's older traditions of family and church. Falwell's measures were aimed at preserving these values, keeping them sacred. "In a lot of ways, the South has been in a time lag from the rest of the country . . . It's been in a generational backwash." Harrell told me that many of the old structures were still in place, that the church was still a "central" social institution in the lives of Southerners, and that the large open-air crusades or revivals still drew the largest crowds in the Bible Belt. To a great degree, some Southern cities differed little from those in the Midwest or the North, said Harrell. The fear in religious circles was that values of the past and the "southerness" of the South were threatened with extinction. This tension, Harrell asserted, gave rise to the Electronic Church.

These religious leaders' efforts at "exporting" their values to the rest of the country really arose out of this fear of losing a church-based society. They were eager to develop a new credibility outside their own world. In much the same way, Harrell argued that the popularity of Southern literature, country and western music, and stock-car racing was an effort at maintaining older traditional values. For a time, the superstars of religion in the United States were these millionaire southerners. Oddly enough, the Michigan-born Jim Bakker and now Defrocked Assemblies of God clergyman was "the lone Yankee" in this exclusive club.

2 Down the highway some 115 kilometers or 70 miles south of Columbia, South Carolina, it was evident that fundamentalism or evangelism hadn't been dealt a deadly blow by the Bakker scandal. Some 42,000 waved church programs at Williams-Bruce Stadium. Above the Coca-Cola neon scoreboard was the message "I Am The Way The Truth And The Life! Jesus!" In a few minutes the most respected Christian evangelist and fundamentalist in the country stepped forward to begin a routine perfected and utilized a thousand times over to charm audiences and transform them into committed followers.

Then sixty-eight years old, the bushy-sideburned Billy Graham, who had studied under the tutelage of traveling revivalist Mordecai Ham, had come to woo these people who had brought their children, the elderly, and the handicapped, suspecting this might be the last crusade of their southern brother in the Carolinas. The last time he had been there was 1950. Some recalled that moment when the Charlotte-born Graham led an outdoor revival Christian historians regard as a turning point in his long career. He had been on the preaching circuit only a few years, when on the site of this football stadium, the young wavy-haired evangelist attracted some 40,000 after a phenomenal three-week crusade. "It was a crusade that just wouldn't quit," remarked Rev. Mark Jeffcoat, director of public relations for the Southern Baptist Convention. In that moment, Graham sensed what the future brought: massive open-air crusades that over a lifetime would bring more than 100 million to hear his message.

That night in May 1987 when I saw him, his message was no different than on any other crusade. Still, it was one that would never fail to grip his followers. When he strode to the pulpit, an immense Bible draped over his left hand like some animal for the sacrifice in Biblical times, his audience was ready for a good old-fashioned sermon of sin and salvation and good works. Graham, his right arm slowly chopping the twilight air, was like a conductor, and to his believers it was a music they had yearned to hear. That deep, hypnotic, even, and melodic voice reverberated throughout the football field. The message was straightforward, always the same: "Yes, God forgives!" Moments later, Graham had his Carolina audience spellbound — chiding them, cajoling them, joking with them, at times even thundering over the loudspeakers like an Old Testament prophet or a righteous and angry Moses scolding his people. But they didn't mind. It's what they had come to hear, what they wanted.

When he finished, it seemed it wasn't enough. They demanded more, and Graham delivered — praying, cajoling them, making sense of their chaos and dilemmas but scornfully warning, "Jesus Christ *will* not compromise!" Then, standing in a shower of light on a stage bordered with gladioluses and chrysanthemums, Graham urged the thousands who sat mesmerized to walk out onto the open field to give themselves to Christ: "Come up now!

Don't anyone leave this stadium while this is happening. This is a holy and quiet moment!"

They came by the thousands across the lush, green grass: mothers cradling babies, or leading young daughters or sons by the hand, servicemen in fatigues marching resolutely with Bibles tucked under an arm, other men in short-sleeve shirts nearly running, hundreds more making their way across the grass in wheelchairs or slowly inching along on aluminum walkers . . . And Graham recalled for them a night like this almost fifty years ago when, as a teenager, he gave himself to Christ: "It changed my life! I know I was forgiven!"

3 After Heritage USA, Columbia's moment seemed magical — it seemed the essence of evangelism: pure, unsullied, genuine. By contrast Bakker appeared to be a fallen angel and Graham an aging and respectable ambassador for the church, perhaps the apostle John, entirely in favor. Again historians and writers speculate that this may be because Graham had broadened his message to include more than just those in the South. He may have clung to his "southerness" said Harrell, but he had learned to relate to the Midwest, the North, everywhere. Graham's message left few unsettled, or alienated. He had learned the cultural secrets of the rest of the country, including the need to consort with politicians and industrialists. Indeed, Richard Nixon was among his best friends. Years later, he would participate in the funeral of that former President of the USA.

Graham also appeared relevant, far removed from the discordant, exclusive and guarded paranoia of the televangelists. While the others — the Swaggarts, the Oral Robertses, and the Bakkers — may have attempted to blast out their epistles to the world on the picture tube, it seemed that it was only the South that could understand it — life was different elsewhere. One observer maintained: "What they said may make sense to Southerners, because they've heard it all their lives, but to the rest of the country, it doesn't wash!" A waitress at the Ramada Inn with whom I spoke told me that she had been reared a Baptist. She pointed out, "If

you're single, there are only two places where you can meet people: in a bar or in a church!"

To the Columbia-born Jeffcoat, the South, with its family
restaurants, tightly-knit church community, traditionally strong
attitudes about alcohol and morals, presented this image to outsiders. It isn't some far-fetched notion, either, because a drive along
the streets of Columbia or Greenville, a city nearby, will take you
to "four churches on every corner." Protestantism flourishes there
like J.C. Penny stores — one in three people are Baptists.

Larry Ross, public relations director for the Billy Graham Crusades, was less positive about the church-going attitudes. To him,
the South suffered from "churchianity," meaning that although
many attended Sunday services, "they haven't given themselves to
Christ." David Roberts, a steel factory worker who lives near
Lynchburg, Virginia, insisted, too, a temperance-minded South is
an exaggeration: "The teenagers are like anywhere else — if they
can get it, they'll drink it!"

To retired Virginian farmer Ashby Millstead, attending church
is all he has ever known. "I've been going ever since I was a barefoot boy. I don't know anything else." Sometimes, too, the past
rooted in the southern heritage comes back to haunt, as was the
case of L. L. Jordan, a retired truck driver, who turned away "two
preachers from the house . . . I got sick after that, and the doctors
didn't know what it was." He said he started going to church and
recovered: "If any preacher comes knocking now, I sure will let 'em
in." Jeffcoat conceded the South was changing as "transplanted
northerners" threaten the old traditions. However, if you had to
choose "the right place" for a Christian to live in the USA, he
added, then the South might be that setting. After all, most of the
neighbors or friends are churchgoers.

Numbers meant little to Harry Dent, former special counsel to
President Richard Nixon and chairman of the Billy Graham Crusade in Columbia. To him, the South was under attack and the
Bible Belt was in danger of flying apart. "South Carolina is in the
middle of the Bible Belt but the belt has become unbuckled." The
collapse of the credibility of televangelists brought Jerry Falwell

galloping to Heritage USA, and what was at stake was the Bible Belt's own reputation as the "holdout" against the rest of the country, which was sliding into materialism and immorality.

Many regarded the Falwell mission as "divine intervention." Former Los Angeles Rams player Rosie Grier, who had come to PTL in the midst of the scandal to conduct a seminar on drug awareness for teenagers, described the Moral Majority leader as "cleaning house . . . He's doing God's work!" Falwell himself suggested the same thing: "The sovereign is cleaning house . . . the Lord has the right to step in and change everything in a hurry . . . I see myself only as a steward."

Southern reaction generally was that with a deposed Bakker, their own "Southern brother," Jerry Falwell, would return respectability. Columbia's newspaper *The State* actually described the political-talking fundamentalist as "a saint." *The Charlotte Observer* — for years a thorn in the side of the Bakker Empire — acknowledged it "admired" Falwell's beginning.

4 After a week of being in Columbia, we made our way to Lynchburg, Virginia. It was a rainy, windy morning. Falwell was in his element as he stepped inside a jammed auditorium at Liberty University. Thunderous applause made his facial expression appear even more self-satisfied. It had been seven days since he had seized control over PTL. Dressed in the formal attire of a chancellor, Falwell bounced to the podium. At his side was Edmund Meese, then attorney general of the USA. Moments later, the broad-shouldered evangelist, then fifty-three, stood before the 1987 graduation class. In some ways, he seemed like a brother to Graham — Southern-born, Baptist, trusting scripture and good works, and holding unswerving devotion to the ministry. Unlike Graham, Falwell didn't merely count politicians among his acquaintances, he put them into power. He viewed them as a means to attack "lawlessness and moral permissiveness." He even claimed authority behind the man in the White House, boasting of delivering the support Ronald Reagan needed to get elected — from all those who cared about religion and values.

In introducing Meese, Falwell's message was clear to Liberty University graduates — that the White House team running this country was "a team under God," and one that was tackling "the cancers of society." Falwell dubbed Reagan "the greatest president that you've known in your lifetime." The attorney general told Liberty Students that the United States needed "people who believe in God and keep His commandments." While such a message might be out of place on most campuses in North America, at Liberty, where smoking and drinking were forbidden, and where students were expelled for reading *Playboy*, it was entirely appropriate.

Falwell stood to one side of the charismatic movement, rooted more in the territory of Billy Graham — conservative and relying upon the Bible for the answers to society's ills. While he may have seized control over PTL, he was a foreigner to the charismatic movement. So much so that many PTL supporters suspected his "cleanup" was intended to drive them into oblivion. Indeed, as he distributed degrees to Liberty students at Lynchburg that day, some 100 angry PTL "Partners," hundreds of miles away from Heritage USA, congregated in a protest and threatened to cut off their financial support unless Jim and Tammy were brought back.

While Falwell's stated objectives were to force the two Protestant streams of fundamentalism into one, he insisted he would never impose his will or theology on the charismatics: "My personality will be seen and felt . . . I'm not a compromiser, but I think I get along with brothers and sisters in Christ." Critics conjectured that if Falwell succeeded, the "religious right" movement would wind up representing even a greater political force in the country. "As soon as the evangelicals and fundamentalists learn how the system works, and they are learning now, they will be a very, very powerful force," said Dallas Theological Seminary's Norman Geisler.

5 With the 1990s, the last vestiges of PTL disappeared. Bakker was still in jail. Swaggart was ever so repentant, confessing he had more than "lust" in his heart — he had actually been caught sleeping around. As for Falwell, he resigned from the Moral

Majority, feeling it was time to let someone else take over. Today, he continues at Lynchburg, concentrating upon what he always loved to do — to preach. I remember what he said in 1987 when everyone was wondering what would happen to televangelism. Falwell was right: "God's business will go on as though we were never here."

6 A year earlier in 1986 I first met Jerry Falwell, receiving permission to accompany him on a crusade. Falwell seemed out of place, or at least uncomfortable, at the back of his private $4.5 million Westwind jet. He sat there wearing a white shirt and tie. He seemed too coarse-looking to be an evangelist, a man of God — his face slightly pocked and swollen. You got the feeling he should be in a machine shop or on an assembly line, for in a suit he appeared stiff, obviously frustrated, ill at ease. When he stood up, he automatically rolled his shoulders forward as if to throw off some nagging strain, then fidgeted with his shirt, yanked it down over the unsightly swell at the waist. If he appeared uneasy, he wasn't. There seemed to be nothing at which he lacked confidence. He could stride into a private meeting or an auditorium of thousands and take command. As soon as he began speaking, he took charge, and instantly had you under his spell. It was a gift, and he knew it. It's called charisma, and he's made it into a million dollar business. Big business.

I must have called his headquarters in Lynchburg, Virginia a dozen times to line up an interview. At one point, I fired off a letter to him. After waiting nearly a year, I gave up. Then suddenly, a newly-hired publicist telephoned the paper one afternoon. My letter had found its way to his desk. He agreed to the interview, and specified it could take place in a few months, unless I wanted to meet with Falwell that next week when he was in Michigan. He told me I could rendezvous with the religious leader, and fly with him to Battle Creek, Michigan where he would be lunching with the Kellogg family. There was a possibility of a half hour on the way there, a half hour on the return flight, and whatever else I needed back in Detroit. It was an opportunity I wasn't going to decline.

By 1986, this broad-shouldered evangelist, son of a hard-drinking oilman who had nothing to do with church, was considered the "pope" among fundamentalists. He had been chosen by *Good Housekeeping* magazine as "the most admired man in America," ahead of Pope John Paul II, Ronald Reagan, and Alan Alda. He sat at the back of the plane with a Diet Coke at his side. He had just petitioned his nineteen year old son Jonathan to brew up some coffee. He reached over and picked up a leather-bound Bible the size of the New York City phone book and placed it in the cubby-hole lavatory situated directly behind him. He then signaled ahead that he was ready for departure. Moments later, the sleek jet, striped in patriotic red, white, and blue, dubbed by the pilots "Long Underwear" because of the "LU" in its registration, 777LU, roared down the runway of a private airport near Detroit Metropolitan Airport. It lifted quickly into the gray smog, then swerved toward Battle Creek where Falwell would meet with the Kellogg family, dine with officials there, go on a tour of the plant. On his return to Detroit that night, he would address an audience at Temple Baptist Church. A busy day. But not unusual for this man who covered about 8,000 miles a week by jet to keep up with a heavy agenda of private meetings and religious and political rallies.

When I met Falwell, he was fifty-two, only a few weeks shy of his fifty-third birthday. He leaned forward to shout over the screaming engines of the jet. He spent more time in the cramped jet than he cared to, but it's because he preferred to fly in and out of places and then back home for the night. He ruled out the notion of living like a rock star out of hotel rooms in different cities every night. He preferred home and actually yearned for family and routine. "I like to go home . . . I try to every night."

Falwell told me he saw himself as just an ordinary pastor from Lynchburg, and while many have regarded him as just another eager political animal, "what comes first . . . is religion — politics is second." He realized others didn't see it that way, especially those who support the World Council of Churches. He smiled at the ironies perpetuated over this. Time and time again, he had accused the World Council of Churches as being nothing more than "a political machine" that had lost sight of the gospel. He nodded his head, and said, "Yup, I know . . . Some might say the same of me . . . But really, they can't." Falwell challenged his critics at the World Council of Churches to come up with the kind of rigorous schedule that finds him preaching at least three times a week at Thomas Road Baptist Church, the church he transformed from a thirty-five member parish in an old bottling building into a 4,000 seat parish with more than 22,000 churchgoers. In addition, the once powerful leader of the religious right in the United States told me that he personally does his Bible Study Hours for radio and conducts his own evangelism on the Old Time Gospel Hour on television to more than 300 stations across the continent. "Just let them come and see what we do, and they'll know religion comes first."

Later when Falwell slipped on his pin-stripe jacket, a gold lapel pin glinted in the sunlight through the jet's windows: "Jesus First." The same lapel pin can be spotted on jackets of the more than 2,300 employees of Jerry Falwell Ministries. Each one is a born-again Christian, including the pilots who command his jet as it criss-crosses the nation. Such devotion is understandable. To his employees, he's a kind of "self-made prophet." They have no doubt of his sincerity. As he spoke his blue eyes held my attention. He clasped his hands, in a prayerful manner, or as if he was collecting thoughts there, while he answered questions.

During the conversation, everything I had heard about him began to come into focus. This was the man who virtually boasted of personally installing Ronald Reagan in the White House. This was the man who claimed to speak for all good-living Americans. He was also the man who went to South Africa to embrace President P. W. Botha's policies and return with the charge that Nobel Peace Prize winner Bishop Desmond Tutu was nothing but a phony. Despite that, Falwell seemed to believe what he said, and that his statements were firmly grounded in Christianity.

The evangelist's meteoric rise to influence in the USA took place in the 1970s. He called 1973 his "watershed year," pointing out that it was then that the Congress legalized abortion — something he described as no surprise after a decade of "lawlessness and moral permissiveness," during the 1960s. It was then that Falwell decided to embark upon a quasi-political campaign which would have shocked most conservative pastors, "but it was right for the moment." Falwell said, "Twenty-five years before this, I would have repudiated such involvement. I felt government could be trusted to change its own direction and cure its own ills. But not so in 1973. I became convinced this country was on a dangerous bend to the left." The abortion legislation was "the straw that broke the camel's back . . . I realized that what the religious left had always been doing, the religious right must begin doing."

It wasn't until 1980 that Falwell actually formed the Moral Majority. He had joined a small band of evangelical tacticians who had been struggling for three years to build a religious vote. Falwell infused new energy into the group. He became its genius, the one to make the organization flourish and become a force to be reckoned with at the polls. Since those first days, more than 110,000 American churches and synagogues have joined Falwell's Moral Majority, and have endorsed what it stands for: "a pro-life, pro-family, pro-moral, and pro-American way of life." In forming the powerful lobby group, Falwell believed he woke "a sleeping giant" in Americans, a giant that sincerely yearned for the ideals of the New Right.

Falwell himself actually stepped down in November 1987 as the leader of the Moral Majority, although even today it is his name that is still associated with it. At the time of his resignation, he had said it was necessary for him to give up politics and return to the church and television ministry. "My first love is back to the pulpit, back to preaching, back to winning souls, back to meeting spiritual needs." By the time he stepped down, Falwell figured he could be credited, "or blamed," as he put it at a news conference to announce his decision at the Willard Hotel in Lynchburg, Virginia, for registering and turning out millions of evangelical voters for Ronald Reagan in 1980 and possibly helping to defeat several liberal Democratic senators in the process. The man Falwell named to succeed him as president of the Moral Majority was Jerry Nimes, a Falwell associate who is not a minister.

At the time that I spoke to him, Falwell was still riding a crest of popularity. It was before the Jim Bakker debacle, before scandals had wreaked havoc with televangelism. Falwell in 1986 still believed firmly that it was necessary for religion and politics to mix. "We had taught them not to be involved in politics, and now we had to un-teach them."

Long before the Moral Majority was functioning, Falwell was working charismatic magic. He took over a dying congregation with some thirty-five surviving members more than thirty years ago and transformed an abandoned building into a sprawling complex that not only included Thomas Road Baptist Church, but Liberty University, a full-fledged, degree-granting college that's bursting at the seams with more than 7,000 students. Falwell also started the Old Time Gospel Hour and the half-hour Bible study programs that beam out his philosophy to more than thirty-four million homes across North America. Jerry Falwell Ministries, having mushroomed from that abandoned church in his home town, today is a $100 million business. On top of that, Falwell's evangelism took him into the Moral Majority and Liberation Federation with an annual operating budget of some $12 million.

The effect through the 1980s was sweeping and pervasive. It carried the unmistakable stamp of Jerry Falwell and "Baptist" thinking. At Liberty University each professor is a "born-again Christian," said Falwell. Students are prohibited from smoking or drinking — "just like everyone on my staff," Falwell pointed out. Students at Liberty also require written permission from the dean to go out on a date, and all movies shown at the college are G-rated, such as Walt Disney's *101 Dalmations.* "It's not for everyone, just like West Point isn't for everyone," he reasoned.

But while the school isn't for everyone, the way of life Falwell has been selling in America is something he believed ought to be adopted by the general population. It's the way to God. This is the belief that motivates the evangelist who freely and aggressively jousts with politicians and journalists around the world. While

Falwell doesn't find agreement among many sectors, there are others who have found his style attractive. Many large corporations favored his brand of conservatism in the 1980s, though less so in the 1990s. But back then, in the time of Reagan, Falwell stood for enterprise, initiative, clean American values. I couldn't help but suspect this was why he was flying off to the Kellogg empire. But Falwell gave no hint of why he was going there. It was obvious — he was like a politician venturing forth looking for support. Even the jet we were flying in was donated to Jerry Falwell Ministries. Before that, Falwell leased an outdated plane that ate up too much fuel.

When his jet landed at Kellogg's private airport in Battle Creek, Falwell pulled on his suit jacket and checked his watch. "Only four minutes behind schedule." When he emerged into the bright sunlight from the small door of the Westwind, he immediately fixed his eyes upon his hosts. He extended a broad hand in greeting, and jokingly wished he had brought the box tops to support his claim he ate their cereal. Again, he sounded much like any ingratiating politician. Moments later, Falwell was on his way, accompanied by Kellogg officials. While he headed for his luncheon, the two pilots — Tim Vaughan and Dave Jones — borrowed a car and drove to a Chinese restaurant. Plates loaded with rice, sweet-and-sour chicken, ham and potatoes, they bowed their heads and paused for a moment of grace. The two admitted to a unique kind of reverence for Falwell whom they referred to simply as "Jerry." They liked the man personally, admired his work, praised him for his principles, and argued that often he's misunderstood, even by his followers. The two maintained that even if Falwell didn't pay them "competitive wages — but he does — they would still work for him, "and that's because we're doing the work of the Lord."

Three hours later, Falwell was back and the Westwind once again roared down the runway and into the Michigan sky, bound for Detroit. An easy day. No confrontation, or at least, not yet. Back in the Motor City he met with a scrum of reporters who tried to provoke some controversial statement from Falwell. He smiled for them. He knew that then Governor Jim Blanchard had made some disparaging remarks about him, but Falwell just waved off the opportunity to retaliate.

Vaughan wasn't surprised at Falwell's hesitancy to get into a debate. He said mostly the religious leader was "diplomatic," except when it came to matters of principle. He said people mistake this for "a nasty side" to Falwell, when in fact, he is only defending what is right and just. What the public don't see of this religious leader is that he's someone who enjoys having a good time. He's a practical joker. Vaughan told me that often when he's telephoned Falwell, he'll answer with, "Boiler Room!" or "Homicide!" He recalled once at a hotel how the former Moral Majority leader rushed out of his room to toss a stink bomb at just the right moment into an elevator crammed with his staff. "He had come out of the room, shouting, 'Hold the elevator!' And we did, and he threw this stink bomb in . . . then the doors closed . . . and we were trapped." Occasionally the staff gets back at him. On one occasion, Falwell opened his shaving kit to discover a dead bluejay.

To his pilots, Falwell is cool and collected. "I've never seen him angry," said Vaughan. "He does get angry, but it's not in a violent or emotional way. He voices it in a slow monotone . . . You don't know your head's cut off until you try and wiggle it." And when I spoke with Falwell, he told me it was no exaggeration to describe him as "the punching bag of the right." He said he didn't mind it. He felt what he had been forging was a whole new way of life, and it was bound to upset people. His mission entailed the fashioning of a whole new approach to society. That meant outlawing print and film pornography and permitting people the right to "a tuition tax credit" so they could send their children to religious-based schools. It meant creating a society where abortion would be a crime and where homosexuals would be "helped spiritually" but denied certain civil rights.

Falwell's vision also prescribed a society where divorce wouldn't be necessary and where feminists would discover that the "old values" weren't so bad after all. On that plane ride back to Detroit, the religious leader deplored "the American brand of feminism." To him, it was nothing more than "an attempt to create a unisex where there are no differences or distinctions . . . Nature itself denies that . . . I'm a husband and a father of three children, and personally I'm quite happy my wife is different than I am." Falwell also abhorred "inclusive language" in scripture and liturgy where male images of God would be replaced with something more impersonal and less sexist. "I think that's a game that unemployed theologians have picked up to occupy their time. John 3:16 said, 'God so loved the world that He gave His only begotten Son,' not his only begotten daughter!' If he had given his only begotten daughter and she died on the cross for me, I'd accept her, but facts are facts!"

Such statements are inflammatory to some, but back in Detroit reporters seemed more interested in the political side to Falwell, about whom he might endorse in the next election, not about whether he prayed, or whether he believed in Heaven or Hell. He shook his head. He wasn't in Detroit to back any politicians. He told me orthodoxy calls for a particular vision for society, and that dream should never seem outrageous — if it's there in the Bible. Politics, he stressed, was only a means toward an end: "The church is to be the moral conscience of society — government is to do the legislating . . . When the church is functioning in a healthy way, it will be uncomfortable for people in the community to openly ignore God's laws and live sinfully, as for example, with adult bookstores and nude dancers." The kind of vision and crusade that Falwell has brought to his believers veers radically from the mainline churches. He eschews any interest in church unity. "I think Christian unity is wonderful . . . But the organizational unity that is being promoted today is pretty hard to swallow."

Once in Detroit, Falwell was ushered into a room at Page Aviation, just before he was brought downtown. He sat at a large table amid reporters who fired questions at him. They were the kinds of questions he liked. Politics. Scandal. Money. Nothing about religion itself. Outside in the hallway, his red-headed son Jonathan was pacing. He seemed bored. He knew it would be midnight before he would be home in Lynchburg. He said he's lived all his life watching his father do this kind of thing. He was obviously proud. He was also learning firsthand what an evangelist ought to do. After all, that's what he was planning to do — follow in his father's footsteps in the ministry.

7 When I saw Falwell again about a year later at a graduation at Liberty University, he was in the news because he had swept in to save the Bakker empire. But the deal with Bakker had turned sour. It was years before the two would reconcile their feelings for one another. They finally did meet, when Falwell visited Bakker in federal prison in Jesup, Georgia, where Bakker was serving time for fraud in the 1987 PTL scandal.

Bakker had asked Falwell to take over his PTL ministry and Fort Mill, South Carolina, theme park. Bakker later accused Falwell of stealing the ministry. Falwell spokesman Mark DeMoss said the meeting with Bakker was "a pastoral visit" and that the two embraced, prayed and "had almost no discussion about the past." Bakker's lawyer reported that the former evangelist appreciated the chance to smooth over bitter feelings with the former Moral Majority leader.

Falwell is now back in the pulpit, having put aside his involvement in the fundamentalist Christian political group Moral Majority. As he had told me on that plane ride in 1986, "My first love is back to the pulpit, back to preaching, back to winning souls, back to meeting spiritual needs."

CHARLES TEMPLETON
24
THE GIMMICKRY OF GOD

"**M**ost were seedy-looking extroverts given to wearing flamboyant clothes, loud men with braying voices, permanently hoarse from exhorting. Many were failed pastors, men who couldn't endure the drudgery of ministerial pastors. Each had a specialty, a gimmick of some kind to set him apart. Some specialized in faith healing or Bible prophecy. Others traded on a criminal past, or on a life of dissolution which enabled them, at the climax of the campaign, to recount their life story under titles such as 'From the Gutter to God.' Some sang as well as preached, which was an economy for the church calling them.

The sermons of most of these men were little more than 'illustrations' strung together on thin theology; and because a meeting wasn't considered a success unless a good number of 'seekers' came to the mourners' bench, they motivated listeners through fear or sentimentality or by telling horrendous tales of men and women who rejected God and went to hell for it. They received little for their efforts; their travel expenses and a love offering on the closing night." — from Charles Templeton's *The Third Temptation*

Charles Templeton strolled into the lobby of the Royal Connaught Hotel in Hamilton, Ontario. Celebrity face. Celebrity bearing. A blend of his novels' protaganists Rev. Leo Francis McGreer, "film star handsome," and the spellbinder Rev. Jimmy Coulter, in a $500 suit. Tall, straight, an air of cockiness, but smiling a kindly warm greeting. We went upstairs to the second floor lobby. He leaned back in a comfortable lobby chair, lamplight shadowing his face and tie, but not his blue, convincing eyes.

This was Templeton in September 1980 when he was promoting his third novel, *The Third Temptation*, the story of Jimmy Coulter, the renowned evangelist who loses faith in God. Shades of Templeton's own life, but the former evangelist will tell you he was a notch above. However, like Coulter, he entered that world of prayer and preachin' in the 1930s. But it was religion with a difference. Templeton had a deportment and demeanor that really conveyed a touch of class on the sawdust trail — going to tent meetings, grimy little churches, riding through slumbering villages on the road, sleeping on buses and in cars, then going with arms open and spouting silver words like some dazzling Hollywood personality urging people to put Jesus in their hearts. Templeton had found God when he was in his twenties. Like the protagonist in his novel, he left *The Toronto Globe and Mail* and "got religion." In those years at the newspaper, he made $18 a week doing sports cartoons. Good money then, and in time the pictures were syndicated and earned Templeton a minor reputation. But he turned his back on this to become a preacher.

"My conversion was not unlike Jimmy's conversion. . . It was sudden, overwhelming, and I felt like a new person . . . I was changed. I was different for the experience." Also like the character Coulter, Templeton practiced tirelessly in empty auditoriums, and the vocal hesitancy and the slight stammer in his voice vanished. Soon he was the boy wonder of evangelism preaching to tens of thousands. Soon he was the leading evangelist with the Presbyterian Church in the United States roaring across the country trailed by an admiring white-robed choir offering the faithful the Kingdom of Heaven.

Today Charles Templeton is an agnostic. "I make a very big distinction between agnostic and atheist. I am not an atheist. An atheist says there is no God. In my view that is presumptuous. How do you know? Have you examined all the evidence that you can flatly say there is no God? I wouldn't dare say that. An agnostic doesn't say there is no God. An agnostic says, 'I cannot know.' Not, 'I do not know,' but 'I cannot know. By virtue of the fact that I'm finite and God's infinite. You can't prove God.'"

Templeton lost his faith over an extended period of time while preaching. It became obvious to him, and he had to get out. "I came to a point finally where to go on would have meant preaching things I didn't believe." It took him two years to untangle himself from obligations. His life was the church. All his friends and associations were the church. Fleeing it overnight was impossible. But like conversion, Templeton's decision was just as overwhelming, and just as sudden, and obvious, as soon as he could see the reality of it all. It struck him like a bolt of lightning at Harrisburg,

Pennsylvania, where he preached to more than 18,000. On his way back to New York where he resided at the time, he turned to his wife and confided, "You know, I cannot go on doing this. I am like an ecclesiastical mountain goat leaping from peak to peak. Never down on the slopes and valleys where people really lived. It's just not for me anymore."

When Templeton abandoned the preaching circuit in 1957, he was head of the department of evangelism for the United Presbyterian Church in the United States. It was a job he had held for only two years, but he had had enough and wanted out. At that time, Templeton's reputation was gigantic. Having been the chief evangelist for the National Council of Churches from 1951 to 1954, he traveled North America, preaching to audiences of up to 70,000 in places like Soldier Field in Chicago, the Rose Bowl in Pasadena, and Radio City Music Hall in New York.

Since quitting the ministry, Templeton found it hard to detach himself entirely. "I can't help it . . . I spent nineteen years of my life doing this," he told me in an interview over the phone from his Toronto apartment in 1988. Templeton pointed out that some people from that era were still angry and bitter over his actions. By and large, those who were closest to him, don't hold it against him. They understand the reasons. "If I had stayed in the ministry, I would have been a hypocrite. How can you tell other people what to believe when you don't believe it yourself?"

Templeton's old friends realized there was no point in attempting to lure him back to Christianity. "Oh, they're disappointed, and they regret it, but they now know that what I did was the only honest option I had. I loved it when I was doing it, and I didn't want to leave . . . but I couldn't stand up in public any longer and proclaim what I didn't believe."

The fact Templeton still clings to the subject is not just because his life has been so intertwined with religion, but also because the questions religion poses are those each and every person faces anyway. "The most important question in life for anybody — in or out of the church — is 'What's it all about?' What is life all about? What's its purpose? What's its meaning? I think anyone who doesn't think seriously about it is trivializing life. Religion interests me more than just about any other single subject."

After those years of selling religion came showbiz (CBC TV), journalism (executive news editor, *The Toronto Star*), politics (contending for the leadership of the Ontario Liberal Party), then novel writing, and finally his autobiography, *An Anecdotal Memoir*.

In 1980, Templeton seemed alone in scoffing at "the crooks" and "phonies" in the televangelist world. This was years before the combined world of Jim Bakker, Jimmy Swaggart, and Oral Roberts would collapse in scandal, taking with it an assortment of others found guilty of immoral behavior and illegal activities. But Templeton was an "insider" — he knew how evangelists could confound and distort people's minds. The worst of these were the televangelists: "The religion that is preached (by them) is the antithesis of Christianity. It is not Christianity. It uses all the words. But it is really 'Me, first!' . . . With them, everything is what God will do for you. He will bless you! He will love you! He will help you! Love Him and pray to Him and He will solve your problems and solve your difficulties. But Jesus said take up your cross and follow me. He said lose your life and you'll find it. So what they're saying is just the exact opposite of what the New Testament teaches."

Televangelism in the 1980s was big business. At the top of Templeton's list of those to reproach was Oral Roberts: "I find it difficult to understand how a man who is close to God builds a school and a hospital, and calls it 'Oral Roberts University' and 'Oral Roberts Hospital of Faith.' I think the humility that a Christian is supposed to feel would let him put something else other than his own name on it. But that's between him and his Lord . . . if he's religious. I don't know whether he's religious. There are a lot of people in religion who aren't religious." Templeton also pegged Swaggart as probably "the most powerful" and persuasive of evangelists in the 1980s . . . He does things with audiences that are quite incredible. He has the kind of spellbinding skills Adolf Hitler had. And within certain limits, he has a kind of genius."

Besides the rogues, there are those who were sincere. Templeton still believes the greatest among them is Billy Graham. "He's the last great evangelist, you know . . . Billy Graham is a good man, but I think what he says is childish and puerile . . . Billy and I are old friends. We traveled together and lived together. I like him and I respect him. But he knows my feelings. And when he comes to Toronto he phones me up and we go down to the hotel and sit around and talk . . . but we don't talk religion because it's something at which we're at antithetical positions."

Graham wasn't exempt from wranglings over his own faith: "Billy . . . after a real struggle within himself . . . and troubled that I was going away from it . . . went out in the mountains of California . . . and prayed and made up his mind that he was going to be obedient to God and he was going to believe the Bible literally . . . take it literally and not question it anymore because it might lead him into trouble. I thought, of course, this was wrong, and I told Billy this. I told him, 'Not to think is a sin against the Creator. He made your mind. The great commandment is that you should love the Lord thy God with thy whole mind. So that not to think, Billy, is to break the great commandment, that not to think is a sin!' And he said, 'Well, I've discovered that when I preach the Bible, when I don't question, when I say that God says, the Bible says, God blesses me and I see results. I don't know about anybody else, but that's the way for me.'"

Templeton's assessment of Graham in 1980 was right on the mark. Long after Bakker's Heritage USA was washed away in ignominy, Graham remained unsullied, ever the clean-living, shining knight among the evangelists. "He's as straight as a string. Billy got his fundamentalism, his belief in the Bible with his mother's milk. It was nurtured during his growing up on a farm in North Carolina." Templeton believed Graham survived the scandals because he had been so genuine, so straight forward. There was nothing to hide in what he uttered or what he did. His old friend had been doing and saying the same things since they were both on the preaching circuit in the 1940s and 1950s. Little had changed except both have grown older.

The last time I spoke with Templeton was about the time he

was promoting *The World of One*, a novel about the future of tel-evangelism. He pointed out he couldn't resist the temptation to capitalize on the Bakker debacle. Satisfied that the likes of Bakker and Swaggart and Roberts were quickly disappearing in terms of influence, he predicted the emergence of a new evangelist — one like the fictional character of Oscar Gladden in *The World of One*. Once again, he described the evangelists of the 1980s as nothing more than "old-fashioned medicine men; they live off people's fears. They are quacks practicing spiritual medicine without a license, offering remedies they neither understand nor have both-ered to examine." Templeton said he couldn't regard them "as evil men in the usual sense, not men of ill-will, not malicious — indeed, they may be eminently personable — but in their zeal to 'do good' they often do great and lasting harm. They exploit guilt and fear. They warp the mind."

Oddly enough, while Templeton abandoned his own faith, he contended that he never abandoned the one figure to whom he looked for support. "The man Jesus Christ is still the biggest influ-ence in my life. I think he is a spiritual and moral genius. I think his understanding of human beings and the human dilemma is far more profound than anyone else I've ever read . . . But I don't wor-ship him."

REVEREND ANDREW MERRITT
25
MADE IN THE IMAGE OF GOD

I t's a church that says you don't have to be sick, you don't have to be unemployed, you don't have to live in squalor, and you don't have to drive around in a beat-up old car. It's a church that tells you if you want that new house, or car, or job, all you need to do is ask the Lord. This church claims it doesn't have a budget, it doesn't worry about how it's going to pay for the mortgage, the new carpeting, sound system, television studios, or whatever else it needs to function, because it believes that all you need to do is turn to the Lord and ask him for whatever you want. It's a church that will cover the land like Burger Kings.

That's been the message all along from Pastor Andrew Merritt, the dynamic modern-day Billy Sunday who revs up his faithful every week with words that come out loud and clear, words that leave you comforted, uplifted and ready to take on the turmoil and chaos in your life. It's a message that roots out the dispossessed from the neighborhoods and suburbs and brings in the faithful by the hundreds. On any given Sunday, Straight Gate Church, situated on the far reaches of Detroit's downtown core, just west of the Cass Corridor, is bursting with more than 1,400 foot-stomping, hand-clapping parishioners eager to follow the fast-talking, fast-walking Merritt who races up and down the church aisles like a wide receiver for the Detroit Lions.

You can't miss his church as you drive along West Fort Street. There among the factories and gas stations is this three-story brick building with the name of the church in huge letters blasting out its invitation. It literally stops you in your tracks. It's meant to. It's designed to draw you in. For several years now, this is what Merritt has been doing — gathering his congregation from a polluted gray landscape that resembles a movie set for a Second World War film — its buildings blackened and bombed out by a city in an urban war zone.

To the faithful, this tall, lean black pastor is bringing hope. He's a kind of comforting prophet. In fact, he views that as his role. He believes his church has been divinely anointed as "the beacon for the city of Detroit." and the one institution that will at long last bring the real renaissance to the City. To Merritt, it's a powerhouse for the Lord, and to him, it is no hollow prophecy to profess that his church will be a leading element in change for the city.

In 1986, he was shown this former Baptist Church building and returned home to pray with his family that he might know whether he ought to take it over. (He was unaware that an offer had already been made on the property and that it had, in fact, been accepted.) When I met Merritt in the summer of 1987, he told me this story of how another power was at work after he had found the place. He called it "the power of the Holy Spirit." The outcome was that the other buyer couldn't negotiate a mortgage. For that matter, neither could Straight Gate. At least in the beginning. When Merritt approached a local bank, its loan officers challenged him about how he expected to raise the funds for the mortgage, if, in fact, it was granted to the church. "The Lord will provide!" he replied. The banker didn't share quite the same faith in the Lord as Merritt. But the pastor wasn't one to give up. A few weeks later, he secured his backers. Later, when it appeared he might not be able to raise the initial funds for the down payment — he only had a few days left before the deadline — he recounted how he advised his congregation it needed yet another $40,000: "I went out of there that night and I had the money . . . I had $40,000 and $500 more."

Merritt emphasized that money and budgets don't worry him. It's really not his concern. His interest is church work. If money is needed to function, it will be forthcoming. "We don't have budgets. We don't fund-raise. We don't do any of that . . . All of our needs are met, and we have money left over to do what we need to get done." It's this air of confidence that pervades Merritt's talk about this predominantly black "Full Gospel" congregation that draws people from all over the city, and from across the river as far away as Chatham, Ontario, some 50 miles away.

Merritt moved from an upper middle class neighborhood church to this present location just beyond the Ambassador Bridge. To some, it was a mistake. There was fear he'd lose the other congregation, that he was moving into a less-than-safe area. Merritt wasn't afraid. Quite the contrary — he took up the challenge. He sensed that he was "led here." It fit in with his vision of churches springing up in different cities all over the country.

Before going to his service, I met with Merritt in his office earlier in the week. He was suspicious about my motives for interviewing him. "Why did you come over here?" he asked. I told him I had seen him on television in the middle of the night, and thought I should write about him. I explained that I was an insomniac, and because I couldn't sleep, I turned on the television, and there he was. I was intrigued by his message, and considered writing something about his work.

"I don't believe you," he said flatly. He stared at me from across the table, not saying another word. I protested, "Why should I lie?" He opened his arms wide in an ostentatious sweep, and grimaced. Then came a rush of melodramatic words, "Oh, you're not lying . . . That's not what I mean . . . I mean, you say you're an insomniac, and that you just happened to turn on the television because you couldn't sleep."

I protested again, "But I *am* an insomniac!"

He leaned forward, his hands together now in prayer, his eyes shutting, as he said, "Oh, com'on! I think what happened is the good Lord woke you . . . Got you out of bed . . . Brought you to that television set . . . Made you turn it on . . . And there I was . . . And now there you are! Seated across from me . . . The Lord has brought you to Straight Gate!" Moments later, he was blessing me, and offering up prayers. I could see this was the kind of hold he had on his people, this charisma, this way of taking control — not in a manipulative way, but actually in a comforting, caring manner.

When I saw him preach that day in the summer, he taunted his parishioners about the kinds of preachers they'd heard before and maintained his own message was dramatically different. Standing on the steps leading up to the pulpit, he delivered a set of questions in machine-gun fashion, shouting: "What kind of preachers have you been listening to? Tell me, did they tell you that the Lord whupped the Devil? Who told you that you had to be sick? Who told you that you had to suffer?" He chided them, "You ask what's so special about Straight Gate . . . Well, I refuse to walk with preachers who tell people they've got to be sick, that sickness teaches them something. I refuse to walk with preachers who say God ain't do' nothin'! You know, some people wouldn't know God if he walked in wearing a red hat!"

And if words weren't enough, Merritt carried a white handkerchief in one hand that he used to wipe away the sweat from his face, resorting to theatrics, hopping up and down and declaring that the very name "Jesus" made him jump. At other times, he did a kind of "Ali shuffle" that delighted his audience and had them on their feet and shouting "Amen!" And he shouted back, drowning them out: "I believe God is good all day long!" They loved him. They loved his enthusiasm, the histrionics, his words, his message. They yearned for him to ask over and over again, "Who said you were no good? Who told you that? What preacher told you this. . . . You want a house. You want some money . . . There's nothing too good for you!"

Merritt would move down an aisle, and ask a parishioner, "Do you want to pay off your mortgage?" And the man would nod, "Yeah, amen!" And Merritt would say, "You've got it! Paid up!" Then he'd be off to someone else: "George, there! Do you want a new Cadillac? D'ya?" And George would kind of get out of the pew a little, and glance about, then say, "Sure, pastor!" And Merritt would lean forward, and very slowly tell him, "Then, it's yours, George, all yours. Go get the keys." What Merritt meant, of course, was that all you needed to do was ask God for whatever you wished. "You know for some of you, if God gave you a million dollars, you wouldn't know what to do with it?"

A Sunday service at Straight Gate isn't like anything you've ever seen. The first forty-five minutes are spent in song, led by a choir and band reminiscent of the early days of Motown. By the time Merritt was up at the pulpit, some in the congregation were dancing, speaking in tongues or waving their arms. When Merritt was well into his sermon, which might go on for more than an hour, the congregation was simply beside itself. At times, he scolded them "Hold it! Hold it, sister, while I'm speaking!" For them, the service was feeling good. It was commitment. It was not a time to glance at your watch. And to Merritt, the reason was because the message was something they'd come to hear. He knew the experience at the Straight Gate was what was missing in most churches throughout the city. Merritt promised his followers his words would alter the way they felt about themselves, their neighborhoods, their city, their country. It was a message that was exclusively for them, but it was also one that was directed at blacks *or* whites. It was for everyone: "I'm not black . . . I'm not white . . . I'm made in the image of God!"

EDGAR AND SHEILA VANN
26
SINGING FOR SALVATION

The words that kept coming back in the silence of this empty sunlit church were: "That ol' devil's busy tonight!" The only sound was from the radiator singing and hissing under the window, or the tall gentle-looking janitor who seemed to float in the solitude across the carpeted floors of this old building. If he hadn't said, "Make yowself at home!" you might not have noticed him. What was missing here was what happened the night before or what takes place every Tuesday night, Friday night, and Saturday afternoon. Missing was the hand clapping, the foot stomping. Missing was the squeal of young girls who flung themselves on the floor shouting, "Jesus! Thank you, Jesus! Thank ya!" What was missing was Pastor Edgar Vann, Jr., a youthful smiling man with long curls that draped down the back of his suit jacket . . . there pumping the crowd for all its worth, microphone in hand, pacing up and down the sanctuary, shouting, "Let me hear ya' praise the Lord!"

It's hard to believe a church could be so quiet when the night before its floors vibrated and lifted, and it wouldn't have seemed at all out of place if the windows had plummeted from their frames. That church is Detroit's towering Second Ebenezer Baptist Church, to the east of the downtown core, like the opposite book end to Rev. Andrew Merritt's Straight Gate. The night before when I was there some 150 people filed into the pews to sing up a storm. This wasn't the congregation — merely the choir that everyone's come to know in this city, the choir that decided to take everyone and anyone from the age of four to twenty-four.

This choir is not interested in professionals — just ordinary folk from the neighborhood, absolutely anyone who can get out on a Tuesday night to sing their hearts out. That's the only prerequisite. "Are you willing to sing? And are you willing to sing your heart out?" asks its music director, the broad-smiling Sheila Vann, a woman with an abundance of talent, who has been turning the traditional hymns into "gospel," but who will admit without batting an eyelash that she can't read a note of music. "It's a gift — and God gave it to me," she told me that winter day in 1986 after I had seen her choir perform for Bishop Desmond Tutu. She said this almost shyly. For her it was no special gift, considering it was one that God had sprinkled generously on most of the people in her "youth chorale." Like her, few — if any — have a formal music background. Like her, they're simply growing up in a church that's on fire for music.

Sheila's background was in a neighborhood Methodist church that stressed music. She joined the choir at the age of twelve. By nineteen, she had followed Edgar Vann to Ebenezer and started the youth chorale. Within seven years the choir's numbers not only mushroomed to more than 100, but it also took top honors in the Gospel Music category of the Freedom Festival competitions at Hart Plaza in downtown Detroit. This gave them the opportunity to release an album which put the choir in the top ten of the gospel charts in Detroit. The choir went on the road, traveling through the night and day to Milwaukee and Chicago. The choir sang before an audience of more than 12,000 at Cobo Arena at the rally of Desmond Tutu of South Africa. There was no doubt in anyone's mind that much of the success of that rally fell to them — they had the crowd on their feet, clapping their hands and shouting. To Sheila, success means "being ourselves . . .We just go out and do our thing . . . And people know what we're all about."

The night before when I had been there, it was only a rehearsal. Even so, the 150 choir members swayed right from the opening song, and before the evening was out, the church was bedlam — young girls writhed in the pews, some threw themselves down on the floor, or raced up and down staircases.Others crouched and wept and shook in their seats and some bellowed out their songs in frenzied abandon. Sheila Vann confided: "That doesn't always happen at rehearsals, but when it does, it's great and it means they're really up for the Lord!" Again, a broad full smile, and laughter. "They're just giving themselves to the Lord." There was no reason to doubt her sincerity. After all, the floors shuddered with the sound from those hypnotic voices that somehow drew in the curious who might have been lucky enough to be passing by in the neighborhood, and these people came through the front door, nodded to the man sitting at the doorway and headed straight upstairs to the balcony or to the back of the church and listened.

Pastor Vann pointed out these individuals came in for what he liked to describe as "an evenin's fun." That's exactly what it was, maintained the thirty year old clergyman who took over the church in 1977. He had been at his father's Methodist Church across the city and opted to go on his own. He arrived without formal ministerial credentials. It was in the winter. He was "taking a chance — it was a chance for Ebenezer and for me," says Sheila Vann. The church he came to was Baptist, not Methodist. It was also debt-ridden, and the congregation had dwindled to about a hundred. In short, the church had had the life "kicked out of it." No one wished to support it. No one — except those who had remained there — had faith in its future. Almost a decade later, Vann could boast of more than 900 members. He credited the youth chorale as the stimulating force behind the church's revival. He claimed this reckless, shapeless group of "kids" that banded together under Sheila's bidding was what breathed new life back into this old church. People started joining because of it, because of the music they heard spilling out into the street. "They came here because something was happening," claimed Pastor Vann. "It was exciting!"

The love of music wasn't the only factor. It may have been on the surface, but something far more fundamental lay just below. The church offered religion as it ought to be — something rooted in the certainty that when you walked through the front door and up those stairs, life would change for you and stay changed. That promise was always there. Certainly for members of the choir, life has been altered. Its members were those "who come off the street." Many emerged from violence in the home or the workplace. Some sprang straight from gangs, from breaking into homes or stealing cars. Often they came, noted Sheila Vann, because of a girlfriend or an acquaintance. Upon arrival, she pointed out, "they'd see there was something going on here . . . And it was better than what was out there."

Leaning forward in a chair in her husband's office, Sheila Vann emphasized how the church didn't go out and "handpick" the best for its choir. There are those who couldn't "carry a tune . . . and we just put someone next to them who could sing." Sheila claimed anyone could join the choir — no matter how excruciating it was to listen to someone who sang completely off key. The fact was no one was excluded. In fact, the only way anyone is "cut" from the choir is if it involves pregnancy out of wedlock. And this happened, and continues to happen. Often. At least once a year. When it does, if both the man and the woman are in the choir, they're both suspended. "They can sit in the church. They can come to rehearsals. We don't tell them they don't belong. They just can't be a part of the public performance," said Pastor Vann. Sheila Vann added, "When they've had their baby, they can come back into the choir. And they do! They come back and they bring the baby too!" She said no judgment is passed on what they've done in their past. "We're a family here, and we care for one another."

If you look around on a Tuesday night, you will find the grandmas or the young parents at the back of the church rocking the children to the songs. If you look a little further, you might even find that among some of the younger members of the choir are some of the children that made their parents sit out a few concerts.

There's no attempt to make these teenagers "feel guilty," Sheila Vann stressed. "And they don't feel guilty." What ails these youths more than anything is being told they can't be in the choir. One girl successfully managed to hide her pregnancy for eight months, simply because she couldn't bear the thought of being separated from the singers. When she confessed to the Vanns, both she and the father — also a choir member — were suspended. But they were welcomed back a few months later.

Sheila Vann said it is hard to comprehend how important it is for these youths to be in the choir, to feel a part of it, to do what they love. It has resulted in some parents "actually using the choir to punish their kids . . . Telling them if they don't get good marks, they'll be forced to quit." To the Vanns, the choir, too, is seen as "an extended family . . . We care about them and they care about each other." To them, this kind of "togetherness" is what the black church is all about. "It serves the total man," Pastor Vann said.

"We're not just speaking to one side of a person, but to every aspect."

That means meeting the social and economic needs of its congregation and reaching out with assistance in more than just the spiritual elements. The church has established scholarships for its youth, and it also provides clothing and food for the poor. Surprisingly enough, there are few complainers. Many in the youth chorale will show up wearing running shoes on a snowy night. "That's all they have," said Sheila Vann. Or sometimes, all they'll be wearing on a bitterly cold winter night is a thin spring jacket, and they'll lie, "telling me they were in a hurry and just grabbed it when they were going out the door . . . The truth is they don't have a winter coat."

Pastor Vann envisions Ebenezer facing the challenges of the poor. The youth chorale has injected "a lot of joy into their lives." He and Sheila are parental figures to many of the children. "They see us as parents . . . They can talk to us in some cases more than they can talk to their parents." In some instances, even, the Vanns intervene at school when these choir members run into difficulties.

"It's a kind of every-day-a-week church," explained Pastor Vann. "We're always open, and anyone can come here." Such openness is a message to the community that church isn't just for Sundays, but for every day and night of the week. That's why it's not so incredible to believe that he could get some 150 kids out on a cold Tuesday night. "They want to be here!" he said. They want to be there because they see the church "speaking to them, inspiring them." And these kids need to be inspired, said Vann. Ebenezer reaches out to the community with a promise of something real, something precious. If Jesus were to return today, Pastor Vann imagined that He would not head out to Grosse Point (a well-to-do neighborhood near Detroit) to set up a church, "He'd come here, where the church is needed."

The magical thing about the youth chorale, elaborated Sheila Vann, was the unbridled confidence it gives these kids. "They are basically shy and withdrawn . . . Many of them when they first come here just wouldn't sing out." She herself experienced the same thing when she joined the church. She knew their dilemma. They needed to hear other choirs and she knew they needed to sing with other choirs. Once they experienced that, "they began to take off . . . I had to help them to give everything that was in them . . . I had to help them not to be ashamed of their voices." And ashamed they aren't. Not now.

From the silence of the empty church in which I sat came a faint echo of those voices from the night before. I remember what Sheila Vann had told me about the Bishop Tutu rally. One girl — an alto — was suddenly thrust before a crowd of 12,000 and ordered to sing solo. "She told us, 'I knew I would have to do it someday, but I didn't think it would have to be now, and in front of so many people.'"

ERNIE HARWELL

27

A BORN-AGAIN SPORTS BROADCASTER

"**B**aseball is a tongue-tied kid from Georgia growing up to be an announcer and praising the Lord for showing him the way to Cooperstown. This is a game for America." — from Ernie Harwell's *Tuned Into Baseball*

Some people are the masters of small talk — vacuous, superficial, and insincere. But what struck me about this man who chided the score-card hawkers and ticket collectors as he strode through the old stadium was his ingenuousness. Part of that was his smile. Part of it was the fact he knew everyone by their first names, and inquired after their wives and children. And he meant it. He was a gentleman through and through, and made you feel at home — at Tiger Stadium.

It was in July 1985 that I met Ernie Harwell. His voice was synonymous with baseball. That familiar anonymous summer radio voice, so smooth, full, rising and falling without concern. Dependable, comforting. He was then sixty-seven years old. Today he no longer broadcasts games for the Tigers. At the end of the 1992 season, he was forced to call it quits because the Tiger organization decided against renewing his contract. When Mike Illitch bought the team at the end of that season, he delivered on a promise to return Harwell to the broadcast booth — if he wanted to come back. The veteran broadcaster hastened back to do play-by-play for a couple of innings each game, but at the end of the 1993 season gracefully stepped aside to concentrate on doing guest appearances and commercials.

I remember him in that open-air booth high above home plate at Tiger Stadium and surveying the lush green infield spread out before him like the smooth surface of a snooker table. It was unofficial batting practice, long before the fans were let in through the gates to catch sight of their heroes. "Those guys are the ones who need it, and they're working to get out of their slumps," he confided. It was said with compassion, concern. You could discern his love for the game, for the Tigers, for the old ballpark. He savored those moments sitting in the broadcast booth, peering out beyond the mesh to monitor the movements of his team. Beside him was that worn bulky leather briefcase that he couldn't shut anymore for all the books, hats, papers and junk he carted about with him to each game. What motivated and moved this man who'd been in broadcasting for forty-five years wasn't the stitched white baseball that had been the success and failure of teams year after year. It was religion.

Harwell counted himself among the "born-again Christians." He smiled when he said that, and quipped that he hoped he would be viewed as "level-headed." He certainly didn't want to come off sounding hysterical. He had a distaste for preaching. He preferred to shy away from the traps in which evangelicals found themselves caught — that is, the situation of cutting oneself off from the rest of the world, simply because the world might seem evil.

Harwell conceded that it surprised people to learn that he was a born-again Christian — mostly because one wouldn't be able to detect it from his deep devotion to baseball, and from his radio coverage. There wasn't a word about faith, religion or God. That's not to indicate that he was desperately struggling to keep his mouth shut on the subject. He simply realized this forum — covering a baseball game — wasn't the place to proselytize. But when he got the opportunity to chat about his faith or religious belief, that was a different thing, and Harwell rarely held back. Such a forum was in his autobiographical *Tuned To Baseball,* wherein one learns about his involvement in the baseball chapel, or the religious convictions of ballplayers and sportswriters. The book was written at home, on Harwell's archaic Underwood typewriter, during the winter months. It wasn't ghost written or tape-recorded. He did it himself, tapping out the stories from memory, and as always, with in that characteristic self-effacing sincerity.

The Georgia-born Harwell started his baseball career as the Atlanta correspondent for *The Sporting News* when he was sixteen. He became a broadcaster of WSB-Atlanta in 1940 and went on to do the play-by-play for the Atlanta Crackers, the Brooklyn Dodgers, the New York Giants and the Baltimore Orioles. In 1959 he came to Detroit to do the play-by-play of the Detroit Tigers. In 1981, Harwell was inducted into the Cooperstown's Baseball Hall of Fame for excellence in broadcasting. Besides the great moments of the game over his broadcasting years, Harwell believes the most revolutionary moment in his life was his decision to commit himself to his faith. That came during Easter 1961. He was driving from spring training in Florida to the Billy Graham Easter service. "I had been one of those guys who had gone to church all their life, like anyone else, but I had managed to stay out of everybody's way, and I didn't do too many bad things . . . I woulda' found my way to Heaven."

Billy Graham altered his life. Harwell attended the Easter Service. He hadn't the faintest idea why he was there. He remembered hopping into his car at Lakeland, Florida, where the Tigers play in the spring before going north. He can't even remember what prompted him to leave the ballpark to head straight there to the crusade. Least of all, he doesn't know what moved him to be "walking down the aisle to dedicate (himself) to Christ." Fifteen years later at the Billy Graham Crusade in Tampa, Florida, Harwell delivered a testimonial.

To Harwell, religious faith that comes at you suddenly, springs from an emptiness, a wantonness. In the sports world, it is not surprising that athletes are overwhelmed by success and failure, and feel the need to fill the void within them. "I think there is a renewed interest in religion among baseball players — I don't know about other sports. They are making so much money these days, that with all the money and fame, they still have a lot of emptiness in their lives. They're alone a lot of times and they see a lot of people who want to be with them because they're major league baseball stars . . . They always have to wonder, 'How would this person feel about me if I were Rupert Jones (former Tiger), a truck driver, or Darrell Evans (former Tiger), a clerk in a hardware store?' And I think they're a little suspicious sometimes of people. And there is an emptiness there that's maybe more so than an ordinary guy . . . And they're always looking for something."

Harwell is not at all naive about the superstition that nearly rules the lives of ballplayers. Sure, it's there, but he asserts there's a fundamental spirituality in everyone, and that it is expressed in different ways. Sometimes it's not something one can pinpoint, or even fully understand. Harwell admitted baseball has always been "a game of luck," but added, "Well, if I were a true Christian, I shouldn't even wish a guy, 'Good luck!' — I should say, 'God bless you!' But baseball players have always been superstitious . . . I mean there's not too much difference between a line drive that is a double play and a line that that's a base hit . . . A couple of inches one way or another . . . you can be very skillful, you can hit the ball very hard, but if you hit it to somebody's glove, you can say, 'Well, I'm unlucky!' "

Harwell told me he really didn't know whether those who took part in the baseball chapel were superstitious, but ballplayers cling to these eccentricities: "There's stuff like guys touching the base before they go out to the outfield, or stepping on a line or not stepping on a line . . . There's Milt Wilcox (former Tiger) who eats blueberry pancakes on the day that he's going to pitch. Ballplayers are really no different than anyone else in the way in which they embrace Christianity. They take to it with great fervor, and later abandon it, or turn against it. What happens is they get all enthusiastic about it, but when the road gets tougher, they just fall by the wayside. That's something we all have to contend with . . . We just have to keep our minds on the right target."

In his own case, Harwell never veered too far away from religion. Coming from a Methodist background in the south, he always made a point of attending church. But it wasn't until that moment in 1961 that he knew his commitment up to that point had been only casual, passive. "There are times and places for everything. I believe in standing up for my beliefs, but I don't think it's practical or effective to bring it in a lot of instances . . . I think we have to make our own choices when the right time comes."

In the case of his autobiography, Harwell thought it was appropriate to write about his connection to his religious faith: "I thought I should put those things in there, because it was a large part of my life . . . It would have been phony to say that one of my main interests was my relationship with God and then write a book and not put it in there."

TINO WALLENDA ZOPPE
28
PASTOR OF THE HIGH WIRE

Tino Wallenda Zoppe learned the art of walking the high wire from his grandfather, the famous tightrope walker Karl Wallenda, who fell to his death in a stunt in San Juan, Puerto Rico in 1978. Today this middle-aged performer carries on his family's tradition in the circus circuit, skipping, dancing, and riding bicycles on thin cables high above crowds, without the use of nets. But while he's best known for this, others regard him in a different light: as the pastor of the high wire.

That's because Tino Wallenda Zoppe has turned to preaching Christianity. He can be seen and heard from the high wire, where he sits thirty feet above the ground — without the use of a net — balanced on a chair that rests precariously on a five-eighth-of-an-inch cable. From that chair, he delivers a ten-minute homily to a hushed crowd. He speaks to them about "faith." Tino is among hundreds of circus performers who have, like those in professional sports and the entertainment business, become "born-again Christians." Zoppe for his part has taken his beliefs right into the circus ring.

I met the high wire priest a few years ago when he came to Windsor, Ontario. He wasn't part of the circus, and he didn't command a large crowd. About 200 turned out and it was just about dusk when he climbed the rigging to entertain and evangelize. This man, who was born in the shadow of Ringling Brothers Circus in Sarasota, Florida captured the imagination of a few that day on the lawn of Calvary Community Church.

Earlier in an interview, he spoke about the nature of "faith," and how once he believed a certain kind of faith was required to climb a ladder and to perch on a thin wire high above the ground without a net to catch you if suddenly you slipped and fell. Zoppe knew it was faith rooted in knowledge — he had performed this act a thousand times. "I could go through the motions in my sleep. I had faith in myself and faith in the odds. I had done it a thousand times. So why worry?" Now Zoppe has a different understanding of faith. While there may be "risks" in walking the high wire, "It is something I do every day, so it's really not a risk as such."

The real faith wasn't in balancing on a thin wire above a shifting and restless crowd, but in coming to terms with yourself. To him, it was a matter of "trust" and he characterized such trust in a story about how one night after performing a series of stunts on the high wire, he asked an audience whether it believed he could walk along the cable high above the ground with someone on his shoulders. The response was overwhelmingly positive. But when Zoppe invited volunteers to come forward, people actually "stepped backwards." No one dared to "act on that belief" that he could carry someone on his shoulders. Finally, one rather frightened man came forward to volunteer, and told Zoppe: "I'm afraid of heights, but I have seen you perform many times. I do not trust myself, but I will trust you." In essence, Zoppe maintained, that's what faith and religious belief is all about — it means taking risks in living out one's religious beliefs.

Zoppe's no philosopher, no scholar, no theologian. His schooling was done on the run. From the age of two, he had been involved in the circus. Initially, his father and mother, who were bareback riders, introduced him to the life of the circus world. At seven, his grandfather taught him how to walk the high wire. At the time of his grandfather's death, Zoppe was in charge of the Wallenda family. Always an articulate and clever speaker, Zoppe became an accomplished homilist, in spite of such an haphazard life.

The circus-like approach to evangelizing was never out of character, or for that matter, out of line for Zoppe. This art of walking the tight rope was "God-given," and therefore seemed a novel way of attracting new converts. While Zoppe performed in the religious circuit independently, he has also been part of a much larger religious performing group called Circus Maranatha, which books only when it is profitable for the group to break away from other commitments. Zoppe tries to book the engagements in the same areas where he might be doing regular circus work.

While Zoppe's move to doing Christian shows did not evolve as a result of the tragedy in the lives of his own family, it has given him a handle on the meaning of tragedy, of death, of trusting God. Zoppe lives those tragedies each time he mounts the high wire.

They aren't easily forgotten. The first such mishap was in 1962 when two members of the group perished in a fall. A third was left paralyzed. The group had been performing at the Michigan State Playgrounds Coliseum. Six men and a woman balanced thirty feet above the ground to create a human pyramid. Four men had been stationed on the wire, two more on poles supported by the bottom men. The woman was in a chair balanced atop a pole supported by the men on the second level. Zoppe was only a boy at the time of that incident. By 1978 when his grandfather was killed, he had already embraced Christianity. It wasn't until that year, however, that Zoppe began performing Christian shows.

Tragedy itself wasn't a factor in turning his attention to evangelizing. His own life had been one of success and rewards. He was in charge of the family's engagements. In 1971 when he was drawn to the church, Zoppe had been working with his grandfather in shows. "Really, I had enough money for things, and there wasn't anything that I can look back to now and say there was an emotional moment that changed things for me . . . It's just that I felt I needed to change and clean up a little."

Zoppe was drawn into the church when other circus performers invited him to join them for some Bible study. He had very little church background — his father had been a Roman Catholic and his mother a Lutheran. Because of the hectic circus life, regular church attendance was impossible. The effect upon Zoppe was a fostering of an agnostic view. Religion remained insignificant. Seven years after he had been introduced to Bible study, Zoppe's involvement in religious life mushroomed to the point where he helped to organize Circus Maranatha, this ensemble of aerial acts, animal and elephant shows and clowns that combine to present a Christian message. "The message is the same as the one I'm giving, but it's done in a variety of ways."

It was impossible for the circus to operate on a full-time basis, because its performers make a living from working with regular circuses throughout the year, and there's no money in the Christian circuit — at least not yet. Circus Maranatha does more and more bookings each year. So much so that Zoppe has been the subject of a number of television news feature shows, including some on CBS and ABC. When the PTL Club was going full steam in North Carolina, Zoppe was Bakker's guest.

When I reached Zoppe at his home in Florida in the summer of 1994, he told me Circus Maranatha was occupying more and more of his life. He was still doing everything else, especially those acts that were reminiscent of the kind of dramatic stunts for which his family was famous. In September 1993, he strolled on the high wire between St. Paul Hotel and the Landmark Center clock tower in St. Paul, Minnesota one Friday evening as part of the city's Oktoberfest activities. In cavalier manner, Zoppe — in the footsteps of his grandfather Karl Wallenda — took a death-defying walk across a tightrope suspended about 100 feet above a chasm at Great Falls in Paterson, New Jersey. His grandfather had done the same stunt in 1973.

Zoppe, like his grandfather before him, continues to involve his family in the business. His daughter Alinda, and his wife, Olinka, are both part of the act. The story of the Wallendas is well documented. When Karl Wallenda joined "The Greatest Show On Earth" in 1927, he brought his family over to the USA from Germany. He found them jobs in the circus. In 1947, the impetus to create the famous Seven Man Pyramid was because he was concerned about how the family would make ends meet. In spite of the 1962 tragedy, the act continued for another year as part of the Wallendas' repertoire. It was eliminated when circus officials insisted the performers use a net. In 1977, the act was resurrected for the film *The Great Wallendas*. Zoppe recalls how they were able to do it without a net because the family was given "control" over the act.

Zoppe still loves the work, the challenge, the thrill. But now what drives him is evangelizing. That's why he takes advantage of his regular travels to squeeze in Christian performances. The reaction from the circus community generally hasn't been entirely positive. Other performers deem his work "silly . . . or crazy." Far more serious is the reaction from the church community who condemn this activity verging on the sacrilegious. Zoppe has argued to the contrary, claiming his approach is a unique way in which to offer the gospel.

Standing on a chair that straddles a thin wire at dusk outside the Windsor church, he told his audience, "You might think I'm a little bit foolish standing up here talking to you . . . But really every day is like that. You, too, walk a tightrope every day of your life."

CHUCK COLSON
29
FROM WATERGATE TO HEAVEN'S GATE

The battle for respectability is never over. Still, Chuck Colson likes the transition of labels from "hatchet man" to "holy man." He figures he'll always carry with him the stigma of those nefarious activities from the scandalous Watergate era, when he was special counsel to former President Richard Nixon and wound up in prison.

But Colson found religion in jail. Since being released, he has been on the religion circuit, declaring to people how he found God, how those perspicacious years in politics are behind him now. That's when I came across him in Grand Rapids, Michigan. He was there running through the same old gig, assuring people that he wasn't about to return to crime. He knew what they were thinking. Certainly people were "forgiving," but they also live in the real world, where they watch criminals embrace God, then get out of jail, and return to crime.

"It happens," Colson said matter-of-factly. He won't make excuses. He knows better. He did a lot of smooth talking in his time. Part of that tough guy veneer still clings to him. He's brash, calculating, almost icy, and rarely minces words. Perhaps that's why people tend to believe him when he tells them straight out that for for him the persistence of staying on the right track has to be viewed with admiration. Forgiveness will come in its own good time. Colson admitted he's struggled with this dilemma. He realizes many are suspicious of his present activities — writing books, lecturing, praying on television. He laughs. It's true, everyone is "just waiting for me to screw up." Especially when he has moved so swiftly and dramatically from crime to Christianity. He acknowledged this was bound to be regarded as just another way to beat the system.

Since Watergate, Colson has not only become a Christian, he's thrown his energies into founding and developing a "conversion" program for convicts. The program, Fellowship House, started in 1976 and situated in Washington, D.C., has the approval of the Federal Bureau of Prisons. It serves the thirty federal prisons in the States, and is working with prisoners in Canada.

Colson also turned to writing. He is the author of *Born Again* and *Life Sentence*, as well as *Loving God*, published by Zondervan Publishing in Grand Rapids, which sold more than 100,000 copies in the first few months of being in print. Such success he couldn't have imagined during the Nixon Years. In those years, success meant shielding the president. It meant lying. It meant being guileful, insincere, hard-line. Colson knows all about cynicism. He won't shy away from the critics who apply it to him.

"It's a natural response," he argued. A now contrite Colson isn't irked by it. If anything, he regards it positively. One of the great faults of contemporary Christianity, he'll tell you, is its unwillingness to embrace the concept of sin. Colson viewed the Roman Catholic Church's synod in the 1980s in Rome as a laudable exercise, since it struggled to understand the whole nature of sin, repentance and forgiveness. He pointed out that, unfortunately, the rest of the world hasn't been so decisive when it comes to accepting sin as "a reality." A lot of churches find it difficult, says Colson, to teach a Christianity which is conscious of sin and repentance. It isn't popular, acceptable, or agreeable.

On the other hand, for a prisoner, it becomes a daily part of life. Sin behind bars is something that can, and does, plague an individual. It seizes him like a nightmare, drains him. The inmate wrestles with it, runs it through his brain until its weight is numbing. It becomes the sole reference point in his life, everything leading up to and following from that moment. For Colson, the hearings, the trials, the media hype was one thing. Prison meant coming to terms with it all. Colson revealed that prisoners may attempt to ignore the sin, and to put it aside and forget, but will fail in the exercise — it'll return to haunt them. It's better to face up, to apprehend it squarely for what it is, to stare God in the face, and ask for forgiveness. It's an epistle Colson never tires of. It's the subject of *Loving God,* the book with a prescription for trying to live "a holy life."

When I spoke with Colson, he was fifty-one. In the 1970s, he had been indicted at the height of the Watergate scandal for both the Daniel Ellsberg break-in and the Watergate cover-up. In a plea-bargaining arrangement in 1974, however, he admitted guilt to obstructing justice by trying to smear and defame Ellsberg before the Pentagon Papers trial. Colson was sentenced to a one-to-three-year term, but spent only seven months behind bars, with most of his term in custody at Maxwell Air Force Base near Montgomery, Alabama. When he was released, the papers quoted a different man: "I'm very grateful to the Lord that this could happen."

Many concluded Colson had pulled yet another fast one. This time, he wouldn't fool the public. Colson shrugged. He knew what he had gone through, and what he believed. His conversion after Watergate occurred when a friend, businessman Tom Philips, confessed how he had been converted. Later that same evening, he read C.S. Lewis's *Mere Christianity*. This was about two years after Watergate. Colson was quoted by Associated Press as explaining that his conversion hit him like "a torpedo . . . I could just see my whole life — I felt unclean. That night I couldn't get the keys into the ignition because I was crying so hard . . . I felt as helpless as a thief nailed to the cross." He maintained that it lifted the pressure from him, the weight of that sin, more than any court room, or presidential pardon.

Colson's belief is that the acknowledgment of sin is what is missing from Christianity today. He emphasized that while it may be humiliating to have one's crime "exposed in the blinding light of the courtroom," it is worse as a prisoner because you are "locked in the midst of every form of evil and depravity." In the comfortable world on the "outside," Colson maintained that sin becomes a concept, something to be viewed philosophically, objectively. It becomes less threatening, harmless. What minimizes the importance of sin in the life of a Christian, Colson argued, are "the miracle workers." He branded "the born-again Christian movement" as the culprit. Colson stated that sin is regarded by many born-again Christian clergymen as something that can be wiped away quickly, easily and without pain. To Colson, Christianity is not something a person can sign up for overnight. It's a learning process. Initiation.

He scoffed at the electronic church, and branded its leaders scoundrels. He maintained that those who believe that by merely flinging open the Bible, and accepting the first words they stumble upon as a revelation that will serve them as a guide for the rest of their lives, are bound up with superstition, not with the Holy Spirit. Born-again Christianity may be correct in judging the Bible as the revelation of God, and that it should be taken "literally for what it offers, but there's a risk in taking scripture out of context . . . It can't be, and shouldn't be," Colson said flatly.

Colson insisted that although real conversion may come quickly in a kind of On-the-Road-to-Damascus style, as described by the apostle Paul, a degree of learning, initiation, or a process of understanding and revaluation, is still required. This best describes Colson's situation. Eager to live a "holy life," he couldn't ignore that such a course was difficult amid a fast-living American culture that offered specious solutions to life.

To him, Christianity itself has been ailing in North America. Being a Christian has meant "confronting secular values." The born-again Christian movement is partly responsible for the erosion of religious life in North America. It is just another "false front" for what real religious values are all about. Colson decried the kind of television evangelism that hawked Bibles and blessings. These sharks were capitalizing on a need in America for something more fundamental and spiritual. People, Colson emphasized, are being taken in blindly by a culture more intent on making money from religion than saving souls. Unfortunately, he added, a lot of money is pouring into the coffers of these individuals and overnight money-making churches. Unfortunately, not many are receiving the spiritual satisfaction they seek.

"What I'm talking about is something more realistic — it's a sober look at Christianity," Colson explained. He acknowledged that he was quoted repeatedly for being a born-again Christian, when actually he preferred a different definition. Conversion seized him in a rush, but unlike many who postulate that life changed, was transformed in fact, over night, for him life has metamorphosed gradually. "The hound of Heaven was at my back," Colson contended, "but I found that I had to grow slowly with more knowledge."

For one, he didn't have the "tools" with which to turn back a whole lifetime of being outside Christianity. Colson said he subscribed "to a kind of Christianity where I went to church at Christmas, and that was it." It meant learning his faith; it meant digging down and researching every aspect of Christianity to come up with the means by which he could deal with the crisis in his life. In retrospect, it didn't surprise him that he would approach his search in this way. After all, his life had been devoted to this approach — being a scholar, lawyer, and counsel to the president of the United States. So, for Colson, although there was the "convincing element" from the start, the content and language of that conversion were foreign to him. "I mean, I had no religious life at all before this."

He claimed the kind of false Christianity being aired on the networks was nothing more than "cheap grace." It didn't fascinate or interest him. Colson sought the bedrock of Christianity, and in prison it wasn't hard to find that "one's spirituality was there for the asking." What many fail to understand is "just how deep Christianity is in the prisons." More than 30,000 have gone through the program in which Colson is involved. He said they emerged from the two-week training courses "with a sense of real conversion." In a way, it was not hard to comprehend why this trend was happening, Colson explained, because "around them everything is lies and people are cheating and stealing." What is also not easily recognized is the pain that can result in embracing Christianity. When prisoners return to prison "carrying Bibles, they are ostracized and ridiculed."

BENJAMIN SPOCK
30
ON THE PEACE TRAIL

It was a hot, hazy summer morning in Detroit, and the tall, scruffy-bearded man strolled into the new peace center at Central United Methodist, a sprawling church in the downtown core. He was there to examine the "peace memorabilia" on display. When he swung around to survey the room, you realized he was probably the tallest man in the crowd. But there's no doubt he was very much aware that his moral and political stature loomed even taller than his physical height.

Dr. Benjamin Spock was the man who, back in 1946, wrote a book that to date has not only sold more than forty million copies in thirty-nine countries but virtually has set the guidelines for family care all over the world. The author of *Baby and Child* is a broad-shouldered, good-humored man with an affinity for the sardonic and a voice that can boom through a room and never fail to grab your attention.

In the early 1960s, the obliging, easy-going pediatrician decided to swap his reputation as a doctor for that of a peace activist. It wasn't entirely voluntary, and it wasn't entirely premeditated. It's just that as a pediatrician, the children for whom he had such affection were suddenly in danger, unless he embraced political activism, a brand of activism he knew would land him battles with the government and the courts. Even after he was slammed in jail, Spock continued the work he had begun when he joined the National Committee for a Sane Nuclear Policy. In his eighties, he was still jetting about the world speaking to audiences and accentuating his support for measures that would "protect children from fallout radiation." Now at ninety-one, he's still voicing his views on a number of issues, not only the the arms race, but even the impact of television on children.

Somehow you wouldn't expect a man like this to talk politics when he appears so entirely congenial, even bored by the whole idea of anyone seeking political office. The day I met him, he slumped in a chair in the corner near the peace center's front door, and in that instant seemed far more interested in the life about him than in talking. At one point when he spotted a long line of school children on the street outside, he beamed, abruptly stopped chatting about Lyndon Johnson and Ronald Reagan, and remarked, "Oh, look at that! Aren't they wonderful? Children. So full of trust . . . It's terrible that we have to turn them into greedy and sour and suspicious adults!" The expression on his face was one of genuine empathy. He worried about the kind of day these children were going to have.

But Spock was not off track. The subject was clearly that of politics and responsibility. On the matter of responsibility, Spock wasn't sure whether he'd admit to defining this solely as the domain of religion, simply because it involved morality. He'd rather stick to the presumption that accountability involved common-sense understanding of morality, something far more humanistic and less zealous and pietistic. Spock also preferred to circumvent as far as possible the assertion that denominational religion ought to play a role in the political arena at all. But in saying that, Spock meant he didn't want his country's political debates governed by the kind of exclusionary or chauvinistic type of religion that claims to have all the answers. He's always been opposed to that. He relegated such religious involvement in politics to the sort of fundamentalism that emerges out of Jerry Falwell's Moral Majority or the electronic evangelists.

Spock has always been more of a humanist than anything else. He was raised by "an excessively moralistic mother who made life painful" for Spock and his brothers and sisters. "She also built fires under us. She was always getting us to keep trying to do good." In essence, that may be at the foundation of what he believes and what guides him. He related a story to me from the First World War period of how his mother had wanted him to wear a castoff suit of his father's: "It was most inappropriate for a fourteen year old, like myself, to wear this kind of suit . . .This suit was loose, floppy and dark, dark gray . . . And there were no cuffs . . . I said, 'I can't wear this suit to school . . . everyone will make fun of me!' And my mother said to me, 'You ought to be ashamed of yourself, worrying about what people think of you . . . Don't you know that it doesn't make the slightest difference what people think of you? All you have to know is that you're right!' When I found myself indicted by the Johnson administration (in 1968), tried and sentenced to two years in jail, then, I thought, well, this is what my mother must have meant."

For the past four decades, Spock has been nurturing this kind of attitude toward politics. Not so much that he's "right" in his beliefs, or that he holds all the answers, but that there's a fundamental "good" to be achieved in society. And if you believe that, Spock insisted, then it means fighting against a society that continues to embrace a far more "materialistic" way of life. At stake are the old traditional family values that have been abandoned. "It means fighting for what you believe to be right," Spock maintained.

The solutions are ever clear in his mind — they lie in the political field. For that reason politics has become something of an obsession for Spock. He knows it, but has always felt entirely justified in making this his life's work. If anything, he has felt duty-bound to devote himself to it. He said so many Americans care very little about their country, and this was evidenced by the meagre turnout at elections. What bewildered Spock, however, was how Americans hold fixed political beliefs, but fail to exercise their vote. For example, some seventy to eighty percent of the people endorsed the proposal for a nuclear freeze, but then turned around and elected a president (President Reagan) "vehemently opposed to it."

To Spock, it seemed the only political activity that "stirred Americans to action" were proposals to introduce new taxes or plans for cuts in social assistance. When it comes to fighting the government over the proliferation of nuclear arms, Americans "feel impotent to resist the trend. If a nuclear weapon went off somewhere and killed a hundred thousand people, then that might suddenly wake them up and tell them that nuclear arms are much too dangerous and that we are being defeated by our own weapons." Then again, it might not, Spock seemed to suggest when he shook his head in disbelief. "Yeah, maybe not."

Spock's conversion to the peace movement wasn't sudden. It took a lot of persuasion. He had supported John F. Kennedy in 1960 because he was convinced that a missile gap existed between the United States and Russia, and that his country had better close that gap. In spite of his public support of Kennedy, the National Committee for a Sane Nuclear Policy continued to pester him. The committee, which had been calling for test-ban treaties between the two superpowers, had wanted someone of high profile at the leadership of their ranks. Spock was approached three times by the committee's organizers. He turned them down, arguing that he knew nothing of radiation. He also preferred "to reassure parents — not scare them!" Finally in 1962 he was induced to join, as co-chairman: "They persuaded me, saying that if we didn't have a test-ban treaty, more and more children around the world would die of cancer and leukemia or would be born with mental and physical defects . . . So I do it primarily as a pediatric issue."

In 1964, two years after joining the National Committee for a Sane Nuclear Policy, Spock was approached by the Lyndon Johnson campaign committee for public support. Spock enthusiastically agreed to this because Johnson had promised not to send troops to fight in an Asian war. "I said I would support him as a citizen, as a pediatrician and as a spokesman for the peace movement." Spock was surprised by a telephone call two days after the election from the president who assured him with these buoyant words: "Dr. Spock, I hope I proved worthy of your trust."

Three months later, Spock denounced Johnson for turning Vietnam into "a fighting war, bombing North Vietnam and sending troops that eventually reached half a million." Spock wrote hundreds of letters of "scathing condemnation" to Johnson. None were answered by the president personally.

During the course of the war, Spock was indicted for his anti-war activities. In 1968 he was arrested along with four others, including the chaplain at Yale University. "And when you're arrested for civil disobedience along with a clergyman, it gives you the feeling you can't be all wrong." His arrest took place about a half a year after he had retired from a twelve year teaching stint at Western Reserve University Medical School. "I went from being a full-time professor at a medical school to being a full-time rabble rouser." Over those years of associating with the peace movement, Spock became far more cynical, far more wrathful than ever before. He has never stopped believing that "things can be accomplished." It seems time has proven him right.

Even when I met him, Spock felt that his optimism arose from the occasional story he stumbled across about mild-mannered people tackling bureaucrats who tried to muscle their way past the lives of ordinary people. Spock cited the case of "a little gentle, middle-aged woman," who operated a nursing home and learned that Oklahoma Public Utilities was going to build a nuclear power plant. This woman, who had never been politically involved in anything, hired a lawyer, and the two of them challenged the city on the safety of the plant. After a long, drawn-out battle, the public utilities "surrendered" to her, said Spock. "If one gentle, middle-aged woman can do this — she had to sell her nursing home, use up all her savings and borrow money — if one gentle woman can do this, then other people should be ashamed of themselves when they say they are discouraged because they wrote a letter to the president and it didn't do any good. I heard people say this during the Vietnam War. They said, 'I wrote a letter to the president, and it didn't stop the war!' "

Spock's message broadened in the 1980s to indict American society as "sick . . . and getting sicker, and I don't see any improvement." He maintained Americans failed to recognize the failure of their own society. Many believed they were "better off than any other country, and since we measure things in materialistic terms we think that this means we're better off. But that's not true."

Spock's concern was an old one — the sanctity of the family. He was hard pressed to predict a rosy future for the traditional American family. To this day, he believes there are just too many factors going against it, from the most obvious, like the rapid divorce rate and the sudden rise of step-families, to violence in the family and the subtle movement of a society that no longer values "the old neighborhoods" where people helped one another. What was happening in the United States, and in Canada, Spock conjectured, was a reversal that has created a situation where, by the end of the 1990s, statisticians predict step-families in the USA will exceed the number of regular families.

There will also be more divorces than marriages.

Spock endured the agonies of being a stepfather to an eleven year-old-daughter who wouldn't smile and wouldn't talk to him. Time was the factor that finally brought a truce between them. "I think she learned after a while it didn't mean she lost her mother to me." The writer and peace activist learned, too, he wasn't the "patient" person many deemed him to be. "I lost my patience with her again and again . . . I bellowed at her, which made things worse. Of course, that's what convinces stepchildren that the stepparent is a louse." Like many other stepchildren, his daughter regarded him for a long time as nothing but "a brute."

Another factor contributing to the breakup of the family is that more than half the mothers of pre-school children in the country work outside the home. This means old family values are in peril of being lost. Spock insisted that although he felt women had "just as much right as men to careers . . . we have to solve the problem of who is going to take care of the children." He asserted that the wealthy may be able to bring in people to supervise and teach their children or to send them to properly-run day care centers, but those on modest incomes often have to settle for something second-rate. The pediatrician said the government ought to subsidize day care as has been done in Europe. Unless that is effected, "emotional depravation" will continue to grow.

It isn't just divorce, or the sharp rise in step-families, or that preschoolers aren't being properly cared for — there are other factors affecting families and creating new tensions. Spock noted that "fierce over-competitiveness" in American society has created the false ideal of a nation of "super kids."

The pressure is being felt now by nursery schools across the country — parents are demanding that teachers instruct their children how to read before they're kindergarten age. Spock deplored the whole notion of rating children this way. He maintained that life has to unfold for children in a simple, easy manner. Games shouldn't be turned into achievement exercises. He'd like to see an end to "little league" baseball. He'd like to see "frizbee" replace it as a national sport. But then, Spock groaned, knowing his country as well as he does, the Americans "would corrupt that, too."

NORMAN VINCENT PEALE
31
A PRESCRIPTION FOR LIFE

Norman Vincent Peale wasn't surprised by the impossible. He wasn't overwhelmed by miracles. He wasn't awed by the fact people could change their lives and wrench themselves out of poverty or depression and become successful, wealthy, happy. Naturally, you would have expected him to say that to you, since he made his money from telling people that they ought to believe in themselves.

Peale, who died Christmas Eve, 1993, at the age of ninety-five on a twenty-acre farm in Duchess County north of New York City, was called "the apostolic therapist of positive thinking." The old-fashioned preacher and philosopher had become a millionaire, virtually on the strength of one book, *The Power of Positive Thinking*, which came out in 1952. Today, it has sold nearly eighteen million copies in fifteen languages. And with it, Peale established himself. He went on to write some forty books, and to become the most sought after speaker and lecturer in the world. Not so well known is the irony that in the 1950s, when he was working on *The Power of Positive Thinking*, he nearly gave up on publishing the book because the publisher disliked it. So discouraged by this reaction, Peale re-worked it, but then threw the manuscript into the trash. His wife, Ruth Peale — obviously far more *positive* than he — rescued the book, and personally delivered it to the publisher.

I spoke with Peale in the summer of 1983. I was intrigued by a man whose life seemed to spell success. I felt a little devilish asking him a question I'm sure others have wondered about. Was he ever depressed? How did he handle it? How far does this power of positive thinking go? He didn't really give me a satisfactory reply. Sure, he got down at times. He was only human. It was normal. But it was what you did with those emotions, how you approached the *whole* of your life, not just those low moments isolated in time.

Peale was eighty-five when I interviewed him. He was still writing and preaching. In fact, he continued to work as pastor of the Marble Collegiate Church in New York City for another year before stepping down and devoting his retirement to more writing, and occasional lectures. He confided that he didn't view himself as some sort of magician who believed in some brand of Christian wizardry to correct the evils of the world. He felt he was pretty down to earth, and stressed he didn't think it all that extraordinary for a person to put their mind to the task and change their life around. He also thought all this talk about "born-again Christianity" as something new and vibrant was really misleading.

The movement itself, Peale pointed out, had existed since the early days of Christianity. "People were talking about being 'born again' when I was a small boy," said Peale. He believed it was President Jimmy Carter who popularized the movement in the United States. Its basis lies in the New Testament, in John 3:3, where the scripture exhorts people to salvation by saying, "Ye shall be born again!" To Peale that has always meant nothing more than "renewing" one's self. Unfortunately, in many cases, the idea developed into "a flippant phrase."

Peale's prescription for society was nothing more than dressed-up scripture. He knew this and touted it as such. Peale rewrote the gospel so people could relate to it in every day, contemporary terms, not couched in any archaic, symbolic, or historical manner. In Peale's terminology, the born-again theory simply meant believing in one's self. Curiously enough, this was the thrust of the first chapter of his best-selling book thirty years ago. But the theory was not a simple one, Peale told me. It came down to more than the making of a decision — it meant commitment, an act of will that could take a lifetime to achieve. The results would be steady and forthcoming. That you could be sure of, Peale promised.

Throughout his life Peale never abandoned those theories. They were developed long before he sat down to write *The Power of Positive Thinking*. Peale was among the first in America to make that link between religion and psychiatry. Working with psychiatrist Smiley Blanton, the two began counseling parishioners at the Marble Collegiate pastorate. Their caseload grew rapidly, eventually leading to the formation of the American Foundation of Religion and Psychiatry, which treated some 600 patients a week with a staff of ministers, priests, rabbis, psychiatrists, psychologists, and social workers. It also provided training programs for pastoral counselors.

In those early years, Peale began to write. Before publishing *The Power of Positive Thinking*, he released *The Art of Believing* and *You Can Win*. His first bestseller was *A Guide To Confident Living*, published in 1948; it went through some twenty-five printings. With Blanton, he also produced *Faith Is The Answer*. During that period in the 1940s, Peale also edited a spiritual newsletter, *Guideposts*, which he distributed himself after the Second World War. Its contents were mostly testimonials from celebrities, successful businessmen, and movie stars. The circulation of this newsletter eventually exceeded two million. Peale sold copies of his sermons during the war through The Foundation for Christian Living, an organization run by his wife, Ruth. It was *The Power of Positive Thinking*, however, that electrified people. It established Peale as a household name.

It was true he was among the first of America's religious leaders to utilize the mass media, both electronic and print. As early as 1935, Peale delivered self-help sermons on a weekly radio program called *The Art Of Living*. By the mid-1950s, especially after *The Power of Positive Thinking* had come out, he was also being heard on some 125 stations across the USA, reaching an estimated audience of five million.

Son of a Methodist preacher and born in Bowersville, Ohio, Peale wasn't always fond of following in his father's footsteps. When it came time for his schooling, he chose journalism. After graduation, he went to work for the old *Detroit Journal*. This was during Prohibition. His beat was covering everything from socials to murder trials in Windsor. After Detroit, Peale enrolled in Boston University School of Theology. He remembered how the term had already begun when he forwarded his application. He decided to let fate take its course — if the request wasn't honored, he'd resolve to let go of the nagging notion of becoming a preacher. The university accepted him, and with his $500 savings, Peale was back in class. He remained there until he earned a Master of Arts and a Bachelor of Sacred Theology. While studying, Peale also worked as a student pastor in several churches.

The seeds for *The Power of Positive Thinking* actually were planted long before theology school. In his sophomore year in college at Ohio Wesleyan University in 1920, one of Peale's teachers pulled him aside and asked why he was so shy and reserved whenever he was invited to respond in the classroom. "He said to me, 'Why do you get so red in the face, and can't articulate when I ask you a question? I know you know the answers. You're nothing but a scared rabbit.'"

The professor advised Peale that since he was the son of a clergyman, he must have some religious faith, and that perhaps he should pray to overcome his problem. Skeptically, Peale prayed. "I expected a miracle, but it didn't come. But gradually ideas started coming to me from others on how to change my life. And I did, eventually."

Peale's first church was in Brooklyn, New York. When he went there, the congregation totaled forty members. From a friend at the gas company, he wangled a list of new people moving into the neighborhood and made a point of inviting them to attend his church. At the end of a three-year stint there, the membership swelled to more than 1,000, requiring the building of a new church. Peale then moved to Syracuse. He was back again in New York in 1932 in the midst of the Great Depression to preach at Marble Collegiate, a member of the Reformed Church in America. Peale remained associated with the church for the rest of his life. Up until the early 1980s he still preached at its Sunday services. Peale watched the congregation grow from 600 to more than 5,000 over the fifty years that he was involved in its operation. When he was preaching, some 2,300 jammed the church's pews — many hearing the message in overflow rooms over closed-circuit television.

Peale certainly had his followers, but he also had his share of critics. Many accused him of "vulgarizing" the gospel and becoming nothing more than just another Amway salesman showing people how to become successful. Peale rejected this. At the basis of his theories were the gospels. He contended that the way one ought to live was outlined clearly in scriptures: "It's all there, all laid out in the Bible." Peale told me, "You should live a decent honorable life, and never try to get into trouble . . . Have a loving, caring attitude toward other people and people will love you and trust you . . . this worked in 1850 . . . It worked in 1900 . . . and it worked in 1950 . . . and it will work in 1983 . . . and so on." Such an attitude always drew venom from ecclesiastical circles. His approach was too simplistic. Peale wouldn't argue with the criticism: "Sure, it (*The Power of Positive Thinking*) was written in simple language because I was trying to reach people who were not in the church."

A greater controversy than the style of his writing arose in the 1960s when Peale presided over the Protestant "Citizens for Religious Freedom." This group questioned whether a Roman Catholic president — John F. Kennedy —would be subject to control by the Vatican. A ludicrous notion, confessed Peale, but argued that the times were different then. And it was something that worried thousands of Americans. Peale resigned in embarrassment from the organization, confessing to the media: "I made a mistake." When I asked him about that controversy, Peale disclosed that the experience was "harrowing," maybe the worst of his life. But it didn't paralyze him. The old preacher made a complete about-turn. During the 1980s, he was a staunch supporter of ecumenism, even hoping for the day when the "old hostilities" would disappear.

The thing that bothered Peale the most in the 1980s and 1990s was the rise of conservatism in North America. Peale knew thousands were embracing religion and the Bible, but he had witnessed this phenomenon before. It was nothing but a trend, part of an "historical cycle," where one generation rejects religion "and the spiritual concepts of living," while another seeks these electrifying elements in their life. The 1960s generation that rejected Christianity for a free-wheeling style was now "learning it (Christianity) all over again." Peale suspected faith in religion was never stronger.

Working against this faith in religion are the tremendous forces in North American society slowly eroding the sanctity of the family. Peale believed that because of relaxed attitudes toward marriage and raising children, family life had taken a beating. He predicted a sharp rise in single-parent families. He also felt if faith on the surface appeared to be stronger — and it seemed that it was — it was because "this moral decay" in society left few options for people: "We are at the bottom again . . . This is the most hopeful spot to be in . . . At the bottom, the only direction is up . . . Humanity gets sick of evil after a while just like a dog that turns on its own vomit."

PAUL-ÉMILE CARDINAL LÉGER
32
PRINCE OF POVERTY

The slightly stooped man stood in the doorway to his office. The look on his face was that of someone far from being content with himself and the world. He made you a little uncomfortable because you knew he'd made the effort you hadn't. You knew he'd been to Japan to work in the missions, to Africa to live among the lepers, and you knew he was now selling off all the jewels and gifts given to him by dignitaries and princes of the church over the years. You knew too he'd kept to the promise he made on Christmas morning sixty-one years ago, when he was nineteen. Paul-Émile Léger had made a decision to become a priest, to give himself to the world. He felt drawn to the mysterious reaches of the church, to a greater understanding of God and to the idea of service to the world. He never fully understood what that service meant until much later in life, until he had quit one of the highest positions in the church to become a missionary in a leper colony.

It was in the tiny village of St. Anicet, fifty kilometers or thirty-one miles southwest of Montreal, near Valleyfield, where life revolved around the store his father owned and around the church where both he and his brother were altar boys, that he made an early commitment. It was there where the influences in his life stopped at the sacristy and the daily rosaries in his family home.

That day I met him in December 1984, he stood in the doorway of a room that was one of a maze of rooms and hallways in a church basement in Outrement, a suburb of Montreal. He had much to muse over. Outside this large stone church, just around the corner, was a gaudy stretch of sex film theaters and bars. It wasn't all that long ago that he had gathered the support of the community to outlaw the advancement of these businesses in the city. This was a man who felt called to do something more vital. Long ago, he resolved to embrace the greater world, the world beyond the petty complaints of affluent charlatans. He decided he could no longer raise a penny for the poor unless he could shoulder some of their problems. When I met him, he told me that he was finally content that he had learned a little of that. Still he welcomed the intimate, firsthand experience of sickness, famine, and starvation. Paul-Émile Cardinal Léger, brother of former Governor

General Jules Léger, was eighty years old when I met him. He died in 1991.

That afternoon in wintry Montreal, the cardinal told me life hadn't stopped for him. He was up early each morning to say mass in the old seminary building where he lived with other retired priests. After that, he made his way down to 130 rue de l'Epée, to the very modern and streamlined basement offices of this old stone church. He was at his desk by 8:30 a.m. He rarely left the building until 3:30 p.m. He brought lunch with him, and ate it at his desk as he read.

The basement operations comprised Cardinal Léger and His Endeavors and Fame Pereo Institute for Lepers, two agencies that still raise money for the Third World. The Cardinal admitted he was cynical about those who gave money. He had witnessed every form of giving, but knew no matter what was offered, or why it was donated, it was going to help in some way. Still the cardinal was not happy. He said there were those who dashed off a check without much meaning — they felt a slight pang of guilt, a little discomfort at the sight of the corpses of children wrapped in dirty rags and images of crying and hungry infants clamoring at the breasts of their mothers. But were they really prepared to do anything about it? He didn't think so.

But Cardinal Léger wasn't one to criticize, unless he had solutions. It seemed this was his life's work. He dreamed solutions. He dreamed of the smoke and wounds of Africa. He remembered the bush communities in Cameroon and the names of lepers — young teenage girls and boys — to whom he brought comfort and for whom he built a hospital. It was something he never wished to forget. Indeed, he regretted ever leaving the place. "But I had to — I was sick," explained Cardinal Léger.

The solutions the Montreal cardinal offered that day were the kind he dreamed of that Christmas in 1923 — to be of service. It wasn't that he was asking young boys to enter the seminary as he did. There was something else people could do. Those studying medicine, for example, could offer six months of their time to work in Ethiopia. But what if you couldn't go to Africa? Then make the sacrifice, retorted Cardinal Léger. He provided the example of a man holidaying in Florida just as the Ethiopian crisis broke in the news. He said the man forwarded $700 to him — "half of what he was going to spend on his holidays . . . Now that's giving!" The cardinal emphasized how this man willingly cut his vacation in half to help the Third World. And with that explanation Léger's piercing eyes prompted you to draw a conclusion in your mind: the measure of giving depends on how much it hurts you to do it. To this the cardinal added: "If a person has to ask, 'What can I do?' then he's not going to do anything."

Léger told me that what must occur is a willingness to give and to serve. That's what he did in spite of all else. However, he quickly eschewed any identification of himself as "Some kind of model . . . No! No! No! I do what I do, and that's all." There's a tremendous credibility in what he espoused. After all, the man made a name for himself helping the Third World. In a 1964 sketch in the *New York Times,* the writer called Cardinal Léger "a tireless foe of poverty." That was long before he made his decision to live in Africa.

That decision to leave everything behind in Canada to go into the Third World was actually formulated during the Second Vatican Council. There among the other red-hatted princes of the church who were changing the liturgies and reshaping the Latin Church, the Montreal archbishop took his first hard look at Africa. All around him at the Vatican Council were bishops and cardinals from Africa, Asia, and South America. In 1963, the Montreal cardinal took a detour on his way home to make a month-long tour of the African leper colonies. On his return to Canada, he arranged to have money sent to those colonies. Soon Léger began urging the church itself to shed its pomp, ceremony, and aloofness, and to shell out to those who suffered. He then began the persistent harassment of the Vatican to dispatch him to Africa to work among the lepers. The Pope pleaded with him to "wait a month." Léger told me, "He asked me to pray and said he would also pray, and then he'd make his decision . . . and finally he did!"

The Vatican announced November 9, 1967, that the Pope had given in to Cardinal Léger's pleas to work among lepers in foreign lands. At sixty-three, Cardinal Léger resigned as Archbishop of Montreal and left for Cameroon. Until then, Paul-Emile Cardinal Léger had been considered one of the most influential princes of the church. His decision to shed the red hat was one of the most dramatic gestures of his life. He knew that. He also knew that he was one of the rising stars in the Roman Catholic Church. In fact, in 1963 — the same year he went on his tour of Africa — his name was mentioned as a possible papal candidate.

Missionary work wasn't new to the cardinal from Montreal. In his first years as a Sulpician priest on Kyushu, the southern island of Japan, he opened a seminary and learned Japanese. He returned to Canada to teach sociology in the Sulpician seminary in Montreal. His next assignment came after the Second World War. He was sent to Rome where he aided Pope Pius XII in finding food and drugs for war-torn Italy. To Léger the scene was like the Third World where people endured starvation and ruin. In the midst of such tireless work, the cardinal said the Pope "adopted" him as a kind of son. "He was like a father to me." Six year later, when still in his forties, Cardinal Léger was elevated to Archbishop of Montreal, and was given the red hat of cardinal by Pope Pius XII.

Behind such influence, there was someone who wasn't willing to accept pomp and authority. Then again, he often used it to his advantage — that is, when he needed to wield the kind of heavy-handed decisiveness that would enable the poor to benefit. In one wing of the church building in Montreal, there was a room crammed with gifts given to him from dignitaries and officials from around the world. These included a jeweled miter that had belonged to Pius XII and a gold cross given to him by Pope John Paul. Cardinal Léger made the decision to sell these gifts to raise money for the poor. "What am I going to do with all this stuff? I don't need it."

He meant that. Over the years, the cardinal learned to pare down the material things he owned. This didn't come easily. He recalled the day, just two weeks before Christmas, when he left for

Africa. He was on a plane from New York, alone. For the first time in his life he felt overwhelmingly isolated. For seventeen years he had had half a dozen secretaries pampering him, waiting on him hand and foot. Wherever he traveled, he had a chauffeur or an aide. "That night I felt profoundly that my decision was very personal, that no one could understand what it meant to me."

When he arrived in Africa, there wasn't the reception he had been accustomed at home, or when he traveled to other lands. To greet him was an archbishop, himself alone. The cardinal gladly followed the prelate into the bush. Not until he arrived at Youande in Cameroon about two weeks later, on Christmas Eve, did Léger make his decision to stay there to work. During that first year the cardinal confirmed 12,000 children. "I used to take my car in the morning, half past six, go into the bush to try and find my way to a small village." Unlike Montreal where he had a chauffeur, Léger drove himself. "I was the taxi," he pointed out, recounting how along the road he would pick up travelers who were walking. "I always had five, six or seven people in the car."

Cardinal Léger knew instantly he had entered a different world — a humbled one. At night, after supper, he soaked in the purity of solitude, its close embrace. It was something he had never experienced before. It awed him, silenced him. "Darkness would come at six every night, and there was no electricity, and I would read by a kerosene lamp. I was in a room that was very humble — and it wasn't very neat . . . I lived the ordinary life of a missionary, nothing spectacular."

Those years molded Cardinal Léger. While his mission may have been far from Africa when I met him in Montreal, he had laid the foundation that provided more than a million dollars a year to adult literacy projects and mobile clinics in Cameroon, nutrition programs, housing and treatment centers for tubercular patients in Haiti and Peru, medical dispensaries in the Upper Volta and Zaire, and the purchase of artificial limbs and braces in Bolivia.

The thing that disturbed him was that no one had bothered to show much interest in this work in all that time. As soon as the Ethiopian crisis broke, said the cardinal, people were shocked and overwhelmed by the numbers who died. "But this has been going on for years, and we've been telling people about it for years . . . It's going to be worse in Chad and other areas." When he spoke like this, the shadow of the old man in the cardinal seemed to disappear and give way to a renewed vitality. He believed ardently in his dreams, and anyone who bothered to listen felt compelled to believe in him.

Cardinal Léger found it inconceivable that most could give without a thought of where their money was going. He said they gave as long as they still had "a little for their Christmas presents, a little for their friends for the weekend," but the giving is empty. "Every day I ask myself the same question," said the gray-haired, bushy-browed cardinal. " 'Am I doing something to bring a little piece of bread to all these children who are dying?' "

EPILOGUE
DIARY AT THE ABBEY OF GETHSEMANI
IN TRAPPIST, KENTUCKY

1 The solemnity of the Abbey of Gethsemani is interrupted by dinner as the monks sit down to a feast of beer and pizza. It seems incongruous. But it isn't. It is the feast day of St. John the Baptist, and the monks celebrate feast days with gusto. They take the day off — from work that is — never from prayer. Feast days are jubilant — they're for celebration, like weekends are for the secular world, and the monks look forward to them. The cheese factory, with all its shining stainless steel, shuts down. And the kitchens for the cake-making aren't even opened. Feast days are relaxing, lazy days when the monks spend a day in reflection, prayer or reading.

Naturally, there's always someone who doesn't accept the routine. Beyond the iron gate and behind the stone wall that separates the monastery from the outside world, Br. Ambrose with his long white beard works away in the field. He is devoted to his crops and spends long hours hoeing and watering vegetables. No one really seems to mind.

We are on time for dinner in the guest refectory, but we have pizza, no beer. The first person we meet is Br. Giovanni, sitting behind a desk at the guest house. Pleasant, but not engaging. His clear brown eyes betray his suspicion of visitors. He is part of the old guard — from the days when silence and sign language reigned over Gethsemani. Now when he recalls the old days, he shakes his head at how Gethsemani paid so little attention to Tom. Tom is Thomas Merton, or Fr. Louis — the name he adopted in the monastery. An intellectual, journalist, poet, and convert to Catholicism, Merton, before entering the monastery, had fathered a child and led a libertine lifestyle. Once here, his writings — The Seven Storey Mountain and The Sign of Jonas — established an international reputation for him. It also put Gethsemani on the map.

"We just didn't know what we had here," Giovanni says a little sadly. He telephones the abbot, Fr. Timothy Kelly, who is expecting us. He puts down the phone and directs us to our rooms — just down the sidewalk and around the corner. The abbot will see us tomorrow.

Once inside, the bearded, amiable Fr. Michael emerges from a small office to direct us upstairs to the only air-conditioned rooms — with the exception of the infirmary — in the complex. The monks must endure this stifling heat. At least they've been able to exchange their heavy wool habits for light, washable, polyester gowns. Michael warns us not to go into the enclosed or cloistered areas, but invites us to participate in any of the liturgical services in the church.

Later, Timothy appears at our rooms to introduce himself and advise us that he'll show us the monastery tomorrow. He is slight, good natured, efficient. He quickly outlines the guidelines to be followed while visiting the monastery and tells us a photographer had earlier upset the solitary community. Not relishing publicity for either himself or the monastery, Timothy accepted us from Windsor for "sentimental" reasons. He was born and reared in Amherstburg and went to Assumption College (now the University of Windsor). Since coming to Gethsemani in 1958, he has only been back to Windsor a few times, the last journey being a few years ago, but only for a couple of hours. He admits living a cloistered life cuts him off from the world but, he adds, that's the point of it, isn't it? Timothy is mildly surprised to discover Joe Clark is no longer the Progressive Conservative leader. "I had heard he had a little bit of trouble."

It's not that Gethsemani is completely cut off from the rest of the world — it does receive some journals and newspapers. But those daily newspapers, like the local Lexington paper, certainly aren't in the vanguard of journalism. *The New York Times* would be great, remarks Timothy, but only the book supplement makes it. Do monks have access to a television or radio? "Well . . . not that I know of," Timothy quips, betraying a good sense of humor. Still, the rules are bent easily. Timothy takes a philosophical attitude

toward it and maintains how restrictions can be carried around like a weight that only alienates and frustrates. Living the rule "joyously," in the spirit in which it is accepted, is the model. But the model should never be an ideal that can never be attained — it must be within everyone's reach.

Gethsemani, a Cistercian monastic community, follows the old Benedictine way — integrating work and prayer into a contemplative life. Founded in 1848, Gethsemani was the first of sixteen monasteries in the USA. There is now one in Orangeville, Ontario.

It is the summer of 1983. Humid and hot in Kentucky. Merton has written about it often in his journals. As photographer Tim McKenna and I drove down to the Abbey of Gethsemani — some 400 miles directly south of Detroit, Michigan, down through Cincinnati, and Louisville, to the outskirts of the quaint Civil War town of Bardstown — I read *The Sign of Jonas*, the best of his monastic journals. It's been years since I looked at the book, which I read when I was barely a teenager. I found it among the boxes my brother had carted home from St. Peter's Seminary in London, Ontario, where he was studying for the priesthood. I realize that settling into the lifestyle here is illusory — this isn't what it's like to be a monk. I'm standing on the outside, looking in . . .

At Vespers (5:30 p.m.) we notice what Timothy means by bending the rules. The long, neat rows of monks bow their heads in song and prayer, but not everyone wears the rich white and black gowns. Two wear bluejeans — one with a T-shirt, the other with a white shirt. Are these visitors? They couldn't be, since guests must remain in the balcony at the back of the church — about as far from the altar as the pitcher's mound at Tiger Stadium is from the upper deck box seats along the first baseline. I make a note to ask the abbot about these two tomorrow. I get to sleep way after midnight.

2 Saturday begins before I'd like it to, with the sound of bells. I count them. Twenty-seven. They signal Vigils — choral prayers in the church. It is 3:00 a.m. The night before I had stayed up well past the 8:00 p.m. curfew set for the monks who had gone to bed at Compline. I understand now why they turn in so early. I head for the church, down the darkened hall, through a door, and up a set of stairs. The church is sparsely lit, the monks below, in their individual pews, face one another bowing, praying, singing. Their music has a prayerful, meditative quality reminiscent of the Gregorian chant. It's not Gregorian — it's the psalms, in English. It's also not that hip, quick-paced church music found in many parishes, complete with guitars, flutes, tambourines, and charismatic fury. It's moving and meditative, and I find myself sailing through Vigils on a cloud. This lack of sleep is a contributing factor.

After Vigils, I return to my room — matchbox-small, narrow, barely room enough for a bed, a desk, a small sink. My suitcase is an imposition, its size rendering it another piece of furniture. I skip Lauds — more choral prayer — at 5:45 a.m. and the meditative prayer just prior to mass. Mass itself is at 6:30 a.m. One of the monks brings the Eucharist upstairs to the guests, who are mostly from neighboring farms and hamlets. Here both the wine and bread are offered.

After breakfast at 7:30 a.m., we accompany Timothy on a tour of the monastery. He tells us the founders of Gethsemani were too patient: "If they had gone five miles further, they would have had good farm land." Instead they settled here, where only about 162 hectares or 400 acres are arable. The rest of the 810 hectares or 2000 acres are woodland. This was the kind of environment in which Merton thrived. Given permission to be more of a recluse, he retreated to a small cottage, or a hermitage in the woods. It was there he spent his days praying and working. His work was his writing. Timothy promises to take us there tomorrow. For now, he guides us through both the old and new of the monastery. He leads us up to the remnants of the old dormitories. Today monks have their own rooms with bookshelves, a bed, pictures on the walls, maybe an easy chair. Not what it used to be like. Timothy can't forget the old dorms where monks slept in one large room: each was assigned a small cell and a bed with a straw mattress. Two Gethsemani monks still use them. One cell is impeccably tidy with a small cross draped over the plumped up pillow; the other looks like someone left in a hurry. Timothy prefers the private rooms, if only because one can sleep better. The dorms were plagued with "snorers," and if it became too extreme, those monks would be "relegated to the snorers dorm." One night Timothy incurred the wrath of one particularly loud monk when he yanked the pillow out from under him.

The two who still sleep in the dorms are mavericks, admits the abbot, who believes Gethsemani ought to allow this option of monastic life here. Such freedom permitted Merton to move out of Gethsemani and into the hermitage two miles into the woods. He remained a part of the monastery, yet kept his distance. He was the first in the Trappist history to live the life of a hermit. There are other mavericks among the ex-diocesan priests, former marines, school teachers, farmers, and musicians at Gethsemani. The two who shun the traditional black and white robes, Timothy says with a smile, are "characters." This is said without distaste or annoyance.

At Chapter (community business meeting) Timothy is less solemn than his predecessors. He doesn't assume the role of the tyrannical, paternalistic father. His approach is in keeping with the times that have seen the monastic communities writing their own constitutions and being run democratically. "They don't listen to me," he chortles. When he was first elected abbot, he attempted to change the rising time to 4:00 a.m. but managed to muster only three votes in his favor.

With the radical change in the church, Gethsemani suffered the loss of many members. Some fled the community, but fortunately, replenishment was quick. At one time, there were more than 260 monks at the abbey. Today there are eighty-six — twenty-three are priests. Fewer embrace the monastic life. Then again, Gethsemani, like many other monasteries today, is far more meticulous and discretionary in its selection of candidates. At one time they plucked the young right out of high schools. Today candidates are encouraged to get a degree, travel, hold down a job, and not to come until their mid-twenties.

One of the first places Timothy introduces us to is the cemetery beside the church. Hundreds of white crosses punctuate the brilliant green, grassy slope. The monks are not buried in caskets. The corpses are placed in the ground with a simple cloth draped over them. The novices usually do the digging. "Sometimes when they're digging they'll come across a shoe," explains one older monk who laughs at how unnerving this can be for the young novices. "The crosses are really arranged architecturally — they don't really correspond accurately to where the graves are . . . They're close, but they may be off a little. So it's hard to know exactly *where* to dig."

Merton was an exception. When he died in Asia, he was shipped home in a coffin. Gethsemani decided to leave him in the casket. Over his grave is the same white cross, with the simple inscription: "Fr. Louis Merton, Dec. 10, 1968." Visitors are permitted to visit his grave, situated just beyond the cloistered barrier. There isn't a monument at Gethsemani for Merton. As Giovanni had reported, "He was just one of the monks when he was here." There is, however, in the cloistered area the "Merton Room," where there's a typewriter and a selection of everything he published. It doesn't contain the archives, which are held at

Bellarmine College, Louisville, Kentucky.

The mainstays of Gethsemani are its cheese and cake-making business. The cheese factory is where Fr. Victor — a tough ex-marine with a loud, sharp voice and a good sense of humor — works. He confesses how they wouldn't employ him in the Christmas cake area because there was bourbon in the pastry, and he was an alcoholic. The bakery is situated across the yard. One of the brothers opens the oven for us to see the cakes revolving on layered shelves like a water wheel. Unlike other religious communities, Gethsemani doesn't sell its products on the property. To protect the solitude of the monks, it discourages outsiders from coming. Gethsemani's mail-order business ships more than 56,800 kilograms or 125,000 pounds of fruit cake each year and about 86,400 kilograms or 190,000 pounds of cheese.

The afternoon is spent in the library, reading *The Sign of Jonas*. It is too hot to go outside. Timothy said it wasn't until he moved to Gethsemani and became a monk that he really became conscious of the weather. "Now I get up in the morning, and hope it is not too hot, not too cold." In winter, the church is bone-chillingly cold at 3:00 a.m.. Merton's diaries describe it as "a tinder-box."

About noon, the monks return to the church for choral prayer. Dinner is at 12:30 p.m., and until 2:15 p.m. there is rest, reading, and personal prayer. At 2:15 p.m., again more choral prayer in the church. Besides Vespers at 5:30 p.m. there is choral prayer at Compline after supper, at 7:30 p.m.

Meals for the guests include meat, but the monks adhere to a vegetarian diet. Lots of protein, derived from cheese and milk and supplemented by beans, fish, and eggs. Gethsemani has a large vegetable garden that supplies tomatoes, squash, corn, and potatoes.

3 Again the bells wake me. This time I count thirty-two. This time I stay in bed. I rise for Lauds — at 6:45 a.m. today because it's Sunday. Mass isn't until 10:30 a.m.

Timothy greets us after breakfast. We head out through the fields to check out the property of Gethsemani. He informs us that between choral prayers and chapter, the monks spend time before morning mass in prayer or reading. In the distance, alongside one of the property's many small lakes, we notice a man jogging, bare-chested, wearing shorts.

"That's not one of the monks, is it?"

"Yup," replies a reluctant Timothy.

"Perhaps he has a rosary in his hands," I offer.

"You're being kind," Timothy says with sarcasm.

We're back in time for mass at 10:30 a.m. We are allowed near the altar. I sit with the monks in chairs just to one side. At communion, I join the brothers and walk to the altar. The wine is in a large ornate chalice which probably holds a good 2.5 liters or 40 ounces. Because Timothy is the abbot, he's the main celebrant.

After lunch, more reading in the air-conditioned guests's library. Timothy meets us this time, dressed in jeans and a workshirt. We accompany him to the Merton hermitage. He takes the route Merton would have gone himself — up slopes and pathways through the woods, to the white cottage in the trees. It was there Merton did so much of his writing. But Timothy points out he wrote in other places as well: "Under trees, in the library, everywhere." He knew Merton well, and confirms the details in Monica Furlong's biography of Merton that upon his own entrance to Gethsemani, he was met by a monk who introduced himself as the master of the novices. This affable man inquired if Timothy had ever read anything about monastic life. When he replied that he had read some of Merton's books, the novice master's interest picked up, and he asked the younger monk for his assessment of those writings. "Rather exaggerated," Timothy responded honestly. The novice master agreed that one couldn't believe everything one read. Timothy later discovered the novice master was Merton.

The hermitage is no shrine to Merton. In fact, it is much the same as when he lived there. Although rearranged, the furniture is the same that Merton used. Same desk facing the window. Same altar situated in a small chapel in a side room. The hermitage is still used occasionally by monks who are given permission to spend a night, a week or a couple of weeks there. There's no question that Merton's spirit — at the hermitage, at the grave site and throughout the community's collection of buildings — hangs over Gethsemani. "He's the drawing card." People come from all over the world to visit the Kentucky abbey, and yet to the monks who were here with Merton through the 1940s, 1950s and 1960s, they still refer to him as Fr. Louis. "He was just one of us."

The day has been so hot that Benediction is unbearable. It's difficult to concentrate on what's going on in the church. Fortunately it lasts only fifteen minutes. Tonight I walk to the end of the main road leading into the monastery. Br. Ambrose is still at work in the fields. He probably sneaked out after Compline to check on things. Who knows when he goes to bed? The hills and fields surrounding the abbey take on that blue hue as the prayerful buildings fade into the night sky.

Again a late night. Up reading Merton. He writes how the monastic vocation is "a mystery," that it cannot be completely expressed in a clean, succinct formula. Merton says: "It is a gift of God, and we do not understand it as soon as we receive it, for all God's gifts, especially His spiritual gifts, share in His own hiddenness and in His own mystery. God will reveal Himself to us in the gift of our vocation, but He will do this only gradually."

It occurs to me now what Timothy meant that first day when I spoke to him about what it would be like to be a monk. "The romanticism wears off," he points out. The last person a monastery wants is the romantic. It's because the monastic vocation is solitary and difficult. That's not to say it isn't joyous; it is. But to be devoted to God is a full time activity. If you're full of pretenses and idealism, the whole activity can become a chore, a sham, a bore. The point of it all isn't stamina, or sticking out the duration of one's stay in the monastery, it is the act of enjoyment, the act of loving God.

4 Again the bells at 3:00 a.m. This time I fall asleep before I can count them all. I can't even remember where I left off. Again I am up for Lauds at 5:45 a.m. I am also there for mass. Quietude reigns over the church, accentuated by the soothing choral psalms of the monks. We skip breakfast and are gone by 8:00 a.m., with

Timothy bidding us good-bye. I promise to send tearsheets, and in response, he steeples his hands and rolls his eyes to Heaven, and says, "I hope I don't lose my job for what I've said."

ACKNOWLEDGEMENTS

A woman in her late thirties dropped in to see me one rainy morning, after noticing my name on the Saturday Religion Page. That was the moment when I got the first inkling of what it would be like to cover religion for *The Windsor Star*. This was the end of 1979, and I had just been assigned the job as religion editor for the paper. It was a role that I would maintain for some 11 years. The woman's opening line was: "I just wanted to introduce myself, and tell you if you need any help, I'd be pleased to provide it." I thanked her for the offer, but wondered how she might be of help. "Well, I am in touch with the Supreme Being, and if you need any answers, or if you need to pose any questions to Him, then just call me. I *know* Him, and I can put those questions to Him, and get the answers."

I never took up her offer. Oddly enough, life went smoothly along, and I got a lot of answers to a lot of questions. All without her help. And maybe without divine intervention. Then again, maybe she was pulling strings for me with some unseen power from above. In any case, coverage of religion took me from one end of the country to the other, indeed, from one end of the world to another. Those were exciting times, and it seemed I was always on the road, despatching stories over the telephone lines. It was during those years of covering religion that I also ran into Gordon Sinclair, who was still working for a radio station in downtown Toronto. When I told him what I was doing, he said to me, "Religion? Are you an atheist?" I told him, "No, I believe in God, and I still go to church — at least as often as I can." Sinclair shook his head. "It's fine to cover religion, but it's best to be an atheist, because then you don't have a stake in what you're writing. It's a little like being a Rotarian and covering the Rotary Club. You can't be doing both." While I am sure Sinclair was wrong, the point he drove home was, "Don't be fooled, don't become one of them!" I think that while I was writing about religion and religious figures, I managed to keep my distance, to be objective, and to respond to people and events with levity and without bias.

I want to thank the people I interviewed for their kindness and candor. They made this book possible. I also want to thank Bob Hilderley of Quarry Press for his interest and faith in seeing this book through to completion. In fact, he was the one who suggested it, and kept after me to complete it. I must also acknowledge the support given to me by the Ontario Arts Council by way of a grant through Quarry Press. I must also express gratitude to a few others — Carl Morgan, former editor of the *Windsor Star*, who supported my efforts in religion coverage for the paper; James Bruce, the *Star's* present editor, who offered encouragement when I told him about the book; Michael Dunnell, the paper's managing editor, who guided me through the hoops in my coverage of the papal tour; Denise Chuk, Maureen Williams, and Ute Hertel of the *Windsor Star* Library, who gracefully and diligently helped track down some of the information and photographs; and Grant Black and the entire *Windsor Star* Photo Department. I also valued the insights and instincts of the late Bob McAleer, former managing editor of the *Windsor Star*, who saw the religion page as an integral and vital part of the news. Before he died of a brain tumor, he pressed me not to give up in my attempts for an interview with Jerry Falwell. That story is in this book. It was the last assignment he gave me.

PHOTO CREDITS

Grant Black: 227
Nick Brancaccio: 144, 149, 214
Marty Gervais: 11, 84, 169
Graeme Gibson: 178
Bev MacKenzie: 220, 251
Tim McKenna: 37, 51, 59, 73, 93, 265
Randy Moore: 29, 125, 138
John Reeves: 174
Ted Rhodes: 98
The Wallendas: 232
Mike Weaver: 2, 244
The Windsor Star Library: 238
World Council of Churches: 78